Schleiermacher *on*
Christian Consciousness
of God's Work *in* History

Princeton Theological Monograph Series

K. C. Hanson and Charles M. Collier, Series Editors

Recent volumes in the series

Christian T. Collins Winn, editor
From the Margins: A Celebration of the Theological Work of Donald W. Dayton

Gabriel Andrew Msoka
Basic Human Rights and the Humanitarian Crises in Sub-Saharan Africa: Ethical Reflections

T. David Beck
The Holy Spirit and the Renewal of All Things: Pneumatology in Paul and Jürgen Moltmann

Trevor Dobbs
Faith, Theology, and Psychoanalysis: The Life and Thought of Harry S. Guntrip

Paul S. Chung, Kim Kyoung-Jae, and Veli-Matti Kärkkäinen, editors
Asian Contextual Theology for the Third Millennium: A Theology of Minjung in Fourth-Eye Formation

Bonnie L. Pattison
Poverty in the Theology of John Calvin

Anette Ejsing
A Theology of Anticipation: A Constructive Study of C. S. Peirce

Michael G. Cartwright
Practices, Politics, and Performance: Toward a Communal Hermeneutic for Christian Ethics

Stephen Finlan and Vladimir Kharlamov, editors
Theōsis: Deification in Christian Theology

David A. Ackerman
Lo, I Tell You a Mystery: Cross, Resurrection, and Paraenesis in the Rhetoric of 1 Corinthians

Schleiermacher *on* Christian Consciousness *of* God's Work *in* History

by
ABRAHAM VARGHESE KUNNUTHARA

With a Foreword by
TERRENCE N. TICE

◦PICKWICK *Publications* • Eugene, Oregon

SCHLEIERMACHER ON CHRISTIAN CONSCIOUSNESS OF GOD'S WORK IN HISTORY

Princeton Theological Monograph Series 76

Copyright © 2008 Abraham Varghese Kunnuthara. All rights reserved. Except for brief quotations in critical articles or reviews, no part of this book may be reproduced in any manner without prior written permission from the publisher. Write: Permissions, Wipf and Stock Publishers, 199 W. 8th Ave., Suite 3, Eugene, OR 97401.

Pickwick Publications
A division of Wipf and Stock Publishers
199 W 8th Ave., Suite 3
Eugene, OR 97401

ISBN 13: 978-1-55635-215-7

Cataloging-in-Publication data:

Kunnuthara, Abraham Varghese.

Schleiermacher on Christian consciousness of God's work in history / Abraham Varghese Kunnuthara. With a foreword by Terrence N. Tice.

   Eugene, Ore.: Pickwick Publications, 2008
   Princeton Theological Monograph Series 76

   xvi + 186 p. ; 23 cm.

   Includes bibliography and index.

   ISBN 13: 978-1-55635-215-7

   1. Schleiermacher, Friedrich, 1768–1834. 2. Schleiermacher, Friedrich, 1760–1834—Contributions in doctrine of God. 3. Schleiermacher, Friedrich, 1769–1834—Contributions in theology of history. I. Tice, Terrence N. II. Title. III. Series.

B3097 .K87 2008.

Manufactured in the U.S.A.

Dedicated to my parents,

*the late Mr. K. T. Varghese (1921–1995)
and
Mrs. Annamma Varghese (b.1927)*

Contents

Foreword by Terrence N. Tice / ix

Preface / xiii

1. Introduction / 1

2. The New Creation and the Old / 23

3. Christian Understanding of God's Work through the Being of the Redeemer / 41

4. Christian Understanding of God's Work in History through the Activity of the Redeemer / 61

5. Christian Understanding of God's Work in History in Relation to the Doctrine of Election / 77

6. God's Work in History in and through the Community of Faith / 99

7. Christian Consciousness of God's Government of the World / 127

Conclusion / 159

Bibliography / 163

Indexes / 175

Foreword

IMAGINE A THEOLOGIAN REARED IN A BRANCH OF THE MARTHOMA church—a varied group in Kerala, South India, which has traditionally claimed its founding by St. Thomas and has a long history of ties and breaks with Rome, close involvement possibly from the second century AD with Syrian orthodoxy, associations with the Church of England and more recently the Church of South India—and with an American-type evangelicalism, which had taken on this branch in a troubled time earlier in the century. Imagine his appropriating numerous blessings from much among these Western and Eastern traditions. Imagine too his growing up in a devout Christian family within an enormous sea of Hindu religion and culture, which he also strove to appreciate and understand. Imagine his thriving, though with low economic means, within one of the most literate communities in India and accepting the vocations of pastor and theologian there and his being deeply exercised by questions concerning the meaning of Christianity as God's special formation of a "new creation" in history and concerning the meaning of history itself. Imagine his then taking on a primarily "Reformed" and "ever reforming" point of view, spurred further in this process by Friedrich Schleiermacher, widely reputed to be the father of modern theology.

Imagine, then, that this same passion near the end of doctoral work at Dallas Theological Seminary had drawn him so close to Schleiermacher's thought, in part by brief stimuli from a couple of teachers but mostly through his own independent searching, that he decided to address these focal questions as an Indian Christian with Schleiermacher's help. This he did—and carried out in an unusually attentive, intelligent and "systematic" (not system-seeking) manner.

Early within the decade since then, the eventual Dr. Kunnuthara, currently Professor of Theology at the highly respected Union Biblical Seminary in Bibvewadi, Pune, Maharastra, India, had called me, with some trepidation as I recall, near the point at which his dissertation proposal was to be considered. We quickly found good company in each other, and afterward we twice spent mutually valuable time together in Dallas; I have met his delightful family, and we have become friends. Now Dr. Kunnuthara is well placed to continue these inquiries and to participate in inter-faith dialogue on major issues addressed in this study as Professor at Union Biblical Seminary.

Early on, I saw that he was arriving at a point where he could, in mature young adulthood, expect to experience effective collegiality with scholars from many cultures and sectors of the church for whom Schleiermacher can have become a treasured companion and to exercise leadership among them, not least in his own country. As he has expressed to me, he does not fully agree or know what to do with everything he has learned in his hugely successful attempt to understand Schleiermacher's dogmatic theology, but he has certainly found Schleiermacher to be immeasurably helpful in his own quest. I am honored also to have been a companion in the process for these few years and to be able to recommend this study, which displayed to me a maturity of theological reflection already at the dissertation stage beyond what would ordinarily be witnessed.

In this place, I should like to add a few comments. First of all, I note that Dr. Kunnuthara credits me with putting a bee in his bonnet with the suggestion that a fresh way of grasping Schleiermacher's systematic theology could be that of reading *Christian Faith* (a translation of which I am now completing) backwards. In 1996 I had been entertaining such a possibility myself, also regarding *On Religion*. Both works should be examined partly as a way of obviating a host of misguided interpretations and tenuously attached objections, even attacks. I was also finding this reconstruction to be a stimulating way to carry out inquiries about the nature of religious faith and theology for myself, after decades of close, perhaps all-too-close, familiarity with each of these works. In mid-1997 I briefly reported on some results of my attempted inquires, which had become very exciting and fruitful to me, in a month full of seminars at a number of British universities and was greatly stimulated by them too. By that means I found that there was far more interest in and high affirmation of Schleiermacher there today than I had ever found reason to expect. This experience gave rise to a sense that conditions might well become ripe for a similar incipient reception in India and other former British colonies as well.

I am glad to send this fine interpretation of Schleiermacher's presentation of doctrine on its way, with two further related observations. First, Dr. Kunnuthara's new look, pursued generally in the reverse direction that Schleiermacher himself hoped might be possible someday, is, I think, likely to spawn similar systematic approaches that will likely be stimulative of thinking well outside the bounds of Schleiermacher studies, which, it seems to me, should be their ultimate effect. My own initial attempts, for example, began with inquiry into the nature of the triune God (with which Schleiermacher concluded), then moved to questions that arise from investigating, successively (new questions pushing one back and back through *Christian Faith*), the love and wisdom of God, faith experience in Christian community and in the world more generally by the Spirit, individual experiences of regeneration and sanctification, appropriating of God's grace in the person and work of Christ, the understanding of sin in the light of redemption, presuppositions (in Part I) for grasping fully all these matters in Christian religious self-consciousness in its relation to God, world and self, and finally pursuit of questions that arise afresh regarding what definition and methods for doing dogmatics are proper to its tasks, given what was found phenomenologically under the conditions of faith and life thus (re-) discovered.

This long, demanding process (which Schleiermacher himself undoubtedly went through in his own development, as did Abraham Kunnuthara) would then lead one out into a similarly oriented process of investigating Christian ethics (as Schleiermacher also did), then quite possibly into a re-reversal in an effort to make what one wished to present as clear as possible, given numerous alternative views, habits and objections, as in the present form of *Christian Faith* and the Christian Ethics lectures. Other configurations, of course, would also be useful (e.g., those adopted in Karl Barth's *Church Dogmatics*). I think readers will find Dr. Kunnuthara's resultant focus on theses closely related to the proposition that "God's work in history is identical to God's work in Christ," as well as his way of getting to and explicating this proposition, will be stimulative of allied inquires and positions that can emerge for them.

My second observation is of suggestions that appear here of dialogues carried on, indicated indirectly for the most part in references to Indian thinkers but also directly in Kunnuthara's laying out Schleiermacher's theological positions and ways he got to them. Also, and without adopting a triumphalist perspective, he sees with Schleiermacher a highly evolved presence in Christianity pertinent to all human life—in a somewhat guarded sense one representative even of the highest, "perfect," if not entirely final refinement of religion. Because of how the two men view the nature of God's work in history, in Christ, there emerges a great openness to dialogue concerning the deepest things of faith and life, not as self-chosen superiors but as equal partners in search of understanding "redemption" and the need for it. Ferreting out such suggestions, which are part of the intention of this work though not meant to be openly articulated here, could become a sizeable fringe benefit for readers of it.

Among the major challenges facing both efforts would surely be that of pressing to see in what ways a sense for the eternity, omnipresence and stable, ordered and in general tightly interconnected process of the divine in this world can logically be meshed or correlated with a possibly more advanced sense for still other elements. Included might be the chance, chaos, indeterminacy, and both ecological and process-oriented characteristics that recent developments toward understanding genetic, animate, human and purely physical aspects of nature manifest to many of us today. How, we would ask, might such characteristics be present in ways the divine is revealed in and through the *Naturzusammenhang*, or interconnected process of nature, which both Schleiermacher and Kunnuthara emphasize? As Schleiermacher averred, exegetical and historical, doctrinal and ethical, philosophical and practical tasks are all interrelated, interdependent aspects of such theological work. Each of them, moreover, has its two interlocking sides, that which draws from a knowledgeable sharing of mind and heart in communities of faith (which Schleiermacher refers to as "ecclesial") and that which draws from the knowledge and methods of scholarship broadly conceived (the "scientific" side). Dr. Kunnuthara, in taking nurture from all these sources in his education, prepares himself and his readers to launch out anew in that same twofold process. In such an ever-renewing, ever-reforming effort, God bless(es) us all!

Terrence N. Tice
Denver, Colorado
February, 2007

Preface

My first exposure to Schleiermacher was in 1983–84, during a Master's course in Nineteenth Century Protestant Theology, given by a Barthian professor in an Anglican College. As has been the experience of many who are interested in Schleiermacher, I too, at first, mistook him to be a pantheist because of phrases like "Spinoza . . . was full of the Holy Spirit." An "Introduction" by Rudolf Otto (whom I knew then, basically and probably only through Radhakrishnan) in John Oman's translation of Schleiermacher's *Reden*[1] was sufficient reason to count him (not because of the content of the Introduction, as I did not understand much of it anyway then, but because of Otto's name) as a kindred spirit with many Hindu sages.

Partly due to the arrangement of the course I took in 1984, and partly due to my own limitations, towards the completion of the course I was looking at Schleiermacher through the liberal theology of the nineteenth century. However, I was confused; I had no way of reconciling a "mystic" and "pantheistic" Schleiermacher with a "liberal" Schleiermacher.

For a doctoral course at Dallas Theological Seminary, I happened to read Schleiermacher's *Hermeneutics*[2] and soon enough I found that there is a lot more in him than I had ever imagined. A paper I did on Schleiermacher's concept of "history" (prompted by Wilhelm Pauck's article)[3] brought me to an awareness of a view of history I had never heard of before—organic! I wanted to study more of the man. My professor, Stephen Spencer, now at Wheaton College, directed me to Brian Gerrish's writings on Schleiermacher; Gerrish and Terrence Tice, whose works I also found at that time, gave me a new Schleiermacher I had not known till then—an Evangelical Reformed theologian; Evangelical as compared with Roman Catholic, and Reformed as compared with

---

1. *On Religion*, trans. John Oman, vii–xxiii.
2. *Hermeneutics: The Handwritten Manuscripts*.
3. Pauck, "Schleiermacher's Conception of History and Church History," 41–56.

Lutheran, though seeking Lutheran/Reformed union in his native Prussia. I went back to Schleiermacher's *Christian Faith,* and I started finding their assessment to be true. I was both shocked and fascinated; he was no pantheist after all. His was a pious heart, totally earnest in seeking and expressing the significance of his faith and belief in and through Jesus Christ and the tradition that truly represents Christ. I knew by then where I should go for a dissertation topic. Several years later, the final product revised for publication, is finally presented here.

Schleiermacher presents to me a very different way of thinking through the Reformed faith; I would not copy him, and he would not want me to. In fact, anyone who would ever ape Schleiermacher would be doing a disservice to his spirit, because his "highest intuition," which he gained in Landsberg an der Warthe in his mid-twenties and which rather acted as a "guiding image or organizing principle"[4] for the rest of his life and work, has it that "each person is to represent humanity in one's own way, combining its elements uniquely so that it may reveal itself in every mode."[5] Indeed one should gladly accept the challenge he gives one toward a renewed reflection upon every area of one's dogmatic tradition. Within the framework of our common commitment to the glory of the Lord Jesus Christ, he deserves my utmost possible attention to seek to help clear up misunderstandings and avoid misrepresentations of him and to allow him to infuse me with insights that can aid my development. I have wished most of all to investigate Schleiermacher's account of how a Christian view of history itself comprises the common inheritance of all who enter into Christian community, regardless of time and region. Thus, Schleiermacher's legacy becomes and remains the property of the Christian Church in the East as much as it does in the West.

The present book is a revised version of my 1998 dissertation at Dallas Theological Seminary. I must thank the excellent teaching team of Drs. Lanier Burns, Craig Blaising, and Stephen Spencer, all of whom taught me at the Dallas Theological Seminary and prepared me for this work. My deepest gratitude to Mr. Jerry Reeves and the Dallas Seminary Foundation for sponsoring my studies at the Dallas Theological Seminary with full financial support.

4. Tice, "Schleiermacher's 'Highest Intuition' in Landsberg (1794–1796)," 19.

5. Quoted in the Tice article, 20. On that account it is also clear that Schleiermacher would totally oppose contemporary attempts to clone humans to desired specification even as he would ardently support all scientific advances that could benefit humanity.

At this point a decade later, as the work finally reaches a broader public, I wish gratefully to acknowledge Terry Tice's considerable encouragement and assistance throughout this process, especially recently in my getting the work revised, up-dated and published. He continues to be teacher, mentor and pastor to me, a great support to me in many ways, and my friend. I also want to thank Terry's wife, Catherine Kelsey, Dean of the Chapel at Iliff School of Theology in Denver, for helping to get the final manuscript in good order.

1

Introduction

The Nature, Scope, and Limitations of the Study

WHAT I AM ATTEMPTING IN THIS WORK IS BOTH A METHOD AND A STUDY, giving equal weight to both. The methodological attempt adopted here calls for thinking through the theology of Schleiermacher in a reverse order from how it is done and articulated in *Christian Faith*. The original impetus for the envisaged mode of approach was given by Dr. Tice in a personal letter.[1] For a long time Schleiermacher himself had toyed with the idea of reversing the order of the body of *Christian Faith* but eventually gave that up altogether because of both aesthetic and theological considerations.[2] However, he was convinced that many of the unfair criticisms of his *Christian Faith* would vanish only if that program of reversal could be effected. In his "Foreword" to the second edition of *Christian Faith*, moreover, Schleiermacher complains that certain sad caricatures and misinterpretations of his *Speeches* prevalent at the time are due to a failure on people's part to discern the rhetorical nature of that piece of literature.[3] And by "rhetorical," he means this:

> A presentation is *rhetorical* when it is so ordered that the effect of the individual part is determined by its place in the whole—as opposed to the *logical*, where the place of each part is determined by its organic position in a system. The rhetorical is an attribute of arrangement, not dependent on the quality of the several parts.[4]

1. Tice in a communication to Kunnuthara, 6/25/95.
2. Schleiermacher, *On the Glaubenslehre*, 55–60.
3. Cited in Berkof, *Two Hundred Years of Theology*, 35–36.
4. Quoted from Berkof.

Even though *Speeches* and *Christian Faith* belong to two different genres (the former mostly to rhapsodic and apologetic discourse and the latter to dogmatics), *Christian Faith* too must be viewed in such a way that both in terms of content and style it is meant to reach its climax toward the end of the book; and therefore whatever is said at the end of the book is supposed to re-enlighten whatever has been said before. Schleiermacher earnestly complains that readers, by and large, have taken his "Introduction" (which in fact lies outside the discipline of dogmatics) as the core and have left the second part of the body completely out of consideration, to brand him as a pantheist and worse.[5] "When so many eminent and respected voices warn that my God ought not to be regarded as the God of the Christian faith, I must surmise that the Introduction and the first part must have served as such a strange and unusual brew to intoxicate them that the readers could no longer taste in the second part what is well known and familiar to them."[6] This work is an humble attempt to pick one strand from Schleiermacher's thinking, namely the Christian consciousness of God's work in history, with *Christian Faith* as the basic text, and to look at the issue in a reversed order from the way it is presented there; all is engaged with the explicit hope of understanding Schleiermacher better, on the one hand, and of provoking others to attempt the same on a grander scale and attending to the whole of *Christian Faith* in its entire scope, on the other hand. The recent revival in Schleiermacher studies in the United States and elsewhere and the quality of the minds which are engaged in it are a sure indication that this can and will be done. Sometimes minor changes, and at other times major alterations are made, with Terrence N. Tice, in quotations picked from the English translation of *Christian Faith*, to assure greater clarity, accuracy or gender inclusiveness, the latter of which was a marked tendency in Schleiermacher's thought. The reader may also note that the title of the book is consistently referred to here as *Christian Faith*, and not as *The Christian Faith* as is in the English translation. The German expression, *Der Christliche Glaube* must properly be translated as *Christian Faith* and not as *The Christian Faith*, as if there were but one.

Just as Schleiermacher's doctrine of *Naturzusammenhang* indicates the interconnectedness of everything to everything else in nature, it happens to be the case that every thought expressed (regardless of its loca-

---

5. *On the Glaubenslehre*, 56.
6. Ibid., 57.

tion in the system) through the 751 pages of *Christian Faith* is somehow connected to everything presented everywhere in the book. According to Schleiermacher, an eminent task of hermeneutics is "to understand the text at first as well as and then even better than its author,"[7] given that proper conditions are present. A pre-requisite toward the practical working out of this goal is that the author be known both subjectively and objectively.

> On the objective side this requires knowing the language as the author knew it. . . . On the subjective side this requires knowing the inner and the outer aspects of the author's life.[8]

This would help a long way toward reconstructing in the mind of the interpreter the process of thought that occurred within the being of the author; and one needs such a process to gain an adequate understanding of any author. With regard to *Christian Faith*, as is amply explained in its own Introduction as well as in *On the Glaubenslehre: Two Letters to Dr. Lüche,* the Introduction, in some sense, is an abstraction from both the second part and the first part of the system of doctrine while also delineating the method and definition of dogmatics followed in the whole book; and the first part of the system of doctrine is in some sense an abstraction from the second part, while the second part forms the expression of the interiority of Christian experience, hence the more immediate nature, the cream, the core, and the climax of Christian doctrine. That being the case, it should be an easy logical inference that before putting down the first line of *Christian Faith* in writing, Schleiermacher's foot was firmly set well below the last line of the book. This means that the written form of *Christian Faith* historically took shape in an inverse order from the mental process of creation and construction of the totality of the work. Therefore, for a preliminary recreation of Schleiermacher's thought, a reversing of the process is required of an interpreter; he/she ought to work from the beginning to the end, holding all judgments in suspense until the end is reached and then rework the totality of the book from the bottom up, in such a way that one would re-formulate the process of thought informed and developed as it had happened in Schleiermacher, and in certain respects possibly, eventually understand him even better

---

7. *Hermeneutics*, 112.
8. Ibid., 113.

than he understood himself by further making use of all source materials available to the author and all his formative influences.

If one were to reverse the course of the flow of the thought of a thinker, it would be incumbent upon that person to inculcate the thinker's thoughts in oneself, feel the heart-throb of the thinker, and, as much as possible, subjectively appropriate to oneself the life and experience of the thinker and the thinker's process of the production of thought, and then allow the whole to flow out of oneself in a formative manner that fits the desired pattern. This is what I have tried to do in this work. In spite of one's best efforts to be true to the thinker, when one reverses in oneself the thoughts of a thinker, the results at best can only be the student's interpretation of the thinker, one that takes form from within the framework of language of the student and of the questions the student will be asking, questions that are and ought to be different from the ones the thinker would have asked himself. The student will have to sense and divine the answers for his/her questions from the style, logic and direction of the thinker. This characteristic will be found in plenty in the present study.

These limitations are acceptable, because this is the best that we can do. Our common sharing of humanity being what it is, we are wonderfully created to experience others within ourselves, and therefore, in spite of any limitations, we are also capable of substantially, correctly representing others. Yet another limitation that should be borne in mind is this, that since the method of presentation is different, or is revised, even some of the language will have to be different, and the student must be allowed to have her/his own language take the place of the thinker's and have it flow out of her/him naturally. One more caution needs to be added here. The very way in which I am arranging the chapters and conducting the theological investigation may indeed induce many first-time readers of Schleiermacher—who though they may not be conversant with his theology are nonetheless privy to caricatures of Schleiermacher (which, sadly, are seldom in short supply)—to attribute wrong meanings to themes discussed in the first few chapters. Therefore, I must request all the readers of this work to go through the whole work and then make their judgments.[9]

---

9. And once someone has read this, I hope that person will take it upon him/herself to commit to reading and re-reading *Christian Faith*, as I think it is the most underused of all *treasure mines* in Christian theological thinking.

The main attempt in this study, stated succinctly, is to explore Schleiermacher's theological conception of the Christian consciousness of God's work in history, that is, of redemption history and the total history of the world, each in relation to the other, and in the pattern and method set forth in the previous paragraph. In rediscovery of his definition of terms, however, in certain respects we may well have to depend heavily upon his Introduction to *Christian Faith*.

Yes, for academic purposes, Christian consciousness can entertain the thought of a history within history, related to each other as part and whole; a redeemed mind has a unique way of understanding God's work within history by giving precedence to redemptive history, i.e. viewing the flow of history overall from within the interests of redemptive history. For Schleiermacher, from the point of view of dogmatics, in a way to be reflected in this study, all history should be deemed to be redemptive history because of his distinctive understanding of Christian teleology. History is purposive; it is eschatological, going somewhere. It is this "somewhere goingness" that is the essence of history, and therefore is essential history, hence the predominant power it holds to involve within itself the interpretative key to history.

In Schleiermacher's view, parts are related to the whole and the whole to parts and the parts to each other organically and by a universal nexus of interrelation. The whole process gains its meaning in and through divine causality in a one-way dependence, though also in an actual communion. The world is dependent upon God, time is dependent upon God's eternity, and human causality is dependent upon divine causality.

Through the course of our discussion, though in a very limited way, it is also proposed to have Schleiermacher dialogue with certain Indian thinkers, both Hindu and Christian, and for more than one reason. Regardless of the fact that Schleiermacher and the Indian thinkers that are to be brought to mind here have articulated their thoughts within and in terms of the structural confines of very different traditions that are as far apart, and as unrelated to each other, as may be possible, and as unaffected by each other as can be, still one may be able to find extremely exciting parallels between them. We must respect the difference. It should not be called vain curiosity, however, if persons advocating unrelated and even competing systems of thought were to look into each other's systems. In the process, each advocate could well find illumination and might even put to good use the precision of the others so as to sharpen one's own interpretative presentation. Furthermore, either in terms of familiarity or in terms of persuasion, all those who will ever read this study can, respectively, be divided into two corresponding groupings, namely, those who are nearer to Schleiermacher than to the Indian thinkers considered here, on a sliding scale of comparison with those who are nearer to the Indian thinkers than to Schleiermacher. An ensuing dialogue between the two directions of thinking will be helpful for either side in either measure, so as to understand and appreciate or criticize, whatever is the case, the farther object of consideration more intelligibly; and the process may also possibly help one understand even the nearer side of one's familiarity or persuasion better.

The Nature of Consciousness in Schleiermacher's View

Any sort of consciousness, in Friedrich Schleiermacher's view, is phenomenological (though not in such a way as to be subjectivist, as it were, rather than objectivist). In his view, we have no access to what is trans-phenomenal; and instructional intrusion from outside the interconnectedness of phenomena is an impossibility, even though claims to that effect can be seen all over the world, and in most communities. Thus, for Schleiermacher revelation as "originally and essentially doctrine" does not make either intellectual or religious sense; rather, the meaning and significance of the concept "revelation" is this: "The *originality* of the fact which lies at the foundation of a religious communion, in the sense that this fact, as conditioning the individual content of the religious emotions which are found in the communion, cannot itself in turn be explained by the historical chain which precedes it."[10] Care should be taken not to read more than what is intended in the last clause of this sentence; it only means that we are not adequate to the task of divining and defining the organic connection this particular "originality" has with all its formative factors; but they are there, they are not simply supernatural, they are natural.

In this sense, the Redeemer is revelation to us but in itself the New Testament is not. The sinlessness and the absolute God-consciousness of Jesus can in no way be explained by observable antecedent natural

---

10. *Christian Faith*, § 10. P.S., 50. Tice, who is retranslating *Christian Faith*, suggests that "emotions" is not exactly the right word for *Erregungen* here. "Affections" might work but only in the sense of referring to states of being affected. "Stirrings" would seem to work better if understood as arising, at the same time, both from without oneself and within oneself.

structures, even though we must surmise that there was just enough potentiality within human nature for such an unprecedented, unparalleled, and unrepeatable appearance. The rules of this occurrence are hidden from us; nevertheless they may be accurately conceived as actualized by a divine ordainment. All the history previous to this point was taking the peculiarly required shape in order to converge toward this absolute spiritual peak, so that it could be said that "when the fullness of time had come, God sent his Son. . . ."[11] In Schleiermacher's judgment, however, the formation of the New Testament can easily be explained as the setting forth in speech of how the early Christians were affected by this occurrence, even in its own fullness; hence the unsuitability of the word "revelation" to describe the New Testament even though it is the primary document of the Christian faith.

In Schleiermacher's usage, the word "nature" is very comprehensive; it includes the totality of creation in both its actualities and its potentialities. Therefore, he does not have much use for the distinction commonly made between the natural and the supernatural. His argument is simple: until human beings have reached the limits of the natural, they cannot speak of the supernatural. Humans are part of nature and therefore can never transcend nature. In Christ, as in every other respect, God meets human beings within the conditions of physical and human, historical nature, in and through their world.

> The idea of the world also determines the boundaries of our knowing. We are bound to the earth. All operations of thinking, even the entire system of our concept forming must be grounded therein.[12]

Even the utmost stretch of our imaginative power does not enable us to argue from beyond nature. The positioning of an Absolute Being, however great that Being may be conceived to be, or from whatever angles it may be imaginable, is beyond us, in so far as that Absolute is viewed as alongside nature or in transcendence of nature. This is so whether it exists in relation to nature or even if it is conceived as independent of nature. No matter what, that which can be defined or explained as in relation to creation, whether as Existence or as Emptiness, or even if it is conceivable or is conceived as non-conceivable in relation to creation, is

11. Gal 4:4.
12. Schleiermacher, *Dialectic*, 43.

thus somehow connected to nature. This connection takes place either by a positive relation or in terms of a contrast, and it must therefore be counted as being within the perimeters of the interconnectedness of nature. Whatever else the difference between Schleiermacher and Barth may be, Schleiermacher would largely agree with what Barth says in the following quotation. Barth says:

> We are originally and properly one with what we can apprehend. To apprehend certainly means to possess. But there is no possession without original and proper unity between the possessor and the possessed. Upon this unity rests the secret of our capacity to apprehend in this or that way the world and what is in it. Heaven and earth, invisible and visible, spirit and nature, being and knowing, the world as object and man as subject—all these, however great may be their immanent contrast, are originally and properly one as the creation of God . . . because the mystery of unity underlying all our other apprehension does not exist here, we cannot conceive God of ourselves.[13]

However, we should note that, for Schleiermacher the referent of "supernatural" is utterly inconceivable to us, or is utterly irrelevant to us; or to put it in a better way, whatever "supernatural" that humankind's faculties can postulate is easily and immediately to be conceived as "natural," so that in our experience the supernatural-natural distinction suddenly becomes superficial. Or it is the case that the reach and destiny of human consciousness is ever and always bound within the natural. Imagination and speculation are limited by the natural, or to put it conversely, nature has infinite dimensions in infinite varieties to provide enough room for human faculties to flourish in limitless indulgences, so that it can never exhaust the possibilities nature offers at any and all times as in single or plural directions. Thus, all knowledge remains phenomenological, and all knowledge occurs through a dialectical process among various perceptions and positions. Since no dialectic is possible between what is within the interconnectedness of nature and what is outside it, except by wrongly dragging the supposed outside entity inside, "revelation" as knowledge present in one's consciousness is a resultant product of the impression on oneself by the *Universum* or the "totality

---

13. Barth, *Church Dogmatics,* vol. 2, pt. 1, 189. We will not concern ourselves here with how God is known in Barth's theology, especially in basic areas like this one in which drastic differences exist between the two.

of everything that there is" regarding the particular object of knowledge concerned, coupled with the uniqueness of the way in which the person's active receptive individuality receives it.

Even the God-consciousness we have and feel comes out of (even though it should not be deemed as a product of) the interior dialectic between our self-consciousness and world-consciousness. Chronologically, the first form of consciousness we possess during our beginning stages of life is akin to animal consciousness, in which a distinction between feeling and perception is not discerned. However, as one grows out of that stage the second level of consciousness emerges and thereby the self finds itself posited alongside and over against the Other. Consciousness, thus, evolves and grows out of the dialectic between self-consciousness and world-consciousness. The self understands itself to be part of the world, yet standing in relative contrast to the world, living in it and as a part of it, conscious of its helplessness if strictly alone and of the overwhelming influence of the world upon it and therefore in partial dependence, and contrariwise, also of the unique place it has in the world and the counter-influence it can and does exert upon the world, and therefore existing in partial freedom. Thus, self engages world in the process of growing in consciousness, and yet other stages of development lie before it.

The Consciousness of God

The two constituents of this reciprocal relation, namely, between the self and the non-self (Other) exist in a given state, depending on each other in such a way that together they can be counted as one Unit and can be called "World." Each singular unit of willing/doing centers, or consciousness-centers, within the World, exists in a state of partial freedom and partial dependence in relation to others in some cases and to the World in all cases, in ways such that the World itself ever exists in a corresponding dependent/freedom relationship to each singular willing unit, as to each combination or permutation. The result is that neither any singular unit within the World, nor any partial totality, nor the total totality of the World as such has any absolute freedom. "In any temporal existence, a feeling of absolute freedom can have no place."[14] Therefore, it necessarily follows that no center of influence capable of exerting its impression upon our consciousness in time and space, whether it is the

---

14. *Christian Faith*, §4.3, 16.

totality of existence or a part thereof, can be the object of our absolute dependence, because that center is susceptible to counter-influence.[15] Now, the very consciousness that we come to possess to the effect that absolute freedom is entirely denied either to me or any other willing center or to the entirety of the "World" is itself a consciousness of our absolute dependence. (Care should be taken to note that the logical or intellectual derivation of the consciousness of absolute dependence does not indicate that absolute dependence in itself is essentially knowledge or that its province is noetic; rather absolute dependence has its "being" within the province of feeling, and nowhere else; and what we have produced is only an intellectual abstraction from that actuality). The "whence" of our feeling of absolute dependence is (almost) anthropomorphically referred to as God, or it is to be conceived as a concrete modification of our feeling. Apart from such a modification, a noetic conception of our "feeling" would be an impossibility.

Thus, as individuals, as associations, as humanity, as World, each and all are equally, trans-temporally, trans-spatially, trans-conceptually, absolutely dependent. Evidently, the correlate of our absolute dependence cannot be called an "object," as that would then bring it into the realm of reciprocity. It cannot be called subject either, because as subject it could be subject only in that it would eliminate the realm of reciprocity or count the totality of *Naturzusammenhang* as unreal, rendering the World as illusion.

Schleiermacher, then, has distanced himself equally from pantheism, monism, deism or from the God of the cosmological argument, all of which are alike equally wanting to him.

It is also evident from the above discussion that consciousness of absolute dependence cannot develop apart from the consciousness of partial dependence and partial freedom that we experience always and everywhere; consciousness of absolute dependence (but not the trans-conscious feeling of absolute dependence as such) is a product of the dialectic between consciousness of partial freedom and partial dependence. Furthermore, because the individual exists as individual only in the

---

15. Anyone who is tempted to tell Schleiermacher that it is possible for God or an extra-terrestrial being to exert a natural influence on us without undergoing a counter-influence must be reminded of Schleiermacher's doctrine of *Naturzusammenhang,* which we have already noted in brief.

context of a community, whose language, conceptions and disposition that person is shaped by and shares, and because consciousness is always conceptual and linguistic, the consciousness of absolute dependence that emerges in that person comes as a distinctive modification mediated by the given community he or she belongs to.

Higher manifestations of religions (that is, monotheistic faiths) normally call the correlate or the "Whence" of this absolute dependence "God"; Christians ordinarily know it as "the God and Father of our Lord Jesus Christ." Each monotheistic community of faith recognizes this "Whence" of absolute dependence in a distinctive modification of its own. Therefore, inescapably, God-consciousness is in part a product of the interior dialectic between self-consciousness and world-consciousness. God-consciousness cannot be said to be present in a state of human life where the dialectic has not developed or is suspended after developing to this high level. Moreover, no one could reasonably say that the dialectic can be dispensed with in any conscious state of existence whatsoever.

Schleiermacher was always conscious of being an Evangelical theologian of a Reformed bent, and he was eager to be acknowledged as such, though not as the inheritor of a "frozen" set of doctrines to which he is bound but as a person who pricelessly valued his Calvinistic and Reformation heritage, the principles of which, as he understood them, he tirelessly defended. He also maintained that the Reformation has established a standard for a continuing process of refinement, revitalization and contextualization of every conceptual force. Therefore, assuming the responsibility of re-reading and reforming theological understanding in the light of the development of scientific knowledge is a protestant privilege in his eyes.[16] It is of no little importance that we should compare his conception of the consciousness of absolute dependence with Calvin's *sensus divinitais*. Calvin says: "Since, from the beginning of the world, there has been no region, no city, in short, no household, that could do without religion, there lies in this a tacit confession of a sense of deity inscribed in the hearts of all."[17] This sense of divinity has some source other than oneself; it is implanted in the human heart; it is equally evident that it is the one God, the one and only God, who implanted it. Atheistic arrogance, polytheism and any other religious modification that human

---

16. *On the Glaubenslehre*, 60–65.
17. John Calvin, *Institutes of the Christian Religion*, 1.3.1.

beings create out of this sense of divinity, is a perversion of this God-imprinted reality, and for Calvin culpability is attached to this distortion. Bearing a sense for divinity is something that is inextinguishable from within the human heart even if someone might wish to ignore it.

Edward A. Dowey Jr. makes the following observations:

> Clearly Calvin does not mean by the term a special organ of the soul, but a *sensus* which is a perception or a sensation, an *intelligentia numinis,* and elsewhere a *gustus divinitatis.* Nor does the term "religious a priori" seem an adequate description, because it implies something formal rather than material, and Calvin does not represent this as a formal possibility or a pre-condition of knowing God. This is already *notitia,* knowledge, and indeed religious knowledge. It is a material and existential concept describing an actual, vital knowing relationship of the human mind with God.[18]

Both "*sensus divinitatis*" and "the feeling of absolute dependence" have their source outside of us. For Calvin, God has implanted it in the human heart. For Schleiermacher, the feeling of absolute dependence has God as its cause; however, this causality is ultimately inexplicable, because any possible explanation will necessarily fall short in being anthropomorphic or will necessarily drag God's "action" down from God's realm to the level of contrasts, to the interconnected process of nature, even though it appears exactly there.

With *sensus divinitatis,* one does not need to nor does one have the chance even to ask the "whence" of it, because the content of what is ingrained upon the human heart is that God is, and is the one and only God. With the feeling of absolute dependence too, the effect is similar even though the approach is different. One comes to a feeling and consciousness of absolute dependence only from within the being and the collective experience of a living religious community with its own distinctive understanding of the "whence" of that feeling and the consciousness that flows from it.

Both *sensus divinitatis* and the feeling of absolute dependence are pre-reflective, though again in different ways. For Calvin, it is an innate consciousness, something of which "each of us is a master from his mother's womb." That is, when self-consciousness emerges in a person,

---

18. Dowey, *Knowledge of God in Calvin's Theology,* 50–51.

sensus divinitatis is evidently there as a consciousness by itself and holds fort in the inner sanctuary of the person's heart, throughout that person's conscious life. Likewise and yet differently, the feeling of absolute dependence, in Schleiermacher's thought, is pre-reflective just insofar as its province is precisely feeling, not intellect. Consciousness of this peculiar feeling arises within the individual only in the context of religious community at some stage of development and only with the emergence of actual conscious life-experience or the feeling of partial dependence and partial freedom in the mundane world. However, that which connects all the person's moments of life in its varied determinations so as to hold it all to a unity is this feeling of absolute dependence. In the light of what has been said above, it is difficult to hold that Schleiermacher is going to more of an elemental analysis of human religiosity than is Calvin, because each is going as deep as is allowable from within the approach each takes to the issue. Of major importance for understanding Schleiermacher's approach is his partial laying out of numerous stages of development in religious feeling and consciousness from a primary state of a certain feeling of dependence, for example, within the very limited scope of fetishism, to an all-encompassing feeling of absolute dependence that emerges and further develops among the monotheistic religions.

All along the spectrum, religion exists as an essential feature of human nature. Schleiermacher, however, takes a developmental approach such that an atheist (a Buddhist, Jainist, or a Spinozist) can be validly religious; in fact, to a certain extent all human beings are religious in their own respective determinations. Moreover, as is common with normal human experience in every sphere of life, in religion too there are levels or gradations of religious manifestations, Christian modification of monotheism being the highest, at least thus far. In considerable contrast, Calvin would say that all determinations of the sense of divinity are essentially manifestations of human sinful rebellion against God and are hence culpable; all modify it, modify it to divine condemnation.[19]

Calvin's *sensus divinitatis* is essentially and originally noetic; therefore it is focused and felt individually even though in concrete determinations the individual naturally may follow a pattern held in common with the community the individual communes with. The feeling of absolute dependence is not noetic, though a knowledge of what it points to would

19. Calvin, *Institutes of the Christian Religion*, 1.4.1.

occur when one reflects upon it; it is, for want of a better term, spiritual or religious; originally and essentially it is felt and not known except after the fact. It is concretely realized within the framework of the interconnected process of nature or *Naturzusammenhang;* even though the feeling center is individual, it is never focused individually; it is felt individually in the context of totality and totally in individuality and totally in the conditions of individuality.

Chronologically, for Calvin, it is from the identical noetic base that people diversify into determinate modifications, whereas for Schleiermacher it is from a determinate modification that people concretely merge into the unity of the feeling and associated consciousness of absolute dependence. On the whole, there are a few similarities of intent between Calvin and Schleiermacher, but the differences seem substantial.

Barth's repeated rejection of any possible analogy between God and humans[20] places him closer to Schleiermacher than, say, to some thinkers strongly influenced by Barth, especially when one considers the doctrine of God. Accordingly, in this respect, application of the nomenclature "neo-orthodoxy" to the Barthian revolution is a misnomer; efforts to baptize Barth into strict orthodoxy or into some minor modification of it is a misdirected design. Overall, Barth is more Schleiermacher's child than orthodoxy's. Both of them start with the Anselmian dictum of "faith seeking understanding"; both concede to the study of dogmatics inherent strength to stand on its own legs, and both reject any space for speculation within dogmatics. Both are Kant's disciples in that all three vigorously assert that directly to know God-in-Godself is an utterly unachievable agenda for us. Consequently, both Barth and Schleiermacher would have it that the formula of eternal distinctions within the Godhead should be reckoned useless. Both are equally trinitarian, but in their own distinctive ways. For Schleiermacher, Christian God-consciousness is of God as mediated by the Redeemer within the interconnected process of nature and is thereby a trinitarian God-consciousness. For Barth, the attempt must be made to place emphasis solely on the initiative of God, for true God-consciousness can come only from God. God relates to us by God's good pleasure, through an encroachment upon our territory by God's grace, all done in a trinitarian fashion.

20. Barth, *Church Dogmatics*, vol. 2, pt. 1, 75ff.

However, we should not fail to note the two major differences between Schleiermacher and Barth, one methodological and the other theological. First, due to Schleiermacher's constant insistence upon an eternal covenant between living faith and scientific enquiry[21] and due to his willingness to let the scientific dogmatic products of the community of faith be laid bare before others for open examination,[22] and also because of his missionary commitment and his allied willingness to use apologetics, chiefly in the *Speeches,* to gain a receptive audience for Christian faith, Schleiermacher is willing to explore and explicate the relevance and placement of dogmatics within the broad spectrum of scientific studies. Barth simply refuses to do this. Second, for Barth God's merciful invasion upon humanity through Christ is a gracious relating of Godself in three persons to humanity; whereas for Schleiermacher any reading of humanlike personality in God at any time is thought to be an unwarranted drawing of God into the realm of contrasts. God relates to persons in a personal manner but is not by this token a singular person or three persons.

The knowledge of God, for Schleiermacher, is in some way different from other kinds of knowledge; we know God in and through the world; the fullest manifestation of God is presented and perfected in nature, including that of human history. In the Editor's Introduction to the 1811 Notes of Schleiermacher's *Dialectic,* Terrence N. Tice states:

> We are stirred to sense or know God, he contends, only in and through the world (the *universum*). Thus "God" and "world," though not identical, are correlates; . . . and we cannot know God except under the condition of the world we have, including our own nature.[23]

God-knowledge is unique because God is unique. We do not possess God, we only possess God-consciousness due to God's relationship to us. An individual's God-knowledge is the knowledge of the effects of God's work in the individual mediated through the common experience of God that the individual shares within and through religious community. "No one, for example, can have the idea of God without knowing

---

21. *On the Glaubenslehre,* 64.
22. The Introduction of *Christian Faith* in full.
23. Tice, "Editor's Introduction," *Dialectic or, The Art of Doing Philosophy,* 5.

how this supreme entity can be impressed within a particular, how this supreme entity would relate to the world."[24]

God is not an object of knowledge; only God's relationship to us (or impact upon us and communion with us) is an object of knowledge. "We have no formula for the being of God in Himself as distinct from the being of God in the world."[25] We do get a glimpse of God through this relationship God effects with us; however, this glimpse cannot strictly be called either knowledge or ignorance. Any proclamation of God that is to be operative upon and within us can only express God in relation to us; and this is not an infra-human ignorance concerning God but the essence of human limitedness in relation to God.[26]

The Nature of Christian Consciousness of History

In Schleiermacher's view, the totality of history and the totality of nature are identical in scope. The former we view in a linear fashion and the latter usually in a lateral fashion. However, if we allow these two to meet at crosswires, at all moments and all points, then the totality of one is identical with the totality of the other. Because of their extensiveness, linearly or laterally, the totality of history and the totality of nature are both beyond the human capacity to reach. The interconnectedness of everything to everything else is to be affirmed, viewed from either a linear or a lateral angle.

The totality is extremely complex, thus any study of it should be a study of manageable parts. History, as a discipline of study, generally and always concerns itself with human history, the diverse relations that human beings have with one another and with the rest of the creation. Limited as we are, both temporally and locationally, even the totality of human history is such an unwieldy mass that the study of history can be practiced only perceptively; each unit worthy of a separate perspective will evince its own historical concerns and produce its own historians.

> Every historical mass may be viewed (a) on the hand as one indivisible being and doing in process of becoming, and (b) on the other hand as a compound of innumerable moments. Genuinely historical observation consists of both.

24. Ibid.
25. *Christian Faith*, §172.1, 748.
26. Ibid., §10. P.S., 52.

(a) The first is simply the characteristic spirit of the whole viewed as to its mobility and without a distinct separation of facts. (b) The other is simply the enumeration of its diverse states but without their being conjoined according to their identity of impulse. Historical observation consists in both ways of viewing: (a) the concentration of a congeries of facts into a single picture of their inner reality and (b) the representation of this inner reality in the separating out of these facts.[27]

History as a study is a predominately hermeneutical-critical discipline. Therein it is comprised of an interpretative analysis and presentation of the production and distribution of thoughts and ideas that have shaped the nature of the mass being studied as well as a facilitation for the creation of openings or avenues for the further development of thoughts and ideas and personalities for positive progress, ordinarily within the same mass. History as a chronicle of events is not of particular help.

> It is of interest only to a vain curiosity that wants to know what once was. This kind of history contains everything and nothing, it must contain everything because even the smallest detail fills time, and it contains nothing because it cannot definitely determine anything.[28]

History viewed simply as a cause and effect series would do more harm than good. One cannot separate the present from the past as if they were opposites, and one cannot detach certain parts from the present. Anticipation of future consequences and possibilities also become part and parcel of historical consciousness, in ways that place Schleiermacher squarely in league with the major American pragmatists. In particular:

> What one thus arbitrarily sets aside (from the whole) is then viewed as having been caused not by a similar single corresponding factor but by a part of all single factors of the recent past. What is characteristic of this view is therefore the tendency to attach small causes to great events and hence to consider historical results as accidental, because one has a wrong conception of what is necessary or inevitable.[29]

---

27. Schleiermacher, *Brief Outline*, §150, 78–79.

28. Quoted in Wilhelm Pauck, "Schleiermacher's Conception of History and Church History," 43, citation from Schleiermacher, *Sämmtliche Werke (SW)* I/11, 263.

29. Quoted in Pauck, 44, cited from *SW* I/11, 624.

As history, dogmatics is concerned with the mediate property of the Reign of God. Therefore, those who work in this discipline look at history from the point of view of the redemption effected by Jesus. For Schleiermacher, Christian theology overall is the systematic account of intellectual reflection on the Christian experience of the infinite in the finite realities of life. The infinite keeps continually entering into the finite with no temporal or spatial gaps left. In Christian consciousness, this continual entry is what keeps history together. Because of this entry, the past is present in the present as well as, in certain respects, the future in the past. This view is not intended to discount or stifle human originality and creativity, as on principle Schleiermacher can never do in any case, but what is produced should be seen only as an interpretation or clarification of the universal nexus of interrelation. The present is present in both the past and, perhaps with some alteration, in the future. Both "longitudinally" and "latitudinally" (temporally and spatially) the different points in the movement of the world are organically related in Christian consciousness. History before the coming of the Lord was a set of developments and preparation towards it; after that, it is all a journey towards the fulfillment of the teleology involved. Laterally, the Church is within the world, living against it in a relative engagement between the redeemed and the non-redeemed and especially between blessedness and sin, the former ever expanding, and all points of history are ordained to meet this movement.

Therefore, in Schleiermacher's thought history is organic. The dynamic of this organic nature finds its rationale in the distinctively Christian understanding of God and of divine causality, a conception in which the distinctive realities of the world and God are kept intact, even as the contrast between mundane causality and the divine causality, which are co-extensive in scope but different in nature, is maintained. The vitality of Christianity is present in its totality in every epoch, event and moment of Christian history; therefore determining moments, crucial breakthroughs and observable highlights of history are all equally related to the inner dynamic of Christianity, in such a way that the organic nature of its total relations may present itself ever more clearly before discerning minds. Undue importance should not be given to particular determining moments of history, because it is important that such pivotal points be understood as products of the total movement of the vital life of the totality presenting itself in unique conglomerations, time and again, out of inner necessity. Rather, such pivotal points should be used as hermeneutical tools to understand the vital life-flow of the totality through its richer and not so rich moments and the significance of the one in relation to the other. Accordingly, one will also not see undue glorification of great individuals in Schleiermacher's thought, even when he would not fail to mark certain great individualities in the Church who variously personify the highest religious interest and scientific interest in a fine balance, far beyond ordinary persons in terms of their possible influence on the Church. These individuals he terms "princes of the Church."[30] In spite of their creative genius and distinctive individual spirit, they must be thought of as the ingeniously effectuated flowering of the spirit of Christianity in their own distinctive way in distinctive times, fulfilling distinctive purposes.

The general condemnation of Schleiermacher as an unhistorical thinker[31] is chiefly based on a pervasive feeling among some critics that a certain absoluteness is attributed to Jesus, who happens to be an historical person. (The criticism that Schleiermacher is not willing to subject the story of Jesus as it is variously presented in the New Testament to historical criticism is so far off the mark as to have no inherent merit to it, in any case.) However, it should be pointed out that the supreme status attributed to Jesus is religious, and only religious; it is explicated solely with regard to His God-consciousness. This means that Jesus is seen to have embodied the ultimacy of God-consciousness, without any aberrations or gaps. What is of concern here is a spiritual aspect of reality, one that must not be confused with mundane history *per se*; religion is the realm of the eternal, though it is stirred and stimulated ever and always by the historical. From the perspective of Christian consciousness, Jesus' God-consciousness is the absolute maximum and therefore is the limit-point in Christian religious experience; however, Schleiermacher never puts a limit to the scientific possibilities or progress humans can achieve in historical existence.

Even the ultimate triumph of the Reign of God that Schleiermacher vigorously champions is a judgment call prompted by the prophetic instinct of the theologian. This judgment call is based on observable patterns in the movement of history, in the inner vitality of the mediating proper-

---

30. *Brief Outline*, §9, 5.
31. A very brief survey of this view is given in Wilhelm Pauck's essay, 41–43.

ties of the Reign of God; and these observations reflect a theologically informed perspective. However, one should not take this to mean that the hope of progressive actualization of God-consciousness in the world precludes the possibilities of patches of moral degeneration in history, or temporary triumph of evil over good, or a holocaust (not unthinkable for him, who knew of massive exclusions, persecutions and murderings of Jews). Even a global nuclear annihilation brought upon ourselves by some temporary insanity cannot be ruled out as if it were outside of the realm of possibility, though as a practical matter it would not have been thinkable in his time. As a rule, hindrances to life of any magnitude can occur any time, in personal, national or global life. Species do come into existence and species do go extinct in history, so Schleiermacher would not find any reason to make an exemption for the human species. We humans just simply do not have all the tools to calculate and predict the course of history as to how, when, where and what would happen. His perspective is simply that every effect happening anywhere anytime has sufficient cause behind it created by the totality of the past and the creativity of the present.

There is a tremendously significant passage in the fifth speech of *On Religion* regarding Schleiermacher's conception of history.

> Christianity—exalted above them all, more historically aware and humble for all its splendor—has expressly acknowledged this transitoriness of its own temporal existence. A time will come, it says, when there will be no longer any need of talk about a mediator but the Father will be all in all. But when will this be? I at least can only believe that it lies beyond all time.[32]

The end of history that is talked about is not the general end of history but the end of history from the perspective of mediating properties of the Reign of God. Moreover, even from this perspective, the end of history as it has been known, or the *telos* projected in Christian hope, is the point at which the Redeemer becomes irrelevant to that history, except in retrospect; it is an ideal stage wherein all living human beings at once reach absolute God-consciousness. However, insofar as absolute goodness is seen to be deposited only in Jesus, within the entirety of history, and therefore a total sinlessness due to His absolute God-consciousness is seen to be His possession alone, it may well also be as a result of the

---

32. *On Religion*, 319–20.

Christian faith (a judgment call from within the perspective of the faith) to suppose that no other person can ever reach that goal, not to speak of all humanity! These sorts of dialectic, or paradox even, are regular features of what Schleiermacher calls "prophetic doctrine."

Therefore, good and evil will always be mixed in life's experience as far as we can anticipate it. An absolute end is practically unreachable; the end of history can be envisaged only from certain perspectives. From a Christian perspective, this end would seem unlikely. An end of history considered from the framework of any perspective (even if that framework involves, in some way, the totality of our human stock) does not need to be considered as the end of total history unless the final end of humanity and the final end of the mediating property of that particular perspective are considered to be identical from a given perspective. We may be able to conceive a final consummation of the hope of a particular perspective, but the final end of the historical process, as such, is difficult for the mind to entertain as a thought or image due to the limitlessness of time also imaginable toward some future end of history.

2

The New Creation and the Old

WHAT I WILL BE ATTEMPTING IN THIS AND THE FOLLOWING CHAPTERS is my own reconstruction, from within my own time and place, of Schleiermacher's theological views, which, for him, is meant to be wholly reflective of the understanding he was seeking to attain of the Reformed faith (and the Lutheran also) in his own time and place, which itself, in turn, he always unconditionally placed under subjection to the Christ event as it is reconstructed in the New Testament and lived in Christian community. So, like all good history, this is self-consciously a reconstruction of a reconstruction of a reconstruction.

The Uniqueness of Christ in Christian Faith

The religious self-consciousness of the Christian acknowledges that Christ is the only person in history who is not in need of redemption, as there happens to be no actuality or consciousness of sin in Him. The God-consciousness manifested in Him remains constantly full and operatively total. He has brought about a higher form of life into creation, the original presence of which can be traced to Him and Him alone.[1] He is also unique in that this new life is present in Him in inviolable constancy and at maximal intensity. The assumption that this potency can be surpassed or even matched by any individual or community, be it even in the remotest future, would purport a stance that Christ can be passed and left behind. That would make Jesus comparable to one or more other redeemers, which, in effect, would shatter the bedrock on which Christian faith reposes. Christian faith knows nothing better or greater than an ever-deeper understanding of Christ[2]: ". . . the thought

1. *Christian Faith*, §108.6, 492–93.
2. Ibid., §93.2, 378.

either of a desire or of an ability to go beyond Christ marks the end of Christian faith."[3]

Schleiermacher calls the appearance of the Redeemer the miracle of all miracles.[4] This is an appearance in the realm of spiritual life "that we can only explain as a new creation, as the beginning of a higher development of spiritual life."[5]

> As everything which has been brought into human life through Christ is presented as a new creation, so Christ Himself is the Second Adam, the beginner and originator of this more perfect human life, or the completion of the creation of humanity. This at the same time indicates in the most definite way that it was impossible to attain to this higher life out of the natural order which had its beginning in Adam.[6]

Now, enquiry must be made as to what newness the advent of Jesus in human history has brought about.

The Originality of Christ

> In the corporate life of sinfulness sin propagates itself naturally, so that an unhindered potency of the God-consciousness in Jesus cannot be understood simply as a product of that life. This God-consciousness, manifesting itself in this potency, can have come into existence only outside the sinful corporate life. And since the whole human race is included in this sinful corporate life, we must believe that this God-consciousness had a supernatural origin. . . .[7]

"Supernatural" must not be taken to mean something of an absolutely extra-terrestrial intervention, lest it would suggest that Jesus was not at all human. What is common between Jesus and the rest of the world is His common humanity with everyone else; He is as human as anyone else is. This can be boldly affirmed because sin, the only thing that separates Jesus from everyone else, is not an essential component of humanity.

---

3. Ibid., 379.
4. *On the Glaubenslehre*, 64.
5. Ibid.
6. *Christian Faith*, §89.1, 367.
7. Ibid., §89.4, 365.

Rather, the miracle talked about here is a spiritual reality infused into creation through the person of Jesus, that "cannot be explained by the content of the human environment to which He belonged, but only by the universal source of spiritual life in virtue of a creative divine act in which, as an absolute maximum, the conception of a human being as the subject of God-consciousness comes to completion."[8]

The humanity of Jesus must have been capable of taking into itself whatever of a "supernatural" character that came about in Him historically.

> So that the idea that the divine revelation in Christ must in this respect be something absolutely supernatural will not simply stand the test . . . even if only the *possibility* of this resides in human nature, so that the actual implanting therein of the divine element must be purely a divine and therefore an eternal act, nevertheless the temporal appearance of this act in one particular person must at the same time be regarded as an action of human nature, grounded in its original constitution and prepared for by all its past history, and accordingly as the highest development of its spiritual power (even if we grant that we could never penetrate so deep into those innermost secrets of universal spiritual life as to be able to develop this general conviction into a definite perception).[9]

To explain it as an arbitrary divine act would require a view of God far too anthropopathic, one that moves beyond acceptability for Schleiermacher. Also it would be unscriptural, notably in view of Galatians 4:4, because, "the fullness of time" mentioned there is indicative of a convergence of various historical elements and circumstances as completed historical preparation toward the reception of the appearance of the Redeemer, something that would have been totally unnecessary had His appearance been a product of pure divine capriciousness.

Secondly, it should also be granted that Jesus must have been human enough to pass on the benefits of His unique endowment to the rest of humanity, or conversely the rest of humanity must have had sufficient competency to share the minimum required commonality with Jesus that His grace could impress upon their receptivity. Thirdly, the nature of the "uniqueness" distinctively present in Him must be thought of as

---

8. Ibid., §93.3, 381.
9. Ibid., §13.1, 64.

powerful enough to reach the whole of humanity, or else those who exist outside of the range of His strength will have to look for other redeemers, with the effect that one would have to concede the possibility of a plurality of redeemers.

Had Christ's dignity (person) been deemed such that we would concede the existence of the same in others, even if only in a microscopic measure whereas He possessed it in a super-eminent way, the result would have been disastrous to Christian faith, as then it would have had it that it was not Christ alone who completed the nature of human creation but that He had done it in collaboration with the other minor figures who had any measure of the said dignity. A corresponding assertion is in order with regard to Christ's activity (work) as well. Christian faith requires a categorical affirmation that Christ's dignity and activity are absolutely, exclusively present or produced in Him and are exclusively transferred from Him, that everything of similar nature found anywhere must be seen as invariably having originated in and proceeded from Him alone.

Ideality (instead of exemplariness) must be attributed to Him, for two reasons. To give meaning to "exemplariness" it would be necessary that one concede to the position that human beings are innately capable of imitating Christ, and that we are placed in relation to Him in such a way that He only needs to be imitated. So Christ's "exclusiveness" with regard to the power of transferring His God-consciousness would become superfluous. Insofar as we would admit the capacity for anyone to imitate Christ, we would compel the radical revision of the Church doctrine of the universal sinfulness of human nature. Secondly, if all that Christ brings is susceptible to imitation from within the framework of prevailing human conditions, then Christ has not introduced anything radically new to creation, and He cannot be registered as the second Adam. Then creation is not completed through Him. If ideality or perfection does not exist anywhere, creation remains incomplete.

> And this would be to assert less of humans than of other creatures—for it may be said of all more limited kinds of being that their concept is perfectly realized in the totality of individuals, which complete each other. But this cannot hold of a species which develops itself freely, if the perfection of an essential vital function posited in the concept be actually found

in no individual; for perfection cannot be obtained by adding together things that are imperfect.[10]

The dignity and activity (person and work) of Christ are so intertwined in Christian consciousness that a totally comprehensive treatment of one doctrine is bound to bring out the total comprehension of the other in its scope. However, as a practical matter, Schleiermacher discourages this way of doing Christology, because it "would involve at once both giving up the (traditional) language of the Church and making a comparison between our statements and other treatments of the doctrine more difficult."[11] One may also add that, given our inherent human limitations, an approach from two sides of the same issue would generally help a more comprehensive coverage than one from a single side.[12]

The Nature of the Old Creation

In order to ward off any possible misunderstanding, mention must be made at this point that the single-minded concern here, with regard to old or new creation, is theological reflection on Christian faith, and therefore the talk is just about religion alone and about no other aspect of human life (much as we do recognize that religion, for Schleiermacher, is an essential part of human nature, and hence anything that has to do with religion places concomitant consequences on all other aspects of life). By "old creation" is meant every religion other than Christianity and every self-consciousness or God-consciousness that evinces itself apart from Christianity or Christ's mediation. In other words, Christian

10. *Christian Faith*, §93.2, 379.
11. *Christian Faith*, §92.3, 375–76.
12. The treatment of this dignity-activity relation has an interesting *methodological* analogue in Schleiermacher's hermeneutics, namely in the grammatical and psychological approaches to the text. I am quoting from Karl Barth: For Schleiermacher, he says: "Understanding involves an integration of the two approaches, the grammatical and the psychological, an integration so close that a text cannot be understood psychologically unless it is also understood grammatically and vice versa. . . . The task of understanding is absolutely discharged when each method, pursued independently, leads to the same result as the other and thus renders the other superfluous, that is, encloses it, for example, by achieving a full psychological understanding of someone's words. This demands on the one side full knowledge of the language and on the other a full knowledge of the person. Since neither can be achieved, there will always be in practice an alternation between the two methods." See Karl Barth, *Theology of Schleiermacher*, 180.

self-consciousness is related to all other self-consciousness as new creation is related to old creation.

The old creation is envisaged the way it is only in view of and from the perspective of the new. Those who live outside of the new creation live in the old, in a state of sin. The consciousness of sin that comes out of the law (Rom 7:7) cannot truly be represented as a developed or a real consciousness because, on the one hand, the law can present only an imperfect picture of the truly good, and, on the other hand, it is bereft of any inherent spiritual capacity to help us overcome sin. "It is only from the absolute sinlessness and the perfect spiritual power of the Redeemer that we gain the full knowledge of sin."[13] Sin, in Christian theology, is explained as a derangement of human nature. This, however, can meaningfully be done only after postulating an original perfection for humanity, a postulation practically made possible only because of our awareness of the sinlessness and God-consciousness of Jesus.

The old creation, from the Christian point of view, is sin-tainted, both individually and institutionally in equal measure. Individuals, groups and generations are all organically related to each other in such a way that each single component is a miniature representation of the whole in a unique way.

> What appears as the congenital sinfulness of one generation is conditioned by the sinfulness of the previous one, and in turn conditions that of the later; and only in the whole series of forms thus assumed, as all connected with the progressive development of human beings, do we find the whole aspect of things denoted by the term "original sin." Moreover, the interconnexion of places and that of times condition each other and indicate dependence on each other. And every human being will readily testify that it is only in relation to the totality of things that either the idea of the sinfulness of individuals or one's own sense of sharing it becomes to the person certain and adequate. It is precisely in virtue of this connexion, in fact, that the individual is representative of the whole race in this regard, for the sinfulness of each points to the sinfulness of all alike in space and time and also goes to condition that totality both around each and after each.[14]

---

13. *Christian Faith*, §68.3, 279.
14. *Christian Faith*, §71.2, 288.

Since the old creation can be conceived as a distinct unity in relative contrast to the new creation, we must surmise that the different points or manifestations of the old are distanced from the new by a fairly even margin; this would be true in spite of the fact that certain religious manifestations, on the basis of phenomenological analysis of self-consciousness, are by comparison abundantly advanced as against certain other manifestations that are crude and primitive. Even the historical connection that Christianity has with Judaism does not change this fact.[15] "From the perspective of the peculiar essence of Christianity, the Jewish self-consciousness is no closer than is the pagan."[16] "Pagan" or non-pagan, all are equally in need of redemption, and identical is the path by which each and all traverse to appropriate the new.

Even the Old Testament is only an expression of the old creation, and therefore it too must be counted as redundant as far as the facts of the new creation are concerned; the use of Old Testament materials in the New Testament, in which portions of the former are proclaimed as

---

15. *Christian Faith*, §12.2, 61.

16. Pickle, "Schleiermacher on Judaism," 134. Schleiermacher's arguments for this position, if not followed closely, can lead to profound misreadings of it. Schleiermacher never claims that, developmentally speaking, the religious content or relationship to God in all Judaism or in all of the Old Testament is strictly on a par with that in all non-Christian Gentile religion (or "pagan" religion—the same word). He also never claims that any faith engendered among the Jewish people of "the Book" is valueless, including the "rabbinic" religion of "the law." Nor does his position lead him to either anti-Judaism or sociopolitical anti-Semitism. In fact, Schleiermacher was a champion of the then-unpopular view that complete and equal civil rights should be accorded the Jews, among whom he actually counted some of his very best, closest friends. What he disputed is any supposition that what God revealed in the perfect, ever consistent God-consciousness of Jesus was in itself presaged by what is contained in the Old Testament, as if at its very core Christianity was simply another stage of Judaism. In both thought and practice, Schleiermacher prized all that is genuinely religious, at all stages of consciousness, but he prized above all what lies at the heart of Christian faith and life, itself capable of further renewal and development in communion with God in Christ, always subject to the fundamental condition of "the redemption accomplished in Jesus of Nazareth," Jesus himself being both a Jew and a human being sent for the sake of all human beings. In this sense, for him Christianity is unique, distinctive, called to be truly and finally representative of the best God has in store for all human beings. At the same time, he reserved the right to be respectfully and lovingly critical, on theological grounds, of any so-called manifestation of Christianity, as of any other religious phenomenon, that falls short of that focal vision. Such activity was integral to his calling as a theologian of the Christian church. As an institution, what he called the visible church itself still has a long way to go in his view.

prophecies finding their fulfillment in the latter, is only an afterthought, that is, only a looking back, after the events in consideration had already happened as reported in the New Testament, and finding a point of contact (albeit artificial), for the sake of communication with the Jews. If one were to follow the hermeneutical practice adopted by the New Testament writers as this is present in their attempt to picture certain New Testament events as the fulfillment of Old Testament prophecies, it is equally viable and valid (or non-viable and non-valid) for someone to search and claim and find quotations from religious scriptures other than the Old Testament and to ascribe or attribute to them the same relation to the New Testament that one finds being attributed to relations between the Old and New Testament in classical or popular Christian theology. The passage from any non-Christian faith, not excepting even Judaism, to Christianity is a crossing over from one religion to another religion. (See Rom 2:11–12, 3:21–24, 2 Cor 5:16–17, Eph 2:13–18.) It cannot be said in any sense that Judaism carried the germ of Christianity such that by natural progress it would have developed into Christianity.

In Schleiermacher's judgment, each religion carries some validity where it holds sway; "each religion bears its own eternal necessity in itself, and every beginning of a religion is original."[17] However, from the Christian point of view, all other religious associations operate at a lower level; Jesus is the one "in Whom the creation of human nature, which up to this point had existed only in a provisional state, was perfected . . ."[18] Since all other religious communities are ordained to pass over into Christianity, and also since the stretch of the spiritual dimensions within this community's God-consciousness (as mediated by Jesus) is infinite, and since it will ever remain unsurpassable in history, not least because Christianity itself is open to further development, other religions are related to Christianity as imperfect to perfect.[19] There is no equation possible between what is in its essence perfect and what is imperfect; a collection of imperfect entities, combined in whichever conceivable permutation, can never lead to an edifice that can be called perfect, because such admixtures will inevitably bring over all their inbuilt flaws into the new combination. That being the case, it may not be too much to claim

---

17. Schleiermacher, *On Religion*, 305–6.
18. *Christian Faith*, §92.1, 374.
19. *Christian Faith*, §93.1, 377.

that there is an infinite (unbridgeable) qualitative difference between the old creation and the new.[20]

The Necessity of the New Creation

By "necessity," Schleiermacher does not mean that there is a natural compulsion from within the creation, say a law or a force, that required either an evolution or a supplanting. Since the point of reference here is spiritual life, and since the time frame of Christian theology is after the advent of Christ, a rational "necessity" of the new creation is only our interpretation of the pre-Christian (which means before the point of time at which the Christ-influence is felt on any individual or group any time any where) spiritual aspiration. We also see the issue as a divine compulsion insofar as divine causality is operative in it.

Human beings are rational creatures; life as a passive flow in an unknown current is unworthy of the genius of humanity. For life to be meaningful, human beings must know their aim and destination; there must be plans made and progress achieved as life goes on; we cannot be in an empty cycle and remain properly human.[21]

The "fullness of time" mentioned in Gal 4:4 passively testifies that the old creation, historically, had stretched out to almost its utmost potential before the coming of the Lord Jesus. Yet the imperfectness of the old order was evident before every eye with spiritual insight; wallowing in the same order deprived people of incentive to progress. On the other hand, a graduation from the old Adamic order to something better had been impossible due to the lack of inherent strength as well as the lack of the possibility of the perception of destination, the consciousness of which produced in humanity a sense of frustration of sorts and an eager expectation for something fuller.

Schleiermacher claims that a consciousness of a serious insufficiency to help people overcome sin can be discerned in almost all religions other

---

20. It may be useful to note here that Schleiermacher, unlike Barth, can never employ the expression "infinite qualitative difference" to depict the relation or gap between God and the creation, because that expression (comparative, that is) or such other ones can be used only when the relation that is thought to be defined is between two objects, and two objects with some commonality. God, for Schleiermacher, cannot be an object, nor can there be any commonality between God and creation, though God does reveal Godself, and does this only in and through the world.

21. Schleiermacher, *Life of Jesus*, 11–12.

than Christianity.[22] For temporary expiation of the problem, sacrifices, penances, purifications, mortifications and such are lavishly prescribed in different religions and in different forms; but these inevitably lead to frustrations. The idea that one can overcome sin by self-effort unfailingly creates newer miseries. The idea that misery will eventually disappear on its own is essentially an affront to God's attributes of holiness and justice; hence, new misery and guilt are formed in addition to the old. All that can be done is to admit the state of sin; given the existing fragmented God-consciousness, the removal of the misery of sin is impossible under those conditions.[23] When frustrated challenges and unfulfilled aspirations become an internal welling up in the universe of humanity that could not be contained without inflicting a critical stunting of the vitality of humanity, by a divine necessity as it were, the new creation ought to emerge. "Every unsatisfied longing which still remains . . . is the expression of an inclination towards Christianity; it indicates the likelihood that a Redeemer, in whom is offered not the shadow but the reality, will be accepted."[24]

The Nature of the New Creation

With regard to the creation of human nature, the new creation is a completion of the old creation. "As everything which has been brought into human life through Christ is presented as a new creation, so Christ Himself is the Second Adam, the beginner and originator of the creation of humankind."[25]

The emergence of the second Adam into the corporate life of humanity resulted in the interjection into the existing order of an absolutely powerful God-consciousness. He is both the embodiment of this power as well as its sole distributor to the world. Further, as this breaking forth became a reality in history, He became the property of the natural order and a permanent, resident reality in the world, and thus He subjected Himself and His influence to the laws of and vagaries of historical existence. The creation of humanity is thus understood to be divided into

---

22. *Christian Faith*, §86.1, 355.
23. Heb 10:1–3.
24. *Christian Faith*, §86.1, 356.
25. *Christian Faith*, §89.1, 367.

two stages.[26] Christ is the second Adam (or the second created one), and the corpus of those who appropriate His blessedness (or who are born again) and thus exist in communion with God through Him is called the new creation. New creation is a more comprehensive expression than the term redemption because while the latter strictly describes only a removal of the misery of sin, the former involves that plus the impartation of an originating and continuing blessedness to the recipients' life.

In God's scheme of things, the first creation was ordained only in view of the second; eternally the appearance of the Redeemer was already present in the first creation. In other words, the second creation was implicitly present in the first, or there was a groaning for the Redeemer, even if it existed only at a sub-conscious level or in half-concealed or shadowy forms and made its appearance only in isolated spurts in history, and that too only to minds with the keenest of insights. Nevertheless, it was present throughout the history of the old creation. (Here by old creation is meant all those places where the influence of Jesus is not reached whether it is before or after Jesus' actual historical appearance.)

> . . . in the ordaining view of God everything which belongs to the first period of the world must have a share in the relation to the Redeemer. At the same time it appears the more natural that this otherwise hidden relation should become specially evident at particular points, which is just the assumption that prompts a search for types and prophecies.[27]

There is an amazing similarity between St. Irenaeus' theory of recapitulation (his most conspicuous, distinctive and central Christological thought) and its corresponding portion in Schleiermacher's system of thought. Only, one should suspend, for a moment, their differences in understanding with regard to the mechanics of God's calling of the universe into existence and their differing perceptions with regard to the pre-existence of the second person of the Trinity. Creation and incarnation are always held together in Irenaeus' thought; if creation is the bringing into being of the whole Universe, incarnation is the restoration into wholesomeness of the fallen world, or the summing up of the old Adamic order in Jesus.

---

26. 2 Cor 5:17.
27. *Christian Faith*, §89.3, 369.

> . . . Adam . . . was formed by the hand of God, that is, by the Word of God . . . so did He who is the Word, recapitulating Adam in Himself. . . . But if the former was taken from the dust, and God was his maker, it was incumbent that the latter also, making a recapitulation in Himself, should be formed as man by God, to have an analogy with the former as respects His origin. Why, then, did not God again take dust, but wrought so that the formation should be made of Mary? It was that there might not be another formation called into being, nor any other which should [require to] be saved, but that the very same formation should be summed up [in Christ as had existed in Adam], the analogy having been thus preserved.[28]

For both theologians, God's creation of the first man Adam was an act affected only in consonance with the divine forethought of the second Adam. Christ existed in God's mind, prior to creation.[29] In fact, for Irenaeus, as much as for Schleiermacher, human beings, and, for that matter, creation itself, finds its significance and fulfillment only in relation to Christ. "*Avec Irénée, nous retrouvons la perspective universelle et cosmique; le Christ Jésus récapitule toute la creation et tout le genre humain, tous le ages et toutes les nations.*"[30]

Christ's recapitulating work is a continuing operation that will extend till the end of times, when He "has put all His enemies under His feet" (1 Cor 15:25). For Schleiermacher, the new creation, or the impulses that originated in Jesus and those continuing to proceed from Him, is destined to reach the farthest extent of space and time so that one day Jesus is to become all in all. For Irenaeus, ". . . through the birth of Christ, Creation returns to its purity, the original form of creation is revealed in its perfectly developed form and in Him life enters into the world of death."[31] Schleiermacher has it that the new creation

---

28. Irenaeus, *Against Heresies*, 3.21.10.

29. It is in order here to note that attribution of temporal categories to God is anthropomorphism for Schleiermacher; God is not to be thought of as being limited by temporality. Use of anthropomorphism is acceptable as long as we understand its limitation and do not insist on anything beyond what evidence we have available.

30. Fantino, *La théologie d'Irénée*, 241. Translation: "With Irenaeus, we come across the universal and cosmic perspective: Jesus Christ recapitulates the whole creation, the totality of the human species of all ages and of all times."

31. Wingren, *Man and the Incarnation*, 80.

inaugurates the original possibility of the triumph of the life of the divine Spirit over the life of sin and death.

Thus, for both these theologians, Christ brings something absolutely new to the world through the new creation. Though the two visions diverge in certain details, both do emphasize the cosmic significance of Jesus' emergence and the transformation of the world effected through the perfecting of creation. For Irenaeus, the scope of Christ's recapitulation is universal in the most intensive sense, such that the beginning inaugurated in the birth of Jesus is to culminate in the teleological omega point where ultimately every fiber of the creation is transformed to a glorified level. Schleiermacher's teleology is less ambitious in that the culminating point is not something that is counted as possibly achievable in time. The content of the transformation envisaged is also more modest; it is the reign of God in God-consciousness, in conformity to the likeness of Jesus, in the minds and hearts of all humanity. The ethical, sociological, scientific and other such benefits that would definitely accrue with this transformation are considered to be just a bonus or a fringe benefit of the process.

Just because Christ brings the "new creation" as something absolutely new into the universe, this does not give one the liberty to characterize the new creation as an organic unity over against the old. True, one can imagine a gathering of all the spiritual impulses that have originated and proceeded from Jesus and create a mental picture of its totality (existing both within the historical Church and outside of it) and call it a unity. However, the human beings that act as the substrata of all these traces of spiritual impulses are realized in, are related in multifarious ways to the totality of creation (the old and new), so that a practical isolation of the new creation to form an organic unity apart from that totality is deemed impossible. However, this is not to diminish the significance of the absolutely "new" that Jesus has introduced into the world. It is still active with respect to all the rest and is fully expected to be effective there to the end of time.

The new corporate life also comes into being with exceptional force and power of attraction. Just as a powerful magnet would attract iron filings around it to itself, creating simultaneously a magnetic power within those same attracted objects such that they are imbued with the strength required to attract their neighboring objects to make the reach and influence of the original magnet felt to the widest extent, so the new creation ever attracts objects and in the process expands; and the strength of the reach of Christ is universal in scope. Those objects that do not have magnetic properties or susceptibility to Christ are worked upon so that this susceptibility may be created in them as well.

The initial divine activity in Jesus is supernatural, but only in the following way. "His peculiar spiritual content, that is, cannot be explained by the content of the human environment to which He belonged but only by the universal source of spiritual life in virtue of a creative divine act in which, as an absolute maximum, the conception of the human being as the subject of God-consciousness comes to completion."[32] With the new creation emerging in and with Jesus, it becomes an established fact in the world of human beings and becomes natural. The absolute God-consciousness of Jesus is a "veritable existence of God in Him." Further, because of this He mediates all existence of God in the world. He bears with Him the whole new creation. This is Jesus' unique contribution to the world of human beings.

Now, in the past, the course of Christianity has itself been regularly and variously influenced or thought out in terms of non-Christian traditions, and this process continues today in various parts of the world. For a Christian of India, this process is inescapable. At this point I find it useful to lay out some allied thoughts of an Indian Christian leader who has lived in a different generation, namely Pandippedi Chenchiah (1886–1959).

Chenchiah's Thoughts of New Creation[33]

Chenchiah, though a man with keen insight and some original thinking, was at best an amateur theologian, or more properly, a critic of the

32. *Christian Faith*, §93.3, 381.

33. Pandippedi Chenchiah (1886–1959) possessed a fiercely independent disposition and a strikingly creative mind. Trained in philosophy and law, he rose to become the Chief Justice of the High Court of Pudukottai. His prominent Brahmin family got converted to Christianity when he was fifteen years of age. Dramatic though his conversion was, Chenchiah always retained his interest in the Hindu heritage and spirituality in which he had been nurtured through his formative years. He was not a systematic thinker; however, flashes of brilliance are evident in most of what he wrote. He was one of the most original thinkers who ever contributed anything to Indian Christian theology. He was the principal spokesman for that generation of unorthodox Christian intellectuals who were caught up in the nationalistic movement under the spell of Gandhi. His thoughts were expressed mainly in the form of responses to other thinkers or through

theological trends prevalent in India during his own time. Therefore, I will not attempt what would likely be an unfair comparison between him and Schleiermacher here. Providing a larger picture of Chenchiah's thought (which will inevitably draw attention to certain divergences on crucial issues between the two as well) is also not a concern here; rather, we will concentrate on Chenchiah's thoughts on "new creation" and see some things there that are strikingly similar to Schleiermacher's thought, which the former came to express free from any influence by the latter.

For Chenchiah, Christianity begins with Christ, and therefore it is Christology that should govern theology, and not the other way around. What is crucial to the Christian is the raw fact of Christ; dogmas, doctrines, worship, rituals, mysteries, and ceremonies only cloud this raw fact. "Viewed as a human effort directed towards a divine objective, Christianity is a religion on a par with other religions. Viewed as an outburst or inrush into history, Jesus is the manifestation of a new creative effort of God, in which the cosmic energy or *sakti* is the Holy Spirit, the new creation is Christ and the new life order, the Kingdom of God."[34] We have heard similar sounds from Schleiermacher.

Jesus is the *adi-purusha* or the first fruits of the new creation; He is the new man, He cannot be explained in terms of the Old Testament or Hinduism. Chenchiah substitutes the usual legal imagery used in Christian theology with biological imagery. "Christianity is not a juridical or a legal problem, but a problem in genetics."[35] Chenchiah also rejects the cross as the center of Christian message insofar as it reduces God to being a judge, and it distorts law by viewing the law as a command and human beings as criminals and Jesus as a sacrifice for propitiation or as a satisfaction for some other legal demand. Propitiation, as a concept, is utterly sub-Christian, in his view; it is unworthy of the genius of Jesus and of Christianity. Mythical representations such as these tend to be of Jewish origin and must be jettisoned in Christian theology.[36] Jesus is a

---

reviews of books, and came through periodicals of very limited reach. He was highly influenced by the philosophers Aurabindo and Henri Bergson.

34. Thangasami, *Theology of Chenchiah*, 172.

35. Job, ed., *Re-thinking Christianity in India Today*, 59. In this perspective, Chenchiah was no more anti-Judaic or anti-Semitic than was Schleiermacher, but he did also reject certain Jewish influences in Christian thought on historical-critical grounds.

36. Note the reasons given. These reasons are similar to those of Schleiermacher, though not so systematically worked out. Schleiermacher never rejected the cross, but he

new addition to creation; and being born as "son of man," his dignity and activity are destined to divert humanity into a higher level of existence. Jesus is the crown and culmination of creation. An interventionist theory of incarnation whereby Jesus is thought of as invading history for a few years and then going back after achieving a specific purpose, or restoring humanity to the original *status quo,* is no different from the Hindu theory of *avatara.* Rather, our portion in Christ is infinitely richer than that. A system of doctrines based on the concept of a Fall, "hardly had they commenced existence," and the recovery of lost ground through a tragedy on the cross, Chenchiah feels, appalls one's imagination.

Rather, the definitive moment for Christianity is the birth of Christ. Born of the Holy Spirit, He brings to the spiritual realm a transcendent order of existence. He is the new entity that stands between God and man; He is the "origin of the species of the sons of God."[37] He is permanently the son of God and the son of Man but not the hyphenated God-Man. Metaphysical oneness with God is an idea alien to the Bible. Reacting strongly against the noted comparativist Hendrick Kraemer, Chenchiah thus says:

> God is God. Man is man. The twain have met in Jesus: not only merely met, but fused and mingled into one. . . . This is the message of Christianity that the Word has become flesh and God has become man. Let there be no Barthian nervousness about it.[38]

Jesus is the proto-type of the new creation, the primogenitor, as it were, of a new species; He is the fulfillment of all earlier evolutions. Chenchiah believes along with Aurabindo that the time has come for an upward mobility for humankind. However, in his thought, unlike that of Teilhard de Chardin, this is not a biological necessity (the biological language used seems fairly certainly to be metaphorical); rather, mankind has to make a conscious effort to receive this "new cosmic creative energy." (This is not very different from Schleiermacher's thoughts on the propagation of the new creation in which the power of the Gospel preached should meet the

---

did not see it as the center or defining event of God's redemptive activity either. Rather, he viewed the cross as a culminating event in Jesus' life, all of which is redemptive. Thus, while he did not refuse to use traditional talk about the cross in the church, he wanted also to issue a corrective to much of that talk.

37. Note that, like almost everyone of his generation worldwide, Chenchiah tends not to be sensitive to gender exclusive language.

38. Job, ed., *Re-thinking Christianity in India,* 17.

required susceptibility in candidates for conversion to be affected.) For Chenchiah, individual conversion alone would not suffice as it would take an intolerably long period of time to take us to the next stage; there should be a communal conscientization. As this happens, the Kingdom of God becomes the new order, the next stage in cosmic evolution. "The Holy Spirit is the new cosmic energy; the Kingdom of God the new order; the children of God the new type that Christ has inaugurated. The Gospel is that God in Jesus has made a new creation."[39]

For both Schleiermacher and Chenchiah, Christ brings something absolutely new to creation; the old is related to the new as promise and fulfillment, because the first was provisional, the second is in itself perfect; the first was ordained only in view of the second, or rather, the second was already latent in the first. Or the new creation is the fulfillment of the old. Chenchiah would term the new as almost, as it were, a biological necessity growing out of the fruition of the old; Schleiermacher would rather term it as divine necessity, rather than anything else. Both take pride in presenting the elevation of creation into a new order as Christ's contribution to creation. Both try to deemphasize any isolated role of the cross in Christian theology and life. For both, the totality of Jesus' life is the concern of Christian theology, and therefore they condemn people's pre-occupation with the cross and any legal and judicial interpretation associated with it. Both have Christology regulating theology. Both reject the authority of the Old Testament. (For Chenchiah, the Hindu *sastras* would serve India better as an ante-chamber for the New Testament than the Old Testament would.) Both have it that Judaism is equally distanced from Christianity as "paganism" is. In fact, if a preference needs to be shown to any non-Christian religion, Chenchiah's choice is not Judaism but Hinduism, as he calls Hinduism the "final fruits of the old creation."

As it is for Chenchiah, for Schleiermacher too, from the viewpoint of Christian doctrine, God's work in history through Christ is this new creation inaugurated in Jesus with all its consequent creative effects.

---

39. Ibid., 57.

3

Christian Understanding of God's Work through the Being of the Redeemer

SCHLEIERMACHER'S DOGMATIC TREATMENT OF CHRISTOLOGY (THE DIGNITY and activity of Christ) follows the traditional trail of the division of the subject into the person and work of Christ. My principal concern in this chapter will be with the person of Christ, and with Christ's significance to history in Christian consciousness. At the very outset, may I make this claim, bold though it may sound, that in Schleiermacher's thought God's work in history is identical with God's work in Jesus! This is what is chiefly argued in the present study; and I believe the truth of it will become clear and evident as this account proceeds.

The Being of God in Jesus

Since Jesus is as human as any human being ever is, Jesus belongs to or is part of God's creation as much as any one else is. The environment into which He was brought into being, which in turn, nurtured Him, was not of such a nature that it could have accorded Him any advantage over other human beings; rather, His circumstances were unique to Him only in the same way as everyone else's circumstance is unique to him or her in his or her own way. Since sin is only a "disturbance of nature," the lack of it in Jesus must not be construed as a deprivation of anything essential from His humanity. Contrariwise, it should be seen as the attestation of His real humanity, or humanity in total purity. He was not provided any special insulation that others did not have against the invasive force of decay and deterioration stemming from evil and sinful surroundings; rather, the facts have it that He was cruelly consumed by the designs and poisoned passion of retrogressive forces in just 33 years' time, ultimately in His being sent to the cross. He was neither less than human nor more than human. He, the sinless human being, is the ideal human being, an ideality into which He wants to elevate the entire species. Since Jesus' ideality is the goal of humanity, and since He is also the truest human being, He is divinely commissioned to represent the whole world of human nature, hence the representative character of His humanity.

Into the ideality that Jesus had, a powerful God-consciousness is found imbued, the dynamics of the divine causality behind which are unfathomable to our puny finiteness. The power of this God-consciousness is absolute in depth and reach; thus, ". . . to ascribe to Christ an absolutely powerful God-consciousness, and to attribute to Him an existence of God in Him are exactly the same thing."[1] With the posting of this pivotal statement, Schleiermacher is parting company with the two-nature theory of orthodox Christology. This is Schleiermacher's explanation of the divinity of Jesus. The traditional view of incarnation will not fit into his system of thinking, mainly for two reasons. (1) He contends that the customary view requires God to be thought of as an entity alongside the world, regardless of the amount and intensity of effort put into explaining the difference between the nature of the being of the Creator and of the being of the creation. (2) The customary view demands distinctions within the Godhead, which Schleiermacher considers to be an intrusion into the sanctity of the simplicity of God. Any kind of intellectual gymnastics to mitigate the damage is ultimately defenseless and therefore useless.

Now we must explore the meaning of the word "divinity" in someone, which is the same as the expression "existence of God" in that person. Schleiermacher's treatment of the issue is given in certain saturated sentences in succinct style.[2] I will attempt to re-phrase and re-arrange them with a view to making it all easier to understand. (1) The existence of God in someone means the relation of the omnipresence of God to that person. (2) Where it exists, it does not exist as a person-to-person relation (that is, God as a person, descending to exist in a chosen human being) because a person to person relation always involves both influence and counter-influence. God is pure activity and can never be acted upon, or counter-influenced. (3) God is God of all, and therefore God's omni-

---

1. *Christian Faith*, §94.2, 387.
2. Ibid., 386–88.

presence that is in relation (i.e., one-way) to the creation (as existence of God) cannot be conceived as manifesting itself in a single piece among many pieces available within nature. That means, omnipresence cannot be bifurcated or distributed in pieces; it can be conceived only as in relation to the totality of nature to which it can be related as its ultimate cause. (4) Since it is the *relation* of God's omnipresence that is being talked about here, the object of the relation must contain within itself a vital receptivity to God's omnipresence. Therefore, insentient objects within nature are excluded as substrata for God's omnipresence. On the same account, even sub-human species are eliminated; we do not count them as being capable of any God-consciousness.[3] (5) Therefore, any God-consciousness is possible only in intelligent human beings. Considering what is said in items (3) and (4), the existence of God has to be thought of as the relation of God's omnipresence to the totality of humanity. (6) The vicious clutch of sin in every individual and individualized religious self-consciousness (leave aside Christ and Christian God-consciousness for a moment) results in this: that sensory[4] orientation dominates their God-consciousness. "If, then, it was able neither to portray God purely and with real adequacy in thought, not yet to exhibit itself as pure activity, it cannot be represented as an existence of God in us."[5] Sensory self-consciousness always forecloses the possibility of pure receptivity, God-consciousness is always patchy. (7) Our mental construction of a total collection of humanity also is not the stratum for "the existence of

---

3. An informative aside here: "Schleiermacher made extensive use of the romantic nature; for him as for Schelling, Coleridge and Emerson, nature was the language of God. But an important difference in the meaning of the word nature distinguishes Schleiermacher from the conventional romantic. For nature meant to him first and foremost human nature, so that it was the universe of human nature that spoke to him the language of God." R. Niebuhr, "Schleiermacher As Prophet," 11–12. Niebuhr's is an astute observation, and a very helpful one at that, but it needs to be balanced and corrected by the following comment from Tice: "This view does not imply, however, that Schleiermacher would have ignored the rest of nature; rather, the rest, however valuable in and of itself, is seen to be an accompaniment of God's relationship to human beings as such."

4. Tice indicates that "*sinnlich*" should be rendered in English as "sensory" and not as "sensuous" as it refers to sensations, which are directed to what is "organic," all of it mediated through the senses. Hence, Schleiermacher can assert both that sensation is essential to all experience and that, preeminently, God-consciousness is not dominated by (oriented to) it.

5. *Christian Faith*, §94.2, 387.

God," because this collection is only a corpus of imperfects; in this corpus we see only a small measure of patchy active receptivity in the corpus; passivity is the norm. (8) That being the case, if there has to be an "existence of God" in humanity, humanity, conceived of as generally sinful and in need of redemption, has to have a representative, an embodiment of ideal human nature, in whom there is absolutely no sin, and in whom there is active receptivity for God in an absolute manner, thus the possibility of redemption. In such a one, the relation of the omnipresence of God, for the sake of the whole of humanity, is possible. (9) Jesus, through His perfect humanity (and He being the only one who has ever had it or ever will have it, uniquely and once and for all), represents human nature in its perfection in Himself, with the capacity and willingness to represent its totality. (10) Jesus, through His perfect vital receptivity to God, and through His perfect God-consciousness, holds, in His person, the relation of the omnipresence of God for the sake of the whole of humanity. He is the vital representative of the whole of humanity by virtue of His being the only truly pure perfect human being. Pure God-consciousness is found in Him alone originally and proceeds from Him alone into the community that He established, which is the Church, visible (imperfectly) and invisible (perfectly). Through the church, this community, in turn, is to extend to the whole world. Therefore, from the perspective of Christian self-consciousness God's work in Jesus and God's work in the world are identical.[6] The existence of God for redemption is seen in Jesus alone. Or He is divine and He alone is divine: "if it is only through Him that the human God-consciousness becomes an existence of God in human nature, and only through the rational nature that the totality of finite powers can become an existence of God in the world, that in truth He alone mediates all existence of God in the world and all revelation of God through the world, insofar as He bears within Himself the whole new creation which contains and develops the potency of the God-consciousness."[7]

6. This proposition is in no way meant to be insensitive to Schleiermacher's understanding of God's creative, redemptive and reconciling work in the world before and outside the "visible Church" and apart from Jesus' presence or influence. Jesus, having made His appearance on earth at the "fullness of time," all history (past and future) are summed up in Him. Since the omnipresence of God in Christ is also eternal in nature, this "presence" involves, either actively or potentially, all people of all times. The matter will keep becoming clearer as our study proceeds.

7. *Christian Faith*, §94.2, 388.

"The existence of God" in a person (which is the same as divinity) is a technical expression used exclusively to indicate the absolute state of God-consciousness, which involves an absolute receptivity to God and an absolutely representative character within the same person. He is the Son of God (not God, the Absolute). Schleiermacher rejects the traditional understanding of Christ as the second person of the trinity, though indeed He is depicted as the central part of a Christian understanding of the triune God acting in history (thus, the structure of *Christian Faith* and his struggle toward a redefinition in the conclusion); one would not see any reference or allusion to worship of either Jesus or the Holy Spirit in his writing.[8] It is supposed that all human beings (apart from Jesus) have, in varying degrees, some partial, disfigured, misunderstood, and misinterpreted God-consciousness. Therefore, with extreme caution, the word "divinity" can be used in an adjectival fashion and never nominatively. "There is certainly something divine in humanity itself."[9] The use of the word "divine" here is far removed from the technical way in which orthodox tradition conceives the word; it is a broadly derivative sermonic usage, it is a preacher's privileged use. Further, it must also be noted that the word *göttliches*, in the sentence quoted above is better rendered as "of the divine," and not as "divine" as De Vries does it. Schleiermacher does not use even *die Gottheit* for Jesus, unless it is in the sense of being a carrier of the divine activity. For him, "divinity" denotes God's active

---

8. Terrence N. Tice affirms this. In a personal note he comments thus: "This is true. In a letter he (Schleiermacher) once strongly admonished his wife against encouraging Jesus-worship, saying that the authentic reference is always to God in Christ, to our communion with God in and through Christ (and he could easily have added: This is what we call the ongoing work of the Holy Spirit)."

One may find in Schleiermacher's sermons expressions that may mislead one to think there is endorsement for Jesus-worship. The word "worship," in the following quotation from a sermon preached by Schleiermacher, is used narrowly; it means only utmost respect and nothing more. "There are so many people in our day who dispute the worth of Christ and his teaching, who undervalue his high calling and divine propose, and who are moved to worship him by neither his teachings nor his blessings." Schleiermacher, "Christ Our Only Savior," in *Servant of the Word*, 28. This message, titled *Daß Christus allein unser Seligmacher ist, und wir keines andern zu warten haben*, was preached on the Third Sunday in Advent, 12 Dec. 1790, and not in 1789 as DeVries has it. See Tice, *Schleiermacher's Sermons*, 37c 2, 9.

9. Friedrich Schleiermacher, "The Redeemer: Both Human and Divine," in the same volume, 37. This sermon was preached on 25th Dec. 1810, on Phil 2:6–7, under the title, *Über die Vereinigung des menschlichen und göttlichen in dem Erlöser, wie sie uns seine erste Ankunft auf der Erde zur deutlichsten Anschauung bringt*. See Tice, 46.

presence in human consciousness. In the fullest sense, divinity as the presence of God in one's relationship to God is ascribed to Jesus alone, but in a secondary sense, it is attributed to Christians who possess a Jesus-mediated consciousness of God. In a tertiary sense, it is used for all human beings, for the sake of whatever consciousness of God they have, because the divine causality is active in history, and by virtue of God's being in communion with individuals and communities in Christ. It is not possible to say anything substantive about God except in relation to God's entering into the world and acting through the conditions of the world. In contrast, for Calvin divinity is God's Godness in Godself, *in se,* but it is also Godness that is relatable to creation, which we can sense and taste. Schleiermacher does not seem to use the expression "the existence of God" to denote an element of the God-consciousness of non-Christians, except insofar as the latter themselves enter into the divine economy of redemption. Properly speaking, "the existence of God" is in any case fully the "property" of Jesus alone. However, to the extent that we bring Christ in our thoughts to the consciousness of God that we possess, in a narrow sense, because of Christ's mediation, that very process becomes an existence of God in us. "He alone mediates all existence of God in the world and all revelation of God through the world insofar as he bears within Himself the whole new creation, which contains and develops the potency of God-consciousness."[10]

Obviously, the perfect humanity and the divinity of Jesus are not to be seen as two distinct pre-fabricated materials fused into one compound in His person. In fact, the perfect humanity and divinity are roughly identical in Jesus; they are only two aspects of thinking almost the same thing from two different angles. "The human and the divine within him are so interwoven that we can hardly distinguish them."[11] Where there is perfect humanity, there one is bound to find "the existence of God," moreover, in the very active sense implied in their being in an active relationship of communion. Historically, and by divine ordination, it is and will ever be found in its fullness only in Jesus Christ.

---

10. *Christian Faith,* §94.2, 388.
11. DeVries, *Servant of the Lord,* 38.

The Person-forming of Jesus

In viewing Jesus as the person in whom humanity is presented in perfection or completeness (*Vollkommenheit*) and therefore is inevitably considered as The Human Being in whom the whole of humanity is summed up, and as the person through whom is mediated the existence of God for all human beings in the world, both in synchrony, it is incumbent upon one who holds such a view to hold that Jesus must have had a human development like everyone else, subjected to the laws of time and movement. This condition mandates that the "existence of God" in Him also must have had a gradual development. Even when it is assumed that He had perfect consciousness of God at all stages of His life, it should go without contention that the perfectness in concern, at each of the various stages of His development, should have been commensurate with the contingent abilities belonging to that particular stage of His life. In His adult stage, it should have been perfect in the most mature sense, so that He could actively and comprehensively represent the totality of humanity and contain sufficient capacities with Him to communicate His spirituality to the uttermost regions of human existence.

The origination of any human being in this world is a unique act of a narrow circle and broad circle at the same time. The individual proceeds from the parents and the immediate society in which the family is placed. This narrow circle provides the person's horizon of thought structure, values and dispositions and religious orientation. Whatever depth or limitedness thereof, or constrictedness and distortions evinced in the particular orientation of the sub-culture, most usually form the specific confines of individuals who are products of the same sub-culture. Accordingly, living in that culture contributes to or creates in the person his or her sinful nature. On the other hand, since each individual is divinely apportioned to represent humanity in that individual's own unique way, it is also true that each individual is a fact of the broad circle of "human nature" in general.

However, there are times when we observe isolated cases wherein individuals surpass the frontiers prescribed by limitations of their culture or sub-culture and show signs of greatness in varying degrees. Some such people show these signs from birth itself, while others grow in time to the same effect. Mahatma Gandhi and Gautama Buddha are two of the better examples. Exactly to the tune of "the kind and degrees of gifts" by which these people exceed their family and descent, is the measure that must be attributed as the distinctive contribution of the second factor in their formation, namely the bigger circle of human nature in general. The how of ways in which these people's lives are embellished by these "excesses" against their immediate circle is not well known to us. So the more ordinarily gifted people are always a product of both their family and descent and human nature in general, the significance of the latter being commensurate with the additional degree in which their gifts stretch beyond the confines of the former. As far as Jesus is concerned, since He is absolutely free from all distortions and sins and parochialism, He can in no way be thought of as the product of the first factor; rather He must be counted as exclusively belonging to the second factor, namely human nature in general. In all essential respects He could be seen to be free from the disturbance of sin passed down from earlier generations that could disturb His constant consciousness of God, and as He developed to be protected by His "touch" with God in such a way that "He can be understood only as an original act of human nature, *i.e.* as an act of human nature as not affected by sin."[12] Until the instance of Jesus, human nature appeared lacking in the ability to be receptive to God in perfect God-consciousness. However, once God's actual implanting of conditions for such a receptivity realized in and after the birth of Jesus, Christians have rightly called the result the new creation, or "the completed creation of human nature." "The appearance of the first human being constituted at the same time the physical life of the human species; the appearance of the second Adam constituted for this nature a new spiritual life, which communicates and develops itself by spiritual fecundation."[13]

The beginnings in and through Jesus and the creation of the new consciousness of God are identical in origin (in terms of time, location and manner), such that each one includes and involves the other one *in toto* and that both are equally capable of explaining each other to the full. Secondly, the implanting of the consciousness of God and the implanting of conditions for its receptivity in human nature (as it is seen in Jesus) are also simultaneous and are capable of mutually explaining each other. Thirdly, just as the implanting of conditions for perfect consciousness of

12. *Christian Faith*, §94.3, 389.
13. Ibid.

God viewed as a fact of history is a harnessing of the spiritual potentiality latent within human nature, the receptivity to it too should be spoken of as harnessing that spiritual maturity which pertains to receptive ability, simultaneously and equally. The capability of the receptivity thus created in the human nature of Jesus for the perfect consciousness of God in Jesus is exactly equal to the task, not more and not less, whichever way we take the measure. Fourthly, saying that the receptivity to perfect God-consciousness as well as the real God-consciousness found in Jesus is an "original act of human nature" and saying that this is an original divine act amount to the same thing. "If the impartation of the Spirit to human nature which was made in the first Adam was insufficient, in that the spirit remained sunk in sensoriness and barely glanced forth clearly at moments as a presentiment of something better, and if the work of creation has only been completed through the second and equally original impartation to the Second Adam, yet both events go back to one undivided eternal divine decree and form, even in a higher sense, only one and the same natural system, though one unattainable by us."[14]

At this juncture, we may interject a few lines to grasp Schleiermacher's perspective with regard to use of the word "nature" in traditional Christology. In the broadest possible terms, "nature" is a universal. It is a matter of gross impropriety for anyone to attempt to bring the divine and the human under the same universal. No co-ordination between the divine and the human is possible without confusion. Not just that,

> If we say that there is in a person a divine and a human nature, then from each of these two points results must issue that cancel each other out. The human nature manifests itself everywhere as a definite, limited consciousness, but the divine nature excludes all that is limited.[15]

Secondly, whichever prevailing meaning of the word "nature" is adopted, division and relation are inescapably assumed in that word; activity and passivity are mixed. In contrast, God is pure activity; passivity is impossible in Him. Thirdly, although "nature" is a universal concept, awareness of it is supposed to be shared by some group or other: thus, this is what we find historically in many general concepts of nature alongside

---

14. *Christian Faith*, §94.3, 389. As earlier, "sensuousness" is changed to sensoriness (*Sinnlichkeit*).

15. Schleiermacher, *Life of Jesus*, 82.

whatever universal concept there may be. The individual belongs to the group by virtue of his or her participation in the "nature" that informs the group. Thus, "nature" limits the individual to his or her distinctive group and simultaneously posts him or her against those who do not share its particular characteristics. However, in Jesus' case, contrary to the use elsewhere, in traditional orthodox doctrine He is called upon to share two natures in Him. Fourthly, life cannot be considered as a unity when there are two natures present in one person. If Christ has only one will, then either His divine nature or His human nature is deprived of a will; hence, one of them, as per choice, is deficient. If it were to be assumed that He had two wills, either there should be conflict between the two or perfect harmony. The former cannot be the case anyway, but if the latter, then one will is always superfluous. Further, even if it is perfect harmony, the harmony can indicate only an agreement, and not unity. Fifthly, it is an equally untenable proposition to say that a divine will and a human will can think the same thoughts and be confined to the same range of noetic reach all the time. "How can a human will will the same thing as the divine will and yet remain a human will, and vice versa?"[16] Sixthly, if a doctrine of the trinity is brought into the picture, confusion increases. Because of Jesus' supposed existence anterior to incarnation, it must be surmised that He possessed His divine nature before He came into this world. If so, do the other two persons of the trinity have separate natures for each? Or is it a single nature that all three share? If the latter is the case, how can a human nature be added to that nature in the incarnation of one person of the trinity, even as the other two persons retain their estate undisturbed? If the former is the case, do we not have the curious scenario of a Godhead having three persons, in essence three divine natures and one human nature? Add to this the awkwardness of having to concede the appending of a human nature to God (that is, to the second person of the trinity), and patched in at a particular point of time at that, and the embarrassment is complete.

Schleiermacher laments that the Reformation did not do anything to clear up this mess; however, since the principle is already in place as his protestant privilege, effecting a doctrinal re-working, he holds, is a divine compulsion within him, geared to redeem dogmatic theology from the excrescences imposed upon it by pagan influences and

---

16. Ibid., 83.

scholastic theology. The Christology of his *Christian Faith* is the product of that compulsion.

The Union of Divinity and Humanity in Jesus

In dogmatics, the Christological formula should be defined in such a way that the existence of God in Jesus is kept intact, while His unity with us human beings is maintained in such a way that He is both the creator and the communicator of redemption. So, in Schleiermacher's revision: "The existence of God in the Redeemer is posited as the innermost fundamental power within Him, from which every activity proceeds and which holds every element together; everything human (in Him) forms only the organism for this fundamental power, and is related to it as the system which both receives and represents it, just as in us all other powers are related to the intelligence."[17]

So, all thoughts, big or small, that occur in Jesus can occur within and only within the structure of His constant consciousness of God (or the divine in Him); and all activities that proceed from Him to so absolutely from the context of the existence of God in Him. This is the rationale that enables us to say that God became human in Jesus, which only means that Godliness in its perfect form became real in flesh and blood in Jesus. Every moment of the Redeemer, viewed in isolation or in unity with the rest, springs out of the divine in Him; and therefore, at every moment of His life He is the incarnation of pristine divineness or Godliness. Every isolated moment of the life of Jesus is a new or unique coming into being of this specific personal existence. Similarly, every activity of Jesus is a new or unique impulse springing from the divine in Him. Alternatively, every activity as well as every moment of Jesus is an equally individual manifestation of the union of the human and the divine.

Christian dogmatics is Trinitarian, but that conception should not be confused with orthodox doctrines of trinity; in fact, the latter should be kept out of all Christological formulations altogether. This is a viable proposition if for no other reason than that the original faith-producing impression Jesus made on the disciples, which they also reduced to thought and expression, was all done apart from any knowledge or thought of a trinity. If one were to insist on conceiving Jesus as the second person of a three-person trinity, the following would be the consequence.

17. *Christian Faith*, §96.3, 397.

Jesus' human nature, then, "... in this way can become a Person only in the sense in which this is true of a Person in the Trinity, so that we are confronted with the dilemma, that either the three Persons must, like human persons, be individuals existing independently by themselves, or Christ as a human being was not such an independent individual—an assertion which gives us a completely docetic picture of Him."[18]

Because we accord a real human nature to Jesus, it goes without saying that He possessed all essentials that are common to all human beings, or that constitute a human being. His organism formed and developed in the way that is common to all. As noted earlier, for Schleiermacher divinity with respect to Jesus the Christ is the same as the relation of God's omnipresence in Him or the existence of God in Him. So obviously, in thinking of the divine-human unity of Jesus, we are not entertaining any notion of divinity as something material being added to humanity, either at the origin of Jesus' life or at any subsequent point thereafter. Divine-humanity is humanity in real life at its spiritual fullness or perfection. While the human nature in Jesus is active in its own realm, with regard to the divinity or "the existence of God" in Jesus, it must be indicated that insofar as it is an activity of God in relationship, and insofar as God is not subject to a counter-influence, it is exclusively a non-causative or non-mundane act of God, it is an eternally operated conditioning for the action of receptivity for divineness within human nature. The presence of God in any person is directly proportional to the person's experience of receptivity to it, and *vice-versa* because those two things are mutually

---

18. *Christian Faith*, §97.2, 399–400. Schleiermacher's argument is terse. So, a few lines of elaboration here may not be out of place. If the trinity is composed of three persons, and if one person out of the three could be separated to assume a human nature, such that that person could walk on earth as a human being, regardless of the nature of their essence or unity, it is conceivable for us that the other two persons of the trinity too are capable of incarnating. Now, for the sake of developing the argument, think of a scenario where all the three persons incarnate at the same time and walk on earth as human beings. To be reckoned as legitimate human beings, that is, non-docetic, the three must be related to each other with an integrity in similar fashion to the relation between three human beings, albeit in an ideal way and without sin. However, on the other hand, the relation between these three incarnate persons must be identical to the relation between the same three persons in their pre-incarnate estate. These two can be reconciled only by saying that the relation between the three persons in the trinity is the same as the relation between three distinct human beings in ideal, sinless settings. Therefore, by dragging the second person of the trinity down to earth in Jesus, we have roughly infused into the Godhead an anthropomorphical three-person communion/distinction. The only way out of this tight corner is to think of Christ in docetic terms, but then that is heretical!

complementary. However, this does not mean that our "receptivity" is a power that is forceful enough to drag the divine down into us. Rather, in God's acting for and toward us, receptivity is awakened; this activity itself is totally God's, it is done according to the divine good pleasure. Jesus' absolute receptivity, viewed as a type of activity that takes place in a relationship of communion, is complemented by God's relation of omnipresence in Him.

The nature of the divine in union with the human in Jesus should be further clarified by two more explanations.[19] Jesus must not be thought of as a human person who is taken up by some external or supernatural force beyond Himself; the thoughts that are instanced in Him are not thoughts belonging to a person called God; they are Jesus' own thoughts as a human being. The divine in Him persists in that as His moments are filled and thoughts are produced in such a way that they occur in His sinless consciousness of God; everything that governs Him and everything that proceeds from Him are from within the nature, power, and ease provided for in this distinctive state. To put it all in different words, we say that Jesus' perfect sinless God-consciousness is, in crux, God's work in history.

The second matter to be clarified is with regard to the nature of *God's work* in history/in Jesus. God's activity in manifesting itself as a concrete dynamic at a destined moment in history cannot be construed as conflicting with Schleiermacher's original dictum that God cannot be dragged into the temporal medium, though God does work in and through it. As God's activity, this is a sovereign eternal activity; since it is intended for us who are finite beings bound in temporality, this eternal activity appears and has to appear in time. The divine causality for this eternal activity is identical with the divine causality for the totality of creation.[20] Jesus' life, being representative in character (perfect human

---

19. In spite of his strong dislike for many terms and frames of reference that traditional Christian theology uses, Schleiermacher, once he has made known his displeasure, retains them in his work, and tries to pack his thoughts into those same receptacles. He does this for several reasons: (1) the convenience of using already existing terms and frames of reference; (2) the difficulty of securing acceptance within the Church for new categories, if those were ever created; (3) the strong sense in him to be part of an ongoing tradition of religious thinking; (4) his desire to compare his thoughts with the products of other theological thinkers in the Church; (5) his desire to interpret or re-interpret the standing creeds of Christian faith.

20. This is an issue that will be dealt with in detail later.

nature, to represent all humanity for receptivity to the divine, and the divine presence, to represent the totality of creation by holding within Himself God-consciousness on behalf of all human beings), the nature of God's eternal activity is interpreted in, by and through His life, for us to appreciate and appropriate. The union of the divine and the human in Jesus is an eternal union. Based on our explanation, it is crystal clear that there is no historical pre-existence of either the divine or the human in the nature of Jesus before it happened historically in the land of Palestine. The divine in Him could not have existed apart from the human or vice-versa; Jesus is an original act of human nature as well as an original act of God. In anthropomorphic language, we can just say that Jesus always existed in the "mind" of God eternally. In Jesus, the eternal work of God comes to take shape in flesh and blood.

Because Jesus' existence, prior to incarnation, is excluded, the credit for the birth of Jesus as sinless and as wholly God-conscious does not belong to Jesus. Since Jesus was born at the "fullness of time," it can be said that when nature's (i.e., humanity's) receptivity was ripe for the Redeemer, the divine decree concerning the coming of the Redeemer became a concrete reality. From the beginning of Jesus' life (stage by stage), He was sinless and fully, adequately God-conscious to the extent that His human development would allow. If we do not concede this point, we will have to struggle with two problems that will destroy Christian faith. (1) If it were the case that Jesus was conscious of His sinfulness[21] at any time, Jesus would not

---

21. At this point, it is imperative for me to fast-forward the beginning student of Schleiermacher to chapter VI, where I deal with Schleiermacher's doctrine of sin. Briefly explained, "sin" is neither the transgression of the known will of God, nor anything in near relation to it. A system of doctrines articulating the ethos of a religion based on a strictly commanding Will of God can at best represent a non-Christian teleological religion such as is to be found in some rabbinic Judaism (see *Christian Faith*, §9.1–2, 39–44). Since, in Christian religion, everything within nature is so viewed as to have been or shaped and conditioned, to facilitate the furtherance of the Reign of God, and therefore, since all helps and hindrances to life alike are thought to be capable of producing religious emotions, a view of "sin" as causing emotional hurt or offense to the Deity, which would result in a divine chastisement or even an exclusion of the offending party from the program of the Reign of God, is not worthy of theological genius in a perfectly teleological religion like Christianity. In Schleiermacher's theology, then, sin is explained only within the view of the Christian doctrine of the Reign of God, or sin is always viewed in relation to grace; one has no meaning without the other. Sin is that stage from which we rise to the estate of redemption by God's grace poured out through Jesus. Therefore, "sinlessness," as attributed to Jesus, always means that Jesus, by birth and through the course of life, was never in a state so as to require redemption for Himself;

have been an original creation of human nature; no new creation. We would have definitely had to look for a Redeemer for Him, at least within that stage of His life wherein He was sinful. (2) This stance would also give us an impression that from a state of sinfulness and less perfect God-consciousness, one can grow his way to full God-consciousness, as Jesus did, which would picture a Redeemer as either unnecessary or as an optional extra, and that would destroy the uniqueness of Jesus in Christian faith and therefore the Christian faith itself.

Therefore, the union of divinity and humanity is to be seen as occurring in Jesus already at the point of the beginning of His existence, the humanity par excellence being the work of and within the totality of human nature, and the divinity par excellence being the work of God, all consequent to the divine decree pertaining to redemption.

Keshub Chunder Sen's View of the Person of Christ[22]

Like Schleiermacher, Sen totally rejects any metaphysical or hypostatic union between Jesus and God. For Sen, Jesus' statement "I and my Father are one" indicates a mystical union between the Father and Son, following Jesus' *kenosis*. The sense of this statement is just this: As and when Jesus totally emptied Himself, God filled that void with Divinity such that the total being in Him was Divine. Or insofar as Jesus' self-abnegation was total, the filling of the Divinity in Him was such that no trace of anything non-Divine remained in Him. Thus it is that Jesus became the "transparent medium" through which we see God.

He is the embodiment of God's grace, the state into which He is commissioned by God, to draw all humanity.

22. Keshub Chunder Sen (1838–1884), arguably the most brilliant Indian thinker of his time, was a third generation leader of renascent Hinduism, a movement that originated and flourished in Kolkatta and irrevocably transformed the face of Hinduism, at least among the intelligentsia of India. Even though he never became a Christian, he was a trendsetter in Indian Christian theology. Of all the outstanding Hindu personalities that came under the spell of Christ, Sen came closest to receiving Christ. Boyd says: "he is the pattern of the Hindu seeker, of one who has found the pearl of great price but is reluctant to sell all that he has in order to buy it." However, some of Sen's disciples did become Christians later. The notable Church leader M. M. Thomas, along with others, maintains that Sen led India and Hinduism in general to a certain degree of discipleship to Christ. Thomas also shows how many of the "original seminal ideas" Sen produced were utilized and developed by Indian Christian theology in the later years. Sen was an independent and original thinker.

> There is Christ before us as a transparent crystal reservoir in which are the waters of divine life. There is no opaque self to obscure our vision. The medium is transparent, and we clearly see through Christ the God of truth and holiness dwelling in him.[23]

For Sen, complete self-surrender, or perfect asceticism, is the best that a human being can do, the highest he/she can go. This is what is evinced in Christ; this is the greatest miracle possible in history; this is the uttermost limit that human mind can conceive with regard to human spiritual progress. Therefore, Jesus' having reached there, he remains the transparent medium in which God dwells, and it is all for the sake of humanity. This is the doctrine of the Divine Humanity of Christ.

Jesus said: "Before Abraham was, I am." Or Christ pre-existed as

> an Idea, as a plan of life, as a pre-determined dispensation yet to be realized, as purity of character, not concrete but abstract, as light not yet manifested. . . . In fact Christ was nothing but a manifestation on earth, in human form, of certain ideas and sentiments which lay before in the God-head. . . .
> Thus it is that Christ existed in God before he was created. There is an uncreated Christ as also the created Christ, the idea of the son and the incarnate son drawing all his vitality and inspiration from the Father. This is the true doctrine of incarnation. Take away from Christ all that is divine, all that is God's, no Christ remains.[24]

Just as Jesus appeared in the fullness of time, it is also to be expected that in the fullness of time India will turn to Christ, he claims. That time has almost come in Sen's view, and it is thus in India's interest that Indians cease to be inimical to Christ. Inasmuch as Christ is the "light that lights every man that comes into the world," the Indians have, unconsciously at least, come under the spell of Christ. Jesus Christ is the Man for others. However, it should also be noted here that in Sen's thinking, it is not the name or the person of Christ that matters but the principles of the "spirit of truth and filial devotion and self-sacrifice." Where these principles are operative, there Christ is.

---

23. Quoted by Boyd, *Introduction to Indian Christian Theology*, 29, from *Lecture* I, 373: Lecture on *India asks: Who is Christ?* (1879).

24. Quoted by M. M. Thomas, *Acknowledged Christ*, 62, from Parekh, *Bramarshi Keshub Chunder Sen*, 99–100.

Scientifically investigated, the doctrine of resurrection may be untenable! However, it does point to one thing, namely, the continuing Humanity of Jesus. Jesus is man first and foremost. Because Divinity dwells in him, his Humanity is perfect. Sen, like Schleiermacher, attributes divinity to Christ but no Deity. To him, Jesus is a product of the spiritual evolution of humankind. Though not in an identical way, Sen's view looks quite close to Schleiermacher's when he teaches that creation is not an instantaneous act, it is an act of the Logos, a continuing process; and it is this continuing evolution of the Logos, superintended and affected by God that climaxes in the emergence of the Divine Humanity of Jesus.

> The New Testament commenced with the birth of the Son of God. The Logos was the beginning of creation and its perfection too was the Logos, the culmination of humanity in the Divine Son. We have arrived at the last link in the series of created organism. The last expression Divinity is Divine Humanity. Having exhibited itself in endless varieties of progressive existence the primary creative force at last took the form of the Son in Christ Jesus.[25]

Christ, for Sen, is universal; He belongs to the East and the West. Unfortunately, he feels, popular western theology propagates a cultic Christ, a "little" Christ, whereas Christ, as reason, love and power, actually exists everywhere, even where the historical Christ's influence has not reached yet. Given this feeling, Sen tried to form an eclectic Church or a Christ-centered harmony of religions formed into what he called The Church of the New Dispensation.

Sen describes himself as a Uni-Trinitarian.[26] Since he refuses to allow essential Deity to the Son and the Holy Spirit, the Trinity he proposes is a functional one, based on the principles of creation and salvation.

> The apex is the very God Jehovah, the Supreme Brahma of the Vedas. Alone, in His own eternal glory He dwells. From Him comes down the Son, in a direct line, an emanation from Divinity. Thus God descends and touches one end of the base of humanity; then running all along the base permeates the world and then

---

25. Keshub Chunder Sen, "That Marvelous Mystery—The Trinity," in *Lectures*, 2:14.

26. Before and during Sen's time, British Unitarians had a substantial influence in Kolkatta.

by the power of the Holy Ghost drags up regenerated humanity to Himself. Divinity coming down to Humanity is the Son; Divinity carrying up humanity to heaven is the Holy Ghost.[27]

Noting a stunning similarity between this view of Trinity and Tillich's is in order here. Tillich says there are two ways to draw trinitarian lines in theology. "The experience of the living God and the experience of the saving God gives rise to the Trinitarian idea."[28] Tillich criticizes Schleiermacher for not using the first option; Tillich believes that without first developing the first option, the second option will become almost useless. "In being bound to the single event it easily becomes superstitious; in being related only to the historical Jesus it becomes only something to be observed."[29]

> The living God is always the Trinitarian God, even before Christology is possible, before the Christ has appeared. He who speaks of the living God is Trinitarian even though he calls himself Unitarian. . . . He (living God) is not a dead oneness in himself, a dead identity, but he goes out and returns. This defines the process of life everywhere. If we apply this symbolically to God, we are involved in Trinitarian thinking. The numbers two or three or four—all of them appear in the history of Christian theology—are not decisive. But the movement of the divine, going out and returning to himself—this is decisive if we speak of a living God.[30]

This is practically identical with Sen's thinking. But one observation needs to be made here. If Tillich makes a methodological bifurcation between living God and saving God, Sen and Schleiermacher will have counted these two identical, at all points of time, in the construction of theology—with the methodological difference that while, for Sen, the saving God is always subsumed in the living God, for Schleiermacher it happens in the reverse order. However, if we are allowed to gloss over

---

27. Sen, *Lectures*, 16.

28. Tillich, *Perspectives*, 113.

29. Ibid., 112. However, with all respect to Tillich's greatness, I must disagree with him in this assessment; I feel that Tillich's criticism smacks of a certain insensitiveness to Schleiermacher's dogmatic method; in Christian theology, the saving God has priority over the living God; and once the saving God is studied, the living God becomes redundant; they are the same.

30. Ibid.

this particular difference, the flow of the Trinitarian thinking of the three theologians looks the same.

Both Schleiermacher and Sen affirm Jesus to be fully human, neither less nor more. Both of them equally affirm the divinity of Christ (over against Deity); for Schleiermacher, divinity is the relation of God's omnipresence to Jesus, or the existence of God in Him, or full and adequate consciousness of God, while, for Sen, it is the Godly filling of the void created in Jesus' absolute self-emptying and self-abnegation. The major difference between the two in this area is that while Sen's "self-abnegation" is pictured as Jesus' own effort, in Schleiermacher's thinking, Jesus' humanity is a product of the "original work" of nature and His divinity is totally God's work. Attribution of "divinity" does not indicate the worship-worthiness of Jesus, for either thinker.[31] For Sen, Jesus is just a prophet alongside of Moses, Mohammed, and others, the distinction being that He is the greatest of all. In contrast, Schleiermacher will have it that Jesus is infinitely superior to everyone else in that He is the communicator of perfect God-consciousness and is the Redeemer to everyone else. For Sen, Jesus is a product of the steady evolution of humanity; Jesus is a stage in that evolution, may even be the highest stage that man can ever achieve. He is still only a model, or the highest gradient into which any human can graduate. Even a remote trace of the Christian doctrine of "sin" is absent in Sen's thinking. True to his Hindu heritage, it is also the case that Sen is not worried about the historicity of Jesus; it is not the person of Christ that matters, it is the principle that is important; whether a person like Jesus ever lived is a matter of indifference. For Schleiermacher, however, we saw that apart from the personal historical life of Jesus, Christianity has no existence. Chenchiah illustrates the difference between Jesus and others by saying that Jesus is to us as we are to animals. Schleiermacher cannot use such a crude illustration, but with adequate qualification he can go with the spirit of what Chenchiah says: "As life is to matter, and soul is to life, so is Jesus to man."[32] (Here "life" is equated with animal life and "soul" with human life.)

So, if, for Sen, Jesus is just one link in the chain of evolution, be it the loftiest, and for Chenchiah Jesus is infinitely superior to other human

---

31. Sen does have reference to Jesus-worship; however, the meaning of "worship" is limited only to paying obeisance. In no way does this reference serve as a promotion of a Christian type of worship.

32. Thangasamy, *Theology of Chenchiah*, 116.

beings, similar to what man is in contrast to animals (Jesus' difference being not a product of aimless evolution but God's creative work, though actuated through an evolution), for Schleiermacher Jesus is the person in whom the omnipresence of God is related for the sake and salvation of the whole world, in whom the existence of God is such that Jesus represents the whole world and mediates the presence of God to the whole world, so that it can be said that God's work in Him is identical to God's work in the whole world.

4

Christian Understanding of God's Work in History through the Activity of the Redeemer

IN SCHLEIERMACHER'S VIEW, BECAUSE THE BEING OF THE REDEEMER is representative in nature and function, the activity of the Redeemer too must essentially evince the same character. Because the being of the Redeemer is God's being or presence in the midst of humanity, the activity of the Redeemer too must essentially be God's activity in the midst of and for the sake of humanity.

The Interrelatedness of the Being and Activity of the Redeemer

The practical relation between Jesus' being and activity is that each one exists totally and exclusively for the other and it cannot be otherwise. Just as one finds a symbiotic relation between the divinity of Jesus and His humanity, each existing independently of the other but mutually conditioned by each other, and totally existing for each other, one may also find a similar mutuality, albeit in a different way, between the being and the activity of Jesus. The slighting of one (or exaggeration thereof) must simultaneously affect the other one to the exact same measure in the same direction. There is no "excess" of the being of God in Jesus that His activity does not require; neither is there any activity in and from Jesus, or required of Jesus, that does not or cannot flow from the power of His human nature and the being of God in Him. Jesus is seen as a singular person, with singular endowment on a singular vocation, doing (and being) everything possible within His powers toward the fulfillment of His calling, for which He is entirely adequate, not more and not less.

We have already noted that Jesus is the original creation and the perfect specimen of human nature. In him converges absolutely all the multifarious facets of the ideality of humanity. It will be helpful to recall, at this point, Schleiermacher's highest intuition at Landsberg (mentioned earlier) that each human being is formed and placed to represent humanity in his/her own unique way. It is obvious from this perspective that, regardless of our sinfulness and imperfection in every conceivable way, no person is an island unto oneself but that in God's world each one is for all and all are for each one; that is, we are all singularly created, uniquely useful and vitally important members of the same organism. It is into this compact structure that Jesus comes as its peculiarly "original work," or as the crown of its creation. Therefore, Jesus, in a supereminent way, is The Man for others. We must also understand that since His humanity is creationally so perfect that it has sufficiently foreclosed the possibility of any betterment (or a teleological pursuit) such that He does not have any useful reason to exist for His own sake. So, all that He is, He is for others. Or the difference between Jesus and me lies in this: that while I exist to represent humanity in my own unique way even as I inch/work toward my *telos* (which is simultaneously for my own sake and for humanity's sake), Jesus' life is to represent humanity in His own unique way even as His work is exclusively geared towards raising humanity to its teleological realization, which is already represented in Him as a single instance. For His own sake, He has nowhere to go; but, on the other hand, because of His integral relation to humanity, it is just that humanity's imperfection is His imperfection by way of participation; it is an imperfection that it is His vocation to correct. As an eighteen-year-old, Schleiermacher wrote from Barby to his father (the context of which will not concern us here): "God, who has evidently created humankind not for perfection but only for the striving after perfection . . ."[1] One should duly infer from this that when there is nothing to strive for, there is nothing to live for. His striving was not to perfect Himself but to communicate His perfection to others.[2]

---

1. Quoted by Blackwell from *Aus Schleiermachers Leben in Breifen* 1, 42–43 (January 21, 1787) in *Schleiermacher's Early Philosophy of Life*, 7–8.

2. One should not feel that Jesus should be conceded the right to live on the merit of His own self, for His own self, in order that He could enjoy the blessings of God's creation in His perfectness. That which smacks of any separation from humanity for selfish enjoyment cannot be construed as a godly thought, and it would be utterly unworthy of Jesus.

Now, if we were to consider the same issue from the side of Jesus' divinity, invariably we would have to come to the same conclusion. We had already noted that the level of perfection of one's humanity is directly proportional to the level of one's divinity. Perfect humanity and perfect divinity coincide. Since creationally the constancy and intensity of God-consciousness in Jesus' being is such that we can say that the omnipresence of God is in Him, an improvement on it is impossible such that He has reason to be here only for the sake of the rest of humanity, whom He is appointed to draw to God. In other words, Jesus' being is only for His activity; the adequacy of His being exactly matches the requirement of His activity—redemptive activity, that is.

This also means that He does not have to have (and should not have) a being or dignity in excess of what His particular activity demands; in fact, He cannot be accorded any more dignity than what His activity requires. An excessive generosity towards either one (i.e. dignity or activity) against the other creates an imbalance between them such that a Christian Christology becomes clearly impossible; a discrepancy between the two will necessarily cast Jesus either as an over-achiever or an under-achiever; and whichever is the case, it inevitably amounts to imperfection. If the strength of His being is in excess of the demands of the call of His duty, then, to the exact measure of the excess therein, it is a waste. If He is thought to have achieved more than His being or dignity is capable of, it can only highlight the lack of the dignity of Christ in such a way that either He is unworthy of being our Redeemer, or that the quality of the redemption He effects is suspect. Further, if Christ were the enfleshment of perfect humanity, or the "original creation" of human nature, how is it logically possible for something to emerge out of its confines that carries a strength in excess of its own capacity? A docetic view of Christ is freakish, it is fundamentally flawed, for Schleiermacher.

The Source of Christ's Activity

By Christ's activity, we mean redemption. In Christ is our *telos*. He is the fulfilled destiny of humanity. The life and work of Christ is both representative and communicative. All that is communicated from Him has its origin exclusively in Him. Now consider this statement from Schleiermacher: "All Christ's activity, then, proceeds from the being of

God in Him."³ It will be grossly blunderous if this is taken to mean that it proceeds exclusively from Christ's divine nature and that His human nature remains passive in this; such a bifurcation is out of place in Schleiermacher's thinking. The quoted statement, rather, is a logical corollary of Schleiermacher's Christology in that no thought or activity can originate in or advance from Jesus apart from the being of God in Him because of the constancy and comprehensiveness of His consciousness of God. If ever something were possible contrariwise, His consciousness of God would be defective to that exact extent of deviation or aberration, with the effect that any thought of the "omnipresence of God" in Christ will be diluted and therefore have to be dropped, with all its attendant consequences for Christian theology. In order to avoid confusion, it must also be remarked here that by "consciousness of God" we mean more than a mere cognitive content; it is living one's life in the presence of God, in relation to God.

The establishment of Christ's being, then, is for the peculiar activity He is called upon to do. However, this language should not be misread to make Christ into a victim of circumstances or a pawn of a pre-determined plan of divine arbitrariness. (1) Christ's activity is a spontaneous outflow of the fullness of His person; it is a free flow, as free as any human activity could be. Had Christ been constrained to do what He did by the highhandedness of a power other than Himself, or even had it been the case that the source of His activity came from the impulses of a willing center other than His own mind, then He should be considered as less than human and unfit to be the Redeemer. However, on the other hand, we must know that we are not equipped to explain and understand the freedom of Christ that produced His exclusive activity; it can only be acknowledged. In this instance, Christ's freedom is not different from any other human being's freedom. Consider the following words from Schleiermacher regarding human freedom.

> . . . creation of such a free agent and the continued freedom of a being created in the context of a greater whole is something which we cannot expect to understand; all that we can do is to recognize the fact. The same is true of the creative activity of Christ. . . .⁴

---

3. *Christian Faith*, §100.2, 426.
4. Ibid.

(2) Inasmuch as Christ's activity proceeds from the being of God in Him, His activity (redemptive, that is) is God's activity; nothing more and nothing less. "Now the being of God in Him as an active principle is timeless and eternal, yet its expressions are all conditioned by the form of human life."[5] Within the interconnected process of nature, therefore, God's timeless and eternal "activity" takes the shape shown in Christ's activity, which is the climax of God's creative activity. Thereby Christ's activity is representative in character, defining every movement, moment and impulse in nature, giving meaning to all of those and calling and enabling it all to be catalytic towards realizing God's ultimate purpose for and in creation. In other words, it is God's activity that has become Christ's activity; and it can also be rendered *vice versa* without any change of meaning. (3) Christ's activity is humanity's activity, though not in such a way as it can be called our own self-redemption. This is because Christ belongs to humanity as much as He belongs to God, though in different ways. There are two ways in which this can be asserted. One, since Christ is human and belongs to humanity as much as everyone else, and He is just so without any infusion or contribution from outside of humanity; as a regular person he is called to represent humanity in His own way, Christ's activity belongs to or is humanity's activity. Second, since Christ is the original organ of humanity, or its ultimate achievement from within, or the emergence of its teleology from within its own inherent powers (freely granted by God) or the fullest blooming of humanity's ultimate potentiality, Christ and His activity belong totally to and is humanity's activity.

Hence, we find Schleiermacher's rendering of Christ's activity in total as one hundred percent His own activity and one hundred percent God's activity by virtue of God's relation to the person of Jesus, as well as by virtue of God's relation to humanity as a whole.

The Manner of Christ's Activity

Christ's activity is personal, it is voluntarily initiated, continued, and completed; it is the act of His sinless perfection stimulated and stipulated by the being of God in Him. It goes forth from Him as a challenge of His personal existence to the objects of His attraction; it does so not just as a moral influence but as a spontaneous outflow of His grace and

5. Ibid.

love to them. It is not an invasion or a violation of fellow beings by the overwhelming power of His personality; it is a challenge of life proceeding from Him in the manner common to all human inter-influence and interaction, even as He retains in Him the utmost respect for others' individuality; it is a faithful persuasion coupled with enabling grace and love for those who are susceptible to His overtures.

The challenge of higher life that Christ issues becomes our own challenge as we are confronted by it, so that we become unhappy with our sinful life and long to be taken up by Christ into His association. Thus, it is both the Redeemer's challenge and our challenge. "These two points of view can be reconciled only by supposing that this challenge is the act of the Redeemer become our own act."[6] The original work belongs to the Redeemer in that He creates the circumstances around us by and through which we become dissatisfied, on our own free will, with our present estate and yearn for the higher life He offers, at which point He assumes us into communion with Him, transplanting us into a new gradient. The precedence that Schleiermacher gives to Christ's work ahead of our own is more Barthian than Tillichian. Tillich, in true adherence to his "method of correlation" throughout the whole of his *Systematic Theology*, always gives logical or chronological priority to the existential question ahead of the "Christ Symbols."[7] In Barth's arrangement of his *Church Dogmatics*, Christology is placed before the doctrine of Sin, explicitly on the argument that human beings lack the knowledge of their own sinfulness because they are already sinful and that only the light of Christ would enlighten them to know their true status before God.[8]

As we are taken up into Christ's community, we put off the old man and put on the new. Sin and the imperfection of individual life are consigned to the safe custody of history; we become the inmates and inheritors of the Reign of God, or the impulses that proceed from the Redeemer become so much our own that we are packed into the corporate life of blessedness.

> . . . if every activity of the Redeemer proceeds from the being of God in Him, and if in the formation of the Redeemer's Person the only active power was the creative divine activity which estab-

---

6. Ibid., 425.
7. Tillich, *Systematic Theology*, vol. 2, 150–65.
8. Barth, *Church Dogmatics*, vol. 4, pt. 1, 358–61.

lished itself as the being of God in Him, then also His activity may be regarded as a continuation of that person-forming divine influence upon human nature. For the pervasive activity of Christ cannot establish itself in an individual without becoming person-forming in him too, for now all his activities are differently determined through the working of Christ in him, and even all impressions are differently received—which means that the personal self-consciousness too becomes altogether different.[9]

Impulses, by nature, cannot originally occur in one isolated individual, even though one may have power to evoke them from him/her. Human impulses are always produced in relationships, and they exist perpetually as travelers on the way. Therefore, we surmise that the authentic development of the Christ-impulse originally ensued from Christ's communication (not just of information but of His total life) to His disciples, i.e., to the first community of faith. Therefore, all the Christian impulses that go forth from the community of faith are Christ-impulses; take Christ away from the community, and all impulses vanish and even the last fiber that holds the community together as Christian is lost. Christ-impulses are always communicated by Christ in and through the community, to the effect that whenever a person or a group of persons is redeemed, it is Christ who absorbs him/her/them into the community. Further, since the manner in which Christ-impulses proceed is always from Christ's communion with the community He established, and since the full fruition of the process in any recipient (which we call redemption) is always the assumption of the same individual into that community, we can say that there is no redemption outside of the Church or Christian community. This does not mean that Christ-impulses do not travel outside of the community; rather, they reach out to all receptive centers in proximity to the community, making their impact according to the measure of the intensity of the meeting between the power of the community's emitting ability and of the susceptibility to Christ of those outsiders which its members meet. Where it is the case that the transmittal of the impulses is sufficiently powerful to transform those outsiders and to absorb them into the community, redemption is a *fait accompli*. However, if that transmittal is less than sufficient, what the beneficiaries get are glimpses of redemption proportionate to the measure of the

---

9. *Christian Faith*, §100.2, 427.

impulses imparted to them; they are in the realm of the influence of grace and are on their way to a fuller realization even as more impulses reach them in accordance with the continued meeting of the spiritual power of the community with the growth of their susceptibility to Christ. No impulse that is transmitted from Christ is ever wasted or can ever be counted as wasted, at any rate.

Now, the manner of the movement of Christ-impulses is always regulated by the physical, spatio-temporal rules of nature. The original occurrence of Christ was certainly supernatural,[10] but the influence emanating from that estate, the initial as well as the subsequent, follows the pattern of normal human communication. The historical placement of Jesus at a particular time and place bids His influence to be furthered only from that point to other points as the physical presence of the Christian community extends to the length and breadth of the human world even as its preaching is met with hearts open to its persuasion.

"Now the being of God in Him as an active principle is timeless and eternal, yet its expressions are all conditioned by the form of human life."[11] So, the influencing activity of Christ does not force its way into the world of people; rather, it meets with human beings who are creationally accorded the dignity freely to chose or reject its advances. Further, "if every activity of the Redeemer proceeds from the being of God in Him, and if in the formation of the Redeemer's Person the only active power was the creative divine activity which established itself as the being of God in Him, then also His every activity may be regarded as a continuation of that person-forming divine influence upon human nature."[12] In other words, the higher life that Jesus brings to people is eternal in nature; it is the work of God. We have earlier noted that for Schleiermacher, the expression "the omnipresence of God in Jesus" means the presence of God in Him actively representing the whole creation. God's presence can only be one of activity, activity of life; and passivity in God would be either deadness or quasi-deadness and is therefore alien to God. So, the

---

10. By supernatural is not meant an incursion into nature by an outside power; it means only that Christ (i.e., His perfection and the being of God in Him) cannot be explained by the natural circumstances that preceded and surrounded Him; it is not naturally explainable, it is the work of the totality of nature in a unique way, a single instance, that cannot be repeated ever.

11. Ibid., 426.

12. Ibid., 427.

expression "God's work in Jesus" must be seen as just a paraphrase of "the omnipresence of God in Him." The person-forming divine activity in Jesus is nothing but eternity in the temporal. Since the activity that proceeds from Jesus into the community can only be the "procession" of the power of the being of God in Him, the person-forming of the redeemed is nothing but the "extension" of eternity into the spatio-temporal, into the lives of people.[13] Since eternal activity is indivisible,

> the total effective influence of Christ is only the continuation of the creative divine activity out of which the Person of Christ arose. For this, too, was directed towards human nature as a whole, in which that being of God was to exist, but in such a way that its effects are mediated through the life of Christ, as its most original organ, for all human nature that has already become personal in the natural sense, in proportion as it allows itself to be brought into spiritual touch with that life and its self-perpetuating organism. And this in order that the former personality may be slain and human nature, in vital fellowship with Christ, be formed into persons in the totality of that higher life.[14]

Because each individual is made for the whole as inviolably as the whole is made for each individual, Jesus, as an individual belongs to the whole; inevitably, then, the omnipresence of God in Him belongs to all. Consequently, since the Christian community of faith is an "extension" of God's work in Jesus, the community belongs to the whole creation, and the whole creation belongs to the community. The "higher life," which connects the community together[15] as one organism, must itself belong to the whole creation. That means that people who never had the privilege to hear the name of Christ as well as people who have heard His name but rejected Him are all in the plan of God; Christ represents all of them. By virtue of the presence of that small measure of divinity in all

---

13. The words "extension" and "procession" are used only in a metaphorical sense, because physical movement and extension are in any case not properties of eternity. We shall deal with the relation between "eternity" and "time" in the seventh chapter.

14. *Christian Faith*, §100.2, 427–28. A reading preferable to "fellowship" (*Gemeinshaft*) would be "communion," or in some contexts "community."

15. Within the community itself, see the manner in which everyone is related to God and to each other: ". . . the establishment and maintenance of the fellowship of each individual with God, and the maintenance and direction of the fellowship of all members with one another, are not separate achievements but the same. . . ." *Christian Faith*, §102.2, 440.

human beings, however imperfect it may be, all are susceptible to Christ-influence, or all are potential Christians; it is not a "never" for anyone, it is only a "not yet." Those who have passed on from the earthly life without ever reaching this "higher life" and those who will follow their suit in the future have simply never had the privilege of a moment in life wherein a sufficient susceptibility to Christ and a sufficiently powerful challenge of the message of Christ together confronted them so as to transform them. Their life was lived out before such a thing could happen historically. However, the omnipresence of God in Christ actively represents them as well.

The scenario may be set forth thus: The totality of God's work in creation is present in Christ, in the omnipresence of God in Him; and the "extension" of the same is found in the community which He established. God's work in Christ and the community involves the whole of humanity, indeed the whole creation, because in Christ and Christianity God's work is represented for the whole creation. Because of the organic nature of the total creation, all human beings and all creation belong to God's eternal and unequivocal concern, the concern one sees in God's work in Christ and Christianity. This is the same as saying: God's work in Christ and God's work in history are identical.

The Method and Means of Christ's Ministration

In order to analyze and elaborate Christ's ministry in thought and words, of all the possible biblical pictorial expressions available to the Church, it chose, because of its historical connections with Judaism, the prophetic, priestly, and kingly figures as presenting the standard.[16] There could well have been better choices; but if these figures are fitting, the Church's tradition with respect to them should certainly be respected, in Schleiermacher's view.

The Prophetic Office of Christ.

The prophetic office in the Old Testament contains three activities, namely, teaching, prophesying and working miracles. Therefore, it is fruitful to look at Jesus' ministry through the eyes of these three aspects.

---

16. Ibid., §102.1, 438–39.

Jesus' teaching is certainly not to be thought of as a purified version of what can be garnered from the general ideas, mandates and guidelines developed through human history; the very concept of natural theology is a myth. "Rather the source of His (Jesus') teaching was the absolutely original revelation of God in Him."[17] Bereft of a consciousness of the world, there is no possibility of a consciousness of God; and this is an unimpeachable axiom even in the case of Jesus. That being the case, Jesus' relation and communion with God and the same with the creation are mutually conditioned. Moreover, inasmuch as the origin of His teachings is averred to be exclusively from His relation with God, the significance of this maxim for Jesus' teaching is this: "In Him the contrast between learning and teaching was only the contrast between the influence of the divine principle in Him upon the receptivity of His spiritual organ (so as to yield a pure apprehension of the human conditions confronting Him in their bearing on human beings' relation to God) and the influence of the same principle upon the spontaneity of His spiritual organ."[18] That is, receptivity and spontaneity are mutually related, in such a way that the former cannot be called purely passive at any time; this would be alien to its nature because of the invariable involvement of the two characteristics with each other. Logically, of course, receptivity precedes spontaneity, and there are indeed moments where one of these states dominates the other; but that is all right, for the fact remains that receptivity is facilitated by the potentiality of spontaneity, and spontaneity's vitality is facilitated always by the actuality of receptivity. Receptivity to God at its maximal comprehensiveness, evinced in Jesus and in corresponding spontaneity thereafter, with all its global ramifications, bear testimony to the effect that God's work in Christ is identical with God's work in history.

The content of Jesus' teaching was determined by the impulses He received from His relation with God; then the impression that was made on Him was translated into communicable form and passed on to His disciples with the effect of establishing the Reign of God among them and beyond. The three parts of His teaching, which are all inseparable from each other, are these: "the doctrine of His person, which is at the same time, in its outward aspect, the doctrine of His calling, or the communication of eternal life in the Reign of God, and in its inward aspect,

---

17. Ibid., §103.2, 443.
18. Ibid., 443–44.

the doctrine of His relation to Him Who had sent Him, or of God as His Father, revealing Himself to Him and through Him."[19]

The revelation of God in Christ is so perfect and inexhaustible that He is the climax and end of all prophecy. No addition to Christ's teaching is possible without sacrificing the special dignity of Christ, and thus of Christian faith.

The second activity of prophetic ministry in the Old Testament is prediction or prophesying; of which two types can be observed. One type was prediction or fore-telling with regard to individual events (on the basis of the Jewish doctrines of election and retribution), used for pastoral purposes such as warning and encouragement. The other type of prophecy was the Messianic prophecy; and when this is properly understood "it always involved the end of those two Jewish conceptions of retribution and election."[20] Jesus, therefore, is the climax and fulfillment of all the prophecies; since His teaching is all about Himself, all His predictions are identical with the scope and concern of His mission; or they are identical with His teaching. The apostolic predictions we find in the New Testament can be interpreted only as an echo of Jesus' predictions. Since nothing essential remains unknown or lacking within the Reign of God, further predictions are unhelpful; rather, they are additions to the gospel and are therefore unacceptable. As the fulfillment of all prophecies, Christ's messianic blanket overlays the whole creation in such a way that God's work in Christ must be thought of as identical with God's work in history.

With regard to the working of miracles too, the same scheme as that laid out above applies. Jesus used his extra-ordinary powers only to do good for people as and when required, but He never used them to produce faith in Him for anyone or to authenticate what He taught of Himself; and this remains true even with regard to John 11:42. Just as in the case of teaching and prophecy, Christ is the climax and end of all miraculous activities too. He is the original and consummate spiritual miracle, and so is the Reign of God, because its total base and being is footed and rooted and subsists in Him.

---

19. Ibid., §103.2, 444–45.
20. Ibid., §103.3, 446.

The Priestly Office of Christ.

Just as in the Old Testament, the High Priest stands before God in ceremonial purity so that God sees people through him, Christ is our High Priest by virtue of His perfect fulfillment of the divine will, apart from whom no human being and no association would be able to be objects of divine good pleasure. "In Christ," however, we forgo self-pride and any thought of being anything by and for ourselves before God, and we willingly allow God to count us as one with Christ through the communion of persons of faith with God established in and through Him. "Each one wishes to appear only as animated by Christ, and as a part of His work which is still in process of development; so that even that which has not yet been altogether united with Him is still related to the same animating principle, because it is yet to be animated by Him some day."[21]

Thus, we are reckoned righteous before God by Christ's own merit. However, this should not be considered in simple transactional terms. We may clarify this point thus: Christ is the object of divine good pleasure because of His perfect obedience or total conformity to the divine will. Yet, He has not made up for or covered our failure by the excess of His merits, because inasmuch as only perfect obedience would satisfy God, Christ's having that does not help anyone else, He has no surplus to spare for us. However, the fact is that God counts us in and through Christ even as we, by virtue of our communion with Christ, have His obedience-impulses created in us (with all the practical ramifications of that action) such that we too become objects of divine good pleasure, though in a secondary sense. The Christ-created impulses in us come to us by grace; God's reckoning of us through Christ is by grace, but there is to be no shirking of responsibility in us. We become aware of and averse to Adamic sin and we share the motive and life-principle of Jesus. Further, those in whom these impulses are yet to be created are also objects of divine good pleasure by virtue of their potentiality for the same, in such a way that they too are seen through Christ and are, in a tertiary style, objects of divine good pleasure. It is as if what Christ is to the redeemed community, Christ and the redeemed community together are to those yet to be redeemed. Thus, once again, through the merit of Christ's 'vicarious obedience' or the perfect fulfillment of the divine will

---

21. *Christian Faith*, §104.3, 454–55. Perhaps "enlivened" and "enlivening" would be the better words here for this life-giving principle.

(which is God's work in Him), God's work in Christ is counted identical with God's work in history.

The Kingly Office of Christ.

His kingdom is not of this world; rather, it concerns the inner life.[22] Christ is the organizer of the organic community of which He is the Lord. Since all the initial as well as subsequent impulses for this community originates and follows from Him, this Lord does not have and cannot have any predecessors or followers. ". . . since He stands to the totality of believers in exactly the same relation as the divine nature in Him does to the human, animating and taking it up into the community of the original life, His lordship too is in the strictest sense a sole lordship, for no one else is in a position to share it."[23] He established the rules and norms for the organism; there are no additions to or subtractions from it by anyone else at any time. He Himself has no amendments or improvements to effect because the original establishment emanated purely and totally from His own perfection. In Him God created a state of affairs whereby all the provisions required for the spiritual nourishment and well-being of His community would incessantly flow from Him, so that the community, thus conceived, does not need to and must not look for these things from any other source. In consonance with the nature of the Reign of God, which is essentially an inner vital relationship of the faithful with Christ and of each one to another through Christ, the kingly authority of Christ is spiritual. By spiritual, we mean life viewed in a religious way. It is acceptance of a complete authority of Christ over persons of faith, individually and collectively. All social relations that the person

---

22. We should watch out here lest we take the statement to mean that Jesus' Reign is concerned only with one aspect of human life and that the rest is up for grabs. No, the spiritual aspect of human beings permeates their whole life in that it is indicative and representative and, in a sense, regulative of their whole being. Accordingly, we should understand the practical limitations of the Reign of God, which is just one spiritual (but visible) organization existing within the context of the general divine government, which is itself comprised of a world of multiple spiritual organizations, which itself exists as a multi-polar world with multifarious relations, within associations of innumerable permutations. In Christian consciousness however, the relation between the Reign of God and the civil government of the world, which springs out of corporate sinful existence (but nonetheless belongs to the general divine government of the world), is that in God's reckoning, the latter is seen through eyes of the former.

23. Ibid., §105.1, 468.

of faith engages in, within or without, and in all moments of his/her life, are, or ought to be, under the control of Christ through the spiritual thread. In the general running of the government of the world, however, there is no functional clash between the civilian authorities and Christ's kingly power; persons of faith, as was the case with Christ Himself in His earthly days, submit to the earthly authorities and participate in the running of the civil government, subject to acceptable norms of public decency and morality, though the perspective they bring is to be formed by that prior relation to God in Christ.

So Christ's kingship is over His community; but inasmuch as the (spiritual) provisions of His kingship are adequate for the whole of history and in teleological terms are expected to reach all in such a way that God would look at the totality of history only through the perspective of Christ's kingship, once again we say, God's work in Christ is identical with God's work in history.

5

Christian Understanding of God's Work in History in Relation to the Doctrine of Election

SCHLEIERMACHER UNDERSTANDS REDEMPTION, OR THE ASSUMPTION OF those who believe into the community of the faithful, to be entirely the work of the Redeemer, thus of God in Christ. The self-consciousness residing in the redeemed that results from this assumption can be described as regeneration and sanctification. It is the commencement of a new life in the new community (or better, the extension of Christ's life in the community into the regenerating self), with creation of a new set of values and dispositions in oneself. Since taking this new direction is conversion, it is also the certain beginning of a life-long process of sanctification. Equally important, this assumption into the community of faith is also the coming into being of the consciousness of a new relationship to God, or the realization of God's justifying act on behalf of oneself actualized in time. This feature needs further explanation.

God's Justifying Decree

In Christian consciousness, justification is God's eternal act effected in time; and conversion is deemed to be Christ's act effected at the same time. Temporally speaking, the two coincide absolutely; one is impossible without the other. The temporal precedence given to Christ's act in Christian devotional expressions, by which act Christ intercedes for the new convert for God's justification, is nothing but poetical. However, ". . . the decision as to *who* in each case is to attain to conversion and *when*, this we have already assigned not to the realm of grace, thus posing it as dependant on Christ, but to the realm of power, taking it as dependant on God, since precisely the latter realm consists in the Father's drawing people to the Son."[1] The occurrence of conversion of people to Christ takes place within the framework of the normal functioning of the divine government of the world and not through any magical, mystical influence or a determination by a capricious or unfathomable extraterrestrial power.

Since the justifying act belongs to the realm of the Father, the claim that there are multiple acts of individual justifications proceeding from the Father in correspondence with the regularity of individual conversions is an untenable proposition. Since conversion is deemed to have occurred at the point of the characteristic modification of the subject's self-consciousness pertaining to the matter, it becomes, in our theological conception, tangible only at its own moment for the individual as well as for the community into which the individual is inserted. That is, by the individual's entry, which happens at a temporal junction, the community of Christ changes the individual, and the individual modifies the community by that entry, each according to the extent of their respective influential power. However, the new and irrevocable impact created through each singular entry in the course of history shall not suffice to sustain a position that from God there is a proceeding of decree or activity corresponding to each entry, even if the decree be deemed to proceed from eternity to time.

> There is only one eternal and universal decree justifying human beings for Christ's sake. On the one hand, this decree is the same as that which sent Christ on his mission, for otherwise that mission would have been conceived and determined by God without a view to its consequences; and on the other hand, the decree that sent Christ forth is also the same as the decree creating the human species, insofar as human nature is first brought to completion in Christ.[2]

God is one, God is eternal. There is no gap or distinction between thought and will in God; rather, thought, will and activity are identical in God. There cannot be deliberation or prevarication in God, both of which demand duration; but there is also no temporality in God; God

---

1. *Christian Faith*, §109.3, 500–1. This translation is somewhat clearer than the one in print. God works in and through Christ, by grace and power, but God is not thereby dependent on a *separate* realm of action by Christ in which discreet acts by Christ determine the fate of individuals independent of God.

2. Ibid., 501.

cannot be subordinated and subjected to the limitations or conditions of God's own creation. Therefore, there cannot be a plurality of decrees in or from God.

No doubt Schleiermacher's forceful assertion concerning the absolute singleness of God's eternal decree is prompted by his disapproval of the popular misunderstanding (among those from within and without) regarding a supposed plurality of decrees, which misunderstanding had been prevalent in the orthodox Reformed tradition. However, the overall orthodox Reformed position and Schleiermacher's are generally at one in maintaining a certain singularity and consistency in the divine decree pertaining to predestination[3] and in holding to the eternal nature of God's decree.[4]

However, one should not gloss over the substantial differences between this tradition and Schleiermacher's views. First, insofar as the focus is placed on decrees of God (plural) and these decrees are considered "the essential internal acts of God" in standard Reformed theology,[5] internal acts in God, for Schleiermacher, are utterly inconceivable to us; we can only speculate, but speculation does not carry us into the realm of God, it can only wallow in wild and baseless imagination and, therefore, is an endeavor beyond the range of dogmatics.

Second, because it is the internal acts of God that are conceived as "decree" and because the internal acts of God are differentiated, the traditional Reformed theology does tend to think of the divine decree in plural form, even if sometimes with the acknowledgment that these are only humanly made distinctions. For Schleiermacher, however, act and decree are singular and identical in God, and there is no distinction possible between general and special decree in God. Schleiermacher wants to preserve the singularity of the decree of God as much as the singularity of God throughout.

Third, while the scope of the decree to predestination, for the standard Reformed tradition, involves both election and reprobation,[6] Schleiermacher utterly rejects a doctrine that condemns a certain sec-

---

3. See Francis Turretin, *Institutes of Elenctic Theology*, 1:332.
4. Heinrich Heppe, *Reformed Dogmatics*, 137–38.
5. Turretin, *Institutes*, 1:311.
6. Ibid., 145–46.

tion of humanity to everlasting damnation; for him, to do so is to read devilishness into the good God.

The one decree is identical to the one act of God's work in history, which is the same as the omnipresence of God in creation, and which is seen in the Lord Jesus. This one decree is identical with God's decree pertaining to the total process of creation and preservation, the completion of which comes in the new creation in Jesus. Jesus is the gathering point of the totality of the old creation and the starting point of the new, such that the omnipresence of God in Jesus evinces a continual presence through the comprehensive stretch of history, viewed as the single divine deed or decree.

Election and Christ

Here we are entering into the domain of Schleiermacher's ecclesiology. Election is the means by which God separates, from the larger ocean of humanity, a community for Godself through Jesus Christ. The new life infused by Jesus into the original Christian community perpetually reaches out into the exterior of its boundaries, with the overt purpose of swelling its own ranks at the expense of the "world." It does so not in such a way as to deplete the "world" but so as to complete it by transferring its own spirituality to the world. Thereby it makes the world as rich as it can be; it moves the world toward its fullness, which is its rightful estate, its birthright.

The contrast between the new community (new creation) and the old creation should not be magnified out of proportion; rather, it may be helpful to break the contrast down into two parts. Even before they knew Jesus, the original community that received Jesus' new life belonged to a larger unorganized group of people who shared kindred impulses with themselves with regard to the expectation of a Messiah and some attendant hopes. The larger community, into the midst of which Jesus was placed by the divine government of the world, reacted to Him in different ways; some jettisoned Him, some remained ambivalent, and some responded positively to His call. Each in his or her own way was influenced by the impulses of Jesus. Ever since that happened, the pattern has been similar; throughout history, the totality of those who come under the spell (in varied measures and under different circumstances, of course) of the life of Jesus, are identified by the biblical expression "the called," out of whom those who submit to His Lordship are called "the elect." The contrast between the "elect" and the "called" is similar to the contrast between the "called" and the totality of humanity. This is a three-tier plan for looking at humanity with regard to Jesus Christ. Jesus can be thought of as at the center of three concentric circles, the innermost being the "elect," the middle one being the "called" and the outer one being the collective basket of humanity.

Barth's placement of the doctrine of election is under the doctrine of God as compared with Schleiermacher, who puts it under ecclesiology. Apart from that, it is safe to say that Schleiermacher's treatment of election significantly prefigures Barth's. In an interesting comment, Barth alludes to his belief that his exposition of the doctrine is fairly original. He says: "It is one of the great puzzles of history that the step which we are now taking toward a true form of the electing God and elected man was not taken long ago, although, as we have seen, many thinkers did come near enough to taking it."[7] Somehow, Schleiermacher does not figure in Barth's list of those who came "near enough." Clearly, Schleiermacher's exposition does not contain any parallel for Barth's forceful assertion of Christ as "the electing God." Schleiermacher basically reserves the concept of "election" for explaining God's act of choosing people to redemption through Christ. Even Barth's affirmation of "Christ as the elected man" also does not neatly fit with Schleiermacher's account; however, an important theological implication of this latter expression certainly fits Schleiermacher's theology. Inasmuch as the Being of God is present in Christ for the sake of humanity as a whole, we can say that Christ is the elected "Man" for Schleiermacher and that everyone who partakes of the fullness of grace through Jesus is elected in and through Christ.

The Act of Election

Election of individuals who are predestined to partake in the redemption effected through Jesus is the immediate refraction of God's activity in Christ, by means of which God blesses the world. Schleiermacher's famous essay on "election" in 1819[8] puts up a stout defense of the general tone of the Augustinian Calvinist rendition of the doctrine of election against the snipes of his contemporary Lutheran theologian, Carl Bretschneider. For

---

7. Barth, *Church Dogmatics*, pt. 2, vol. 2, 147.
8. Schleiermacher, *Ueber die Lehre von der Erwählung*, KGA I.10, 147–222.

Schleiermacher, if Christ were not to be rendered superfluous, if the generally accepted protestant thought regarding the incapacity of human beings for conversion would need to be maintained, if the doctrine of grace were to have any sensible meaning and if the natural heresies of Manichaeism and Pelagianism were to be avoided, then the doctrine of election as propounded by Augustine and Calvin can be seen as a logical necessity.

After having set forth this situation, Schleiermacher, in a long polemic, repudiates certain specific objections to the doctrine raised by Bretschneider, much of which will not concern us here. However, toward the end of the essay, Schleiermacher does make some crucial modifications on the traditional articulation of the doctrine.[9] These recastings are very significant for our thesis, but we may also note that all the significant points of this revision are subsequently better argued and arranged in *Christian Faith*. In any case, before going into the details of the same, it is important that we understand the difference between our acts and God's act, human causality and divine causality. Election being God's activity, it is incumbent upon us to eliminate all the anthropomorphic overtones ordinarily associated with the doctrine. A right conception of the nature of God's act, therefore, is a prerequisite to understanding the meaning of "election."

God's act occurs as the consequence of God's one eternal decree. "Consequence" does not entail chronological sequence, because the decree is eternal; it is contemporaneous with all moments in the sense that it transcends both duration (time) and location (space).[10] It is possible and in fact necessary for us to think of Schleiermacher's "one" as non-representative of a numeral inasmuch as the decree is eternal. The same characteristic applies when we consider the implication of Schleiermacher's monotheistic representation of God. That which is eternal cannot be contained in or represented properly by a numeral, because a numeral, in itself, if applied to anyone or anything, puts that person or thing or entity into a location. God is a locationless One.

While not overlooking the substantial material differences between Schleiermacher's thought and Sankara's, it is possible here to discern a similarity between them with regard to the doctrine of God. I would suggest that the wisdom of the *advaita vedanta's* negative representa-

9. *Ueber die Lehre von der Erwählung*, KGA I.10, 206–22.

10. I will deal with the nature of Schleiermacher's conception of "eternity" later, in chapter 7.

tion of God as "non-dual" instead of "one," may be of help. We know God as non-dual in relation to us through our redemptive estate or our feeling of absolute dependence. That non-reciprocal dependent relation everyone and everything has with the Ultimate causal Ground (whether one recognizes that relation or not is another matter) is a relation to that Ultimate that is non-dual in nature and holds a non-dual willing center. However, in themselves these conceptions provide no explanation of God-in-Godself.[11]

God's decree, therefore, is to be represented as non-dual, non-temporal and non-locational; however, its concretization can take place only historically, spatially and sequentially. Further, note should be made of the fact that here we also reach the limit of logic because of our inability to conceive of or entertain the thought of any sort of gap between the decree in itself and its historical concretization, as there cannot be found any analogy between what is non-dual, non-spatial, and non-temporal and what is historical, spatial, and sequential; otherwise it has no meaning to us, it is non-existent to us. Nonetheless, the latter, that is, history, depends absolutely upon the former, the divine decree. This dependence is analogous to or, more correctly, is the same as the creature's feeling of absolute dependence on the Creator.

Although the word "dependence" is the common term in the expressions "absolute dependence" and "partial" or "relative" dependence, the nature of these two types of dependence cannot be compared or contrasted. In life, we note that all dependences are relative dependences; and Schleiermacher's conception of "absolute dependence" is a construct created by borrowing the feeling of that universal human experience of relative dependence and then elevating it to the religious realm, so that one has a category available for thinking and reflecting there, where otherwise thought and words would fail to reach.

In Schleiermacher's view, there is no spatial or temporal gap between intention or thought and action in God. In fact, in God thought and action are identical. As human beings, we live and move and have our being within the framework of *Naturzusammenhang* (the interconnected process of nature) and in such a way that we always act and are being acted upon. Therefore, our life is a tête-à-tête between activity and passivity. But there is absolutely no passivity in God, for two reasons. First,

---

11. See also chapter 7 on this matter.

a counter-influence on God is an incontrovertibly practical impossibility because of the absence of any counterpoint of reference to God, as God's existence is characterized by absolute non-duality. Second, granting that God is the creator and the preserver of the creation, any sort of absence of activity cannot be acceded to God without nullification of the world. Moreover, this view is placed here on the presupposition that God's activity is exclusively in relation to the world of God's creation, and any thought of knowing a divine activity apart from the world is deemed to be a useless thought. This is true because anything apart from creation with which God can play that we can imagine still has to be God's creation or God's world!

For the sake of thought, grant provisionally that God does multiple activities with regard to creation. Since there is no passivity in God that can come and create any space between these multiple activities, the thought of multipleness will dissipate on its own; God's act is non-multiple as well as non-dual.

It was already pointed out that God's act realizes itself in the mundane world only in an actual historical fashion, in extension and continuity, characterized by change. However, it is gross anthropomorphism to hold that specific historical contingencies can and do proceed directly from God or modify God in any way. Change is a material modification, it is applicable only to the realm of creation. This is yet another reason why there cannot be multiple acts in God; a succession of acts is effectively connected with change. We cannot superimpose historical accretions on God and then expect to retain God as the immutable God of Christian theology. Therefore, God's non-dual, non-multiple thought/act/intention/decree is simultaneously present with all temporal and spatial points of its stretched-out historical realization, manifesting itself in all sorts of multiplicity. This simultaneousness contemporaneity must not also be thought of as a collapsing of the past, present and future into an instantaneous affair in God. By coalescing past, present, and future into an instant, we have not made any advance in thinking, because that which is instantaneous is as temporally oriented and regulated and circumscribed as that which is stretched out in time.

Schleiermacher's attempt here is to take us to the limits of thinking and leave us there, so that we would simply wonder at the greatness of God. His is an attempt to de-anthropomorphize or demythologize theology to the extent humanly possible and equally, at the same time, to help make our theology both as intelligible as possible in a scientific world and as realistic to ourselves as it can be, without compromising on it pastoral and didactic character.

Election is God's act; therefore, the nature of this act is indispensably in consonance with the way God would act. That means the election of the apostles Peter and Paul, and the election of any human being today or any day, and the election of all members of the Christian community of all times, including the aggregate of all future ones, are one and the same act for God. Further, election of any and all, and the running of the divine government of the world is one and the same act for God. In other words, the conversion of any individual to full Christian privileges, or that person's election thereto, is no special and bracketed work of God. Rather it occurs as a natural process proceeding from the divine government of the world taking shape in history, as history.

Two legitimate reservations against this view of God's act need to be addressed. (1) One might wonder whether the individual *per se* is reckoned important and is left to be lost in the ocean of the mass and whether there is no scope for the thought of God's distinctive love and personal care centered on the individual. Schleiermacher would answer that the facts are different. Since there is nothing accidental in God, all human beings are in God's plan, each coming in one's own unique way, unique place, time and circumscribed within a unique set of relations. Since there is no possibility but only actuality in God, the apprehension or thought that someone else would have or could have taken one's own place in the system of things is itself meaningless. Since past, present and future are equally real before God's eyes, and since God is related to each point in it simultaneously by utterly transcending time and space, whatever actually has happened or will happen in the future in its totality is what is real and actual before God. So, no one who has ever come into this world at any time is an optional extra or an unnecessary inconvenience for God. The fact of being thrown into the mass, for Schleiermacher, cannot be indicative of an individual's unimportance in any case. If humanity (of all times) can be compared to a circle, each individual is a small segment within the circle, from each of which the whole circle can be constructed without any extra data, or the whole circle is present in each segment; the whole of humanity is present in each individual.

Because God's relationship to a given individual or group is identical to God's relation to the sum total of all God-human relations, the lesser the importance of one individual, the lesser the importance of everyone else and of the totality itself, equally and originally. The failure or success of any individual is the same of every individual and the whole. God's relationship with humanity cannot be split into pieces; a mental construction of God's relation to each individual as each single piece is acceptable only insofar as one acknowledges that the accumulation of all pieces is no bigger than any single piece and that a part is a predicate of the whole and the whole is a predicate of a part.

Therefore, the feeling that I am lost in the ocean of humanity is out of place in intelligent thinking, because each individual is created with such an inherent value that each is vitally significant for everyone else. This is our human organicity, our species nature. Accordingly, for one to desire or claim special love or care or privilege or divine pandering, leaving others aside, is downright selfishness, it is an unabashed claim for more importance for oneself in contradistinction to everyone else; it contradicts our species-consciousness. It hurts the species as much as it hurts oneself or anyone else. Because all are of equal worth in the eyes of God, God cannot rob a Peter to pay a Paul. Each one should, with contented acceptance of what would come to him or her as the course of the world takes shape in relation to him or her, meet it with the best use of the talents and resources that may be at hand and make the best out of it all to the common benefit of humanity.

Any thought of a special divine intervention of behalf of a favorite individual or group would be a participation by God in partisanship, partiality towards some is partiality against the rest. Favoritism is a human limitation, a failure emanating from human finiteness, and we will not do well to impute the same to God. Moreover, the accordance of exclusive privileges to one or more persons against the rest of the humanity would create significant difficulties for thought. Thus: (a) A divine intervention in the middle of an already ongoing historical process meddles with the thought of the singleness of God's act; the gap between the first and second act creates a vacuum in God, a passivity. (b) One also has to concede that this second act, or whatever subsequent act or acts may follow, testifies to an after-thought in God after the original plan was already set forth. A second "creation" or intervention into the already existing order would mess up the *Naturzusammenhang*, a position inconsistent with our view of God. (c) It breaks the identicality of God's relationship with each and all. (d) By interposing into the labyrinth of human relationship,

God would break the unity of the human species. Rather, God loves me and cares for me and each individual in the species not by setting me up against the rest but by treating me always as one with the rest. Any special consideration for certain people would be a consideration against the rest. Instead, a true assertion regarding God's love for oneself is an assertion of God's love for everyone else, individually and collectively.

(2) One might also wonder what the practical use or meaning would be of a coalescing of an individual's fate as it is displayed in history with God's work for that person or what would be the use of a God whose acts cannot be isolated in contradistinction to the general flow of things. This is one of the many accusations that Bennie Dale Craver makes against Schleiermacher in his 1994 dissertation.[12] We may also observe that a different shade of the same objection can be seen, albeit in a supremely sophisticated form, in Karl Barth's famous *Concluding Unscientific Postscript on Schleiermacher*.[13] Schleiermacher would readily respond to this accusation with his own disquiet with regard to the spirit and content of the objection itself. (a) Schleiermacher has not distanced God from the big or small things of life and of creation any more than the objector has. (b) Apprehension of this sort has never occurred to Schleiermacher personally; rather, he would say, this fear can form only in people who have not experienced the new life in Christ anyway. (c) The presupposition behind the criticism stems from a concept of God akin to that in Deistic thought, the only difference here being that God the "watchmaker" is allowed to meddle with the "watch," as and when called for, for oiling it and repairing it even after the "watch" is made and up to function. (d) Ultimately the God who interferes with creation (i.e., by acting within it with an act/acts apart from the original act of creation) and the Schleiermacharian God who with non-dual non-temporal act completes the work of creation have, at the end of the line, produced the same result. Take our perspective from the end-point of history, all that has happened through the course of the total running of history and the shape of its outcome at the consummation of history would be exactly identical, whether one has chosen orthodoxy's God or Schleiermacher's God! Or God's relation to any part of history, or to the whole thereof, is

---

12. Craver, "Divine Government of the World," 236.

13. See versions two and three of the four versions of the two questions Barth asks with regard to Schleiermacher's theology in "Concluding Unscientific Postscript on Schleiermacher," *Theology of Schleiermacher*.

the same in both views. Schleiermacher's attempt is not to reduce God to a good feeling or a helpful thought for human spiritual nurture but only to "magnify" God by explaining that in God there is no need for or possibility of any *ad hoc* decisions and acts and that the original act of God has sufficiently taken care of the need of order in the universe, and has elected all humans, each in one's own time, and has answered all prayers of all believers of all times in God's own way. Even when someone is convinced that his or her specific prayer for a special request has been particularly addressed and granted by God, all that has happened is that the determined flow of the divine government (within which this particular issue at hand is also included) has taken its course in history; and no change in the will of God has occurred in the process.

To avoid misunderstanding, the use of the present perfect tense in the above two sentences should be balanced by saying that in God past, present and future are identical, and that creation's temporaneity is brought forth and played out by God's eternity alone. A certain reorientation of our usual style of thinking through thoughts on God and eternity is required of us if we are not to misunderstand Schleiermacher. It is easy (and one cannot be more wrong) to read in Schleiermacher's God a certain apathy or aloofness or helplessness, once God has set for the interconnected process of nature and put it in its place. What he is trying to show us is the limit of our thought. In terms of this limit, God and eternity appear not as part of the limit nor as an adjunct to it but as that on which the totality of the limit has its being and movement, which is not circumscribed by or governed by the rules of the limit but which circumscribes and sets/has set the rules that govern the being and nature and the totality of relations within the limit and is therefore necessarily indefinable and indescribable by and through the categories of or available within the limit.

Election and Predestination

At this stage of our exposition, no one will be left to wonder what God's role is in the election of individuals, which happens as the natural flow of history takes its course. God's involvement in each individual case of election is identical to God's involvement in sending Christ (or in the election of Jesus) for the sake of the world. Each one's regeneration occurs at the divinely appointed "fullness of time" unique to the person's placement within the species, and each one's regeneration is a divine predestination to salvation in Christ. The point of regeneration is the moment in life that holds together the period of preparatory grace and the period subsequent to regeneration as pertains to a given person. It is also the moment at which the self-consciousness of all who belong to the circle of the redeemed is created in the person.

Any sadness for anyone's not having been born again earlier than it actually happened is only a sign of immaturity; it is roughly equivalent to being sad for Christ's not having been born earlier than He really was (failing to give His blessedness to more people than was really possible in actuality), which again is equivalent to being sad over the fact of the creation of the world's not having taken place (assuming *creatio ex nihilo*) earlier than it actually occurred, "for that life is in itself eternal, and gains no increment by the duration of time,"[14] and this stands true whether one envisions the concept of life after death as a reality or as an illusion.

Predestination is not to be considered as a previously programmed or as a remote-controlled effect that would automatically have happened at its appointed time regardless of the context of a person's interconnection with human relations and circumstances. An attribution of prior programming can be made for it only insofar as the same can be made for the organized cluster of all intricacies and shades of all human relations surrounding it (with full respect to the human freedom individuals possess singularly and collectively in all permutations, considered in particular contexts). Consequently, the same attribution should be made for the sake of the larger context of the totality of the *Naturzusammenhang* in which the said surroundings in their entirety are placed.

> In every occurrence, the manner and the time of each individual's regeneration is determined by the distinctiveness of the individual's own inner life, or of the individual's freedom and by the individual's relations to the natural and historical development of justifying divine grace, or of the individual's place in the world. Thus, above all, the Reign of grace or of the Son arises only in absolute unity with the Reign of omniscient omnipotence, or of the Father; and since the entirety of the world's order is, like the world itself, eternal in God, nothing happens in the Reign of grace without divine predestination. Thus, all this is given from the outset in and through the self-consciousness of people

---

14. *Christian Faith*, §118.1, 541.

touched by grace; and whether they may then choose to say that their state is a work of divine grace in Christ or that it is a result of divine predestination, each statement implies the other.[15]

The Relative Contrast between Election and Rejection

One principle that overlays the whole of Schleiermacher's doctrine of election is the Christian conception of an absolute equality of all people before God.

> For us, all human beings are in the state of sinfulness in common, in which everything is guilt in common. In this respect all are completely equal and no advantage is to be attributed to anyone in relation to the new life being communicated by Christ.[16]

There is no inherent merit in any individual's seeking to grab God's special attention so that God is drawn to pick that person from among the rest. However, in the divine government of the world, because of the inequality of preaching (as is the case with every other human activity or aspect of life), certain persons and certain peoples do get the advantage of listening to the gospel through the presence and the missionary thrust of the Church in their midst, a privilege which is somehow denied to many others. As to why this discrimination happens, there is only one answer: God willed it to be so.[17] Preparatory grace works within and among these privileged people, leading to the bringing forth of a select number among them as the gospel is proclaimed to them at its maximum power at the point of their maximum susceptibility to the message, so that they are enabled to make their full commitment to Christ. These people are the ascertainable objects of God's election.

Since election cannot in any way be considered as a reward, rejection cannot be construed as a punishment, unless one is willing to attribute baselessness or senselessness to God's thought and action.[18] On the other hand, we note that election and rejection are a fact of life in Christian

---

15. Ibid., 547. Extensive changes are made in the translation, with Terrence N. Tice.

16. Ibid., 534.

17. Schleiermacher, *Ueber die Lehre von der Erwählung*, *KGA* I.10, 211, lines 34–42. Schleiermacher is just following Calvin here. See *Institutes of The Christian Religion*, 3.20.1.

18. *Christian Faith*, §116.2, 535.

faith. Still, serious thought cannot entertain any inference from this fact to the effect that election is seen to be a random sampling of humanity that reflects an arbitrariness or caprice on God's part. Election and rejection are not anything like the Hindu concept of *Bhagavan's lila* (God's play). Two laws of the divine government of the world will explain the establishment of the said disparity.

> Clearly, one such law obviously is this: that what proceeds from a single point spreads only gradually over the whole area. Less obvious perhaps is this: that the state of grace can never be inborn but that at birth even Christian children are essentially the same as all other descendants of Adam. In contrast, any supposed difference would be an exception not explicable by the fundamental fact of Christianity, and obliterate the concept of species.[19]

As an institution and as a movement, the Church of Christ is stationed within the world as an integral part of the world, as one among the many similar sorts of establishments. So, the outward movement of the Church, or the conversion of individuals into the Church, is always bound up with the natural laws of movement. From the one point in time and space where Jesus' ministry was operative, at times

> by changing His locale He widened the circle of His proclamation, while at other times He tarried in one place to consolidate His work. Indeed, even where He was ordered to go away, that fact must have worked to the unmerited disadvantage of many who otherwise would naturally have come to follow Him. All this, however, is rooted in the divine government of the world.[20]

Thus, God does make distinctions. Some nations and peoples never hear the gospel, some others hear but proclamation reaches them with insufficient power, some to whom some attempt to proclaim the gospel is made are denied the privilege through the forces of resistance against the gospel, and to some it is proclaimed with sufficient force so that they turn to Christ. This is the way God has willed it; the divine ordinance with regard to "election" works in the precise way conditioned by the order of nature, in a discriminatory fashion. "If God had not willed this definitely and unconditionally, God would have established either a dif-

---

19. Ibid., §117.1, 536–37.
20. Ibid., §117.2, 537.

ferent order of nature for human life or a different plan of salvation for the human spirit."[21]

Having said this much, Schleiermacher wants to make one clarification. The real and actual contrast between those who are elected and those who are rejected should not be magnified to create a fundamental cleavage between the two, resulting in a permanent split of the species. (1) A permanent divisiveness between two factions cannot be ascribed to "original creation" lest it be said that there are two sets of species. (2) If the contrast were thought to have crept in later, against the appointed plan in the original creation, the original work, i.e., God's work, would have to be called faulty. If a fundamental inequality is created through Christ's entrance, one in which inherent powers of attraction to Christ are evidenced only in one section of the two divisions of humanity, we run into Pelagianism or Manichaeism, depending upon the case. (3) The contrast is in any case not creational; all those who were/are elected, at one time or another would be in the "rejected" category before having been ushered into the state of grace, an earlier period during which they would have had no material difference from the state of all those who completed their course of life in the state of so-called "rejection." So, the contrast between the elect and the rejected can only be a relative one, identical to the contrast between the two periods of any elected person's own life, between the person's "elect days" and "pre-elect or rejected days." It is temporary, it is transient. Therefore, the doctrine of the everlasting damnation of the "rejected" should be utterly abandoned; otherwise, it would obliterate the concept of species. God did not create two kinds of human species; the difference between the two sides must be seen only as a contingency of history, an accident:[22] an "accident" that is well within the original plan of God, in the divine government of the world. If part of the species is deemed lost forever, our sympathy for them arising out of our species-consciousness will convert the blessedness of eternal life to eternal misery. (4) If election occurs regardless of any merit in the object, then election is not a reward. This also means that rejection cannot be regarded as punishment either, unless one is willing to concede blatant contradiction within God. God's attributes of mercy and justice cannot be torn apart and handed out in pieces. If it is mercy, it is mercy for all,

21. Ibid., §117.4, 539.
22. Ibid., §118.1, 540.

and if it is justice, it is justice for all. There cannot be a cleavage between different attributes of God.

> In general terms, it is not to be conceded that there is a divided revelation of the divine attributes, in that they would then be limited and God would be an unlimited Being with limited attributes. Rather, justice and mercy must not exclude each other, but in the same people, mercy must show itself as justice.[23]

Therefore, it is justice for all and mercy for all, this in spite of the relative disparity in the according of redemption.

Someone might well object that even this relative disparity, in which only some come to know eternal life during that allotted period of time of earth, and that too at different stages of life, is in effect a real disparity and therefore is a blot on God's reputation, one that is unacceptable to Christian thought. Schleiermacher will not look for a way around this problem; he accepts this divinely ordered discrimination, but it is just one among many others we observe in life. Exactly similar discrimination can be detected in God's allowing many pre-natal lives to perish in their mother's wombs, leaving only the rest to see the light of independent existence.[24]

Disparities and variations inherently belong to the nature of multiplicity and organicity. However, in themselves disparities of life are never permanent; they always keep fluctuating. In consonance with that observation, we must also say that the elect-rejected disparity too cannot be a permanently entrenched division. We say this with one difference, of course: from the point of the time of one's election, the same person is elect always; all those who are not elect are moving toward their election, each one in one's own time. Moreover, since our species-consciousness is such that each one of us belongs to everyone else, the lessness of one person's good fortune is in effect the lessness of the same for everyone else. If another person is endowed with riches, that too is a blessing within humanity as a whole and is thus, everyone's blessing. Therefore, the disparities, which are indeed real, cancel out each other in the final count. Accordingly, an atomistic view of things is not in any way appropriate in a species-conscious view of life. Thus, the only explanation one can give with regard to the disparity in contention is this: the reason or the

23. Ibid., §118.2, 543–44.
24. *Ueber die Lehre von der Erwählung*, 203, 11, 18–24.

peculiar dynamic in the working out of the natural course of history must be explored either at the beginning of history or at its end, depending upon one's perspective—at the beginning if we depend on divine good pleasure, and at the end if we depend on divine predestination; and whichever is the case, one cannot drive a wedge between the two, for God's good-pleasure and predestination coincide.

Election and the Divine Good Pleasure

Election as God's act is that positive spiritual influence on the functioning of the divine government of the world, forming and furthering the Reign of God, within the organic confines of the universal structure, as an integral part of the whole. In separating certain human beings, name by name, out of the mass into a community of the Christ-centered Church, God brings about this specific modification in the world. Only with caution can we say that it re-shapes the form of the divine government of the world, because with regard to divine causality whatever is actual is what really is; all mere possibilities are excluded. In light of the insistence on the singularity (or better, non-duality) of God's act, the depiction of election as a special divine activity within the larger structure of the universe can be considered as a legitimate set-up only as a concession to our limitations, as a convenience for thought and analysis. This scheme is not meant to posit an act within God's act, it is intended only to express perception in faith of certain highlights regarding the historical ramifications of God's act in governing the world based on God's good pleasure. Election can be asserted as God's act only if we are willing to see it as that high watermark which signifies and represents the fullness of God's total non-dual act. This also helps us make one important inference: that if through election one sees any arbitrariness in God, then the totality of God's work, namely creation/preservation must evidence the same arbitrariness. To put the matter differently, blaming God for an arbitrary election is identical to blaming God for an arbitrary creation!

Given the thrust of Schleiermacher's thinking, it would be easy to surmise that God's choice of Jesus of Nazareth to be the savior of the world can be termed God's primordial election, effected on behalf of the world. Instead he views the union between the divine and the human in Jesus as God's election of the world. Each individuated case of regeneration that follows from the procession of God's grace through Jesus down through all the years is an extension of union of the divine and the human. The exact shape of this extension (i.e., the fullest detailed chronicle of who all entered the Reign of God, when, where and how and of all who produced how much of an influence in all directions etc. to bring Church life, and consequently, total human life to the shape that we see at present) is exactly the outworking of the divine good pleasure; nothing more and nothing less. To say that things could have been otherwise is to imply knowledge that God could have created a different set of human species. Each individual conversion is conditioned by the context in which the individual is placed; therefore, basing election of individuals to regeneration at each one's destined time and place simply expresses a dependence of our thoughts on the notion of God's fore-knowledge, a fore-knowledge that is identical to fore-ordination, thus eliminating the Pelagian wedge that distorts God's omnipresence. Further, if it were conceded that something could happen that God had not explicitly willed, then we could have had to contend with Manichaeism, or the existence of a parallel will alongside God's.[25]

Since each individual is determined by the context of his or her human relations (not robbing from any credit that duly belongs to human freedom), we are able to posit a two-way relation between the individual and the context involved. Each is patterned to suit exactly the peculiar needs of the other in such a way that nothing else can be thought to substitute for one or the other. The only explanation for this twofold relation is that it is a divine ordination proceeding from God's good pleasure. Now, the same reciprocity can be affirmed with regard to Jesus and the whole creation.

> Christ was determined as He was only because and insofar as the entire context was determined in a certain way; and, conversely, the entire context was so determined only because and insofar as Christ was determined in a certain way. To say this obviously means, in taking our stand upon the divine good pleasure, to say that the determination in both cases is what it is simply through the divine good pleasure. Indeed, whenever we conceive of the compass of natural causality as a self-enclosed whole and refer back to its establishment in the divine causality,

---

25. See Ward, "The Doctrine of Election in the Theologies of Friedrich Schleiermacher and Karl Barth," 14–15.

we can reach no ground of determination for the latter except the divine good pleasure.[26]

Election as God's work in history

In our discussion, we have isolated two ways of viewing the fact of election. (1) As a natural happening, it is comprised of some transforming influence that transpires in accordance with the laws governing normal human relations. As such, each instance of election is a distinctive manifestation of relative causality whereby a combination of free thinking and activity intermixes with conditioning influences on the person from his or her context. By willingly yielding to the transforming influence that invades him or her, the individual substratum is modified to produce the person as a new creation, as a unique admixture in relation to the person's old self and as the new life of Christ wrapped in the rest of the conditioning influence. Consequently, both the relative freedom and the relative dependence of the person are also modified to suit the new life that person acquires. The moment of such a personal transformation is also the moment at which a new relationship (the old being dead) for the person with the rest of humanity begins as he or she joins the communion of transformed persons to enjoy its newness and actively to reshape the community and humanity itself to whatever degree or magnitude is made possible by the person's own prowess. The whole process is an effecting of a mutual influence and conditioning. As such, this can be called God's work only as any other happening in the course of history can be called the same.

(2) We have already established that, for Schleiermacher, the total structure of history or of a created entity seen as a single unit is the effect of God's non-dual decree, God's non-dual, non-multiple act. Strictly speaking, this act (which is the same as being a non-dual entity, since act and effect are identical in God) is the expression of God's absolute freedom, and this is the only dwelling spot for the content of the expression "absolute freedom."[27] As against this exclusive freedom, human causality

---

26. *Christian Faith*, §120.3, 555.

27. I am stretching things a little bit here. In Schleiermacher's thinking, even though "absolute freedom" is a concept that can legitimately be attributed to God, the perceptible content of that thought has no meaning to us as it is absolutely beyond any possible experience of any nature. So, Schleiermacher abstains from any talk about "absolute free-

is always conditioned by creational forces near and far, contained within a totality (within which everything is conditioned by everything else) the boundaries of which will ever remain unreachable for us.[28] So, the totality of creational causality can be grasped in our conception only in a negative fashion, as something endlessly stretched out. Yet, since the dynamic within this infinite stretch is such that every isolable part is related in infinite ways to everything else, the mass of the totality should be thought of as a constant, inner set of relations within it being always in commotion, in dynamic interaction, bringing forth creative configurations, positive or negative, ever anew. Parts are always related both to other parts and to the whole, and the whole to parts, thus in an interdependent causality; and this is the only causality possible within the confines of creation. The relation between God and the creation can be best expressed in terms of causality. The exhaustive edifice of relative causality is absolutely dependent upon the divine causality; there is no counter-influence. Since God's subsistence is *absolutely* devoid of encumbrances and as such God lives in absolute freedom, absolute freedom has no analogue in creation. Therefore, there is no analogy between divine causality, which corresponds to "absolute freedom," and human causality, which corresponds to relative and dependent freedom. Election as a contingent happening or as a modification of relationship connected with human relations and activities is, then, to be thought of as one thing among many such things; however, we have earlier hinted at another way of looking at election.

---

dom," as that is not relevant for our existence in any case. (In *Christian Faith*, §41.P.S., 156, there is the mention that God's decree comes from God's absolute freedom. But an exposition of absolute freedom is out of place; it is inserted there only to show the utter contrast between human causality and divine causality.) This is one place where Schleiermacher is a good Kantian. He has wholeheartedly given himself to the argument that God-in-Godself is a conception utterly inconceivable to us. Therefore, "absolute freedom" in itself, viewed as God's estate in itself, is also a meaningless concept for us. My use of it is only a provisional one, an imaginary creation of a counterpoint to "absolute dependence," in order to form a structure for understanding, as a parallel to the relation between relative dependence and relative freedom. In reality the qualification "absolute" placed before "dependence" is to indicate the certain absence and impossibility of a counterpoint; indeed, if there should ever be a counterpoint, it would cease to be "absolute."

28. This is because as beings limited by time and space, we will never be able to stand outside of time and space, that is, not even in imagination, to compare it with parallel entities, and to analyze and study it objectively.

In chapter 3, we established that since the being of God in Jesus is the "omnipresence of God" in Him, as the presence that represents the entirety of God's presence and activity in the world, God's work in history is identical with God's work in Jesus. In chapter 4 we have argued that for Jesus' own sake alone, He never had any need to be in this world due to His all-round perfection and that His being in its entirety, therefore, is for His activity, which is redemption of humanity. In the present chapter, we have said that since election of people toward regeneration is the means by which God carries out God's blueprint for the world, the choice of Jesus to be the bearer of salvation can in a way be called the original or primordial election. Everyone else who is elected is elected in and through Christ. Since election is the means by which God effects Jesus' activity in the world, the election of Jesus in conjunction with the election of everyone else down through the human story can be called God's work in history. In other words, that which God started in Jesus of Nazareth, God completes through extending the influence of Jesus to people through election. To put the matter differently, the divine causality in the election of Jesus is identical with the divine causality in the election of all those who reach regeneration; this divine causality, in turn, is identical with God's work in history.

6

God's Work in History in and through the Community of Faith

THE GOOD WORK THAT GOD BEGAN IN JESUS IS MAINTAINED AND FURTHERED to take it to a future completion through the community of faith that Jesus established. Through the influencing power inherent in the Church, God brings about change in the hearts of people, adds new recruits to the Church, and ministers to one and all who are already within. God does all this through the instrumentality of each person's relationship to the rest and all other relationships and conditioned by each one's station in life (primarily one's "inner life," that is, but by no means excluding one's "outer life," for the former influences and is fully experienced through the latter). In this way God preserves and strengthens each and all, grows the Church in the world, and thereby blesses the world.

The Divine Motive and Means in Redemption

The driving force of God's love is the divine motive in the furtherance of redemption, and the divine means employed is God's wisdom. However, this is the part of our study where we must warn ourselves that we are treading on delicate ground; we are trying to represent divine causality in the structure and language of human causality. The attempt is, as such, inevitable due to our human limitation, but we are intelligent enough to recognize that it is fraught with the danger of anthropomorphic "reductionism." Anthropomorphism is unavoidable to some extent, but a less than careful use of it will lead to untenable propositions and pave the way for atheism, if history is any guide.[1]

---

1. See Ebeling, "Schleiermacher's Doctrine of the Divine Attributes," 127–28.

Election, predestination, and the creation of the Church occur out of a motive (not to be thought of as a fleeting emotion) within God; it is the same motive that prompts God (the present tense is used with caution) to create and preserve. The Christian consciousness of that motive is expressed in the divine attribute of "love," and the practical working out of that love is seen in the divine attribute of "wisdom." God is love; God is equated only with love and nothing else.[2] (Again, care should be taken to note that Schleiermacher is not treating God-in-Godself, nor is he thinking of God as a singular person; what he describes are the attributes that we ascribe to God in our dependent relationship to God, which attributes, however, are as real as our dependence itself.) It may also be helpful here to quote proposition 50 from *Christian Faith*. "All attributes that we ascribe to God are to designate not something special in God but only something special in the way in which the absolute feeling of dependence is to be referred to Him."[3] Love is the essence of God within Christian consciousness; it is the preceding impulse within God that is revealed as motivating God to create and redeem. However, there is no chronological sequence involved in the relation between God's love and God's creation. "Now, in all human causality we distinguish between the underlying disposition and the more or less corresponding way in which it is carried out."[4] This is the distinction that is referred to in making a tentative distinction between God's motive and action. However, we must bear in mind that from the ultimate point of view there is no such distinction in God; they are identical. That being the case, even the distinctions that we make between the different attributes that we ascribe to God are of the same character; ultimately they are unreal.

Schleiermacher equates "essence" and "attributes" in God; thus, hereafter the German word for "essence," *Wesen*, will be more properly translated "nature."[5] All other attributes gain meaning finally and only through love, because love is the single scriptural attribute that is comprehensive enough to act as the causal ground for the self-impartation of God (not a pantheistic one). Insofar as there cannot be any difference between essence and attributes in God, that which is predicated of God

---

2. 1 John 4:16.
3. *Christian Faith*, §50, 194.
4. Ibid., §165.1, 726.
5. Ibid., §167.1, 730.

must be deep and broad enough to contain all attributes that can be ascribed to God. While we may be able to find another attribute "in virtue of which all finite things are through God as they are,"[6] only love provides the motive, so to speak, for God's action. The divine attribute by which the proper designing of aims regarding the divine government of the world is effected is called wisdom. Or, "wisdom is the art, as it were, of realizing the divine love completely."[7]

Since divine love and wisdom are active attributes, not passive or receptive, the preceding impulse in God cannot be affected or influenced by anyone, anytime, anywhere. God's love is not amenable to fleeting feelings; it is not passionate love. Individual, instantiated activities in their isolation do not affect God, because God's spatio-temporal transcendence requires that God be related to all mundane impulses at all places and at all times equally in a non-temporal, non-spatial manner; thus, the best way to understand God's love is to think of God as being related to world history in its totality, the explanation of which can be given only negatively, as neither instantaneously nor durationally related, and neither atomistically nor indefinitely present.

Divine love, in Christian piety, is the communication of the divine nature, and it is realized only through redemption and as a concept; it has relevance for the explication of faith only in its relation to redemption.[8] Those who disagree with this position, seeing a divine love in the general arrangement of nature apart from redemption, are generally those who "tend more to put the distinctive features of Christianity in the shadows than to give them prominence."[9] In any case, Schleiermacher concedes that even among people who are yet to be touched by the grace of God in Christ, their capacity for God-consciousness in its Christian modification qualifies them, as well, to conceive themselves as objects of divine love, notwithstanding the fact that some of them may be extremely negatively disposed to Christ at present.

Redemption is our experience of God's love, and that is the reason we attribute "love" to God. Therefore, insofar as a recognition of God's

6. Ibid.
7. *Christian Faith*, §165.1, 727.
8. The resemblance to views of Calvin and Barth here is ours to observe. Of course, Calvin and Barth would use "revelation" here instead of "redemption" and that too differently conceived in each case. However, the thrust of the thought is similar in all three.
9. *Christian Faith*, §166.1, 728.

love is not developed within the inner life of those who are not yet redeemed, we should say: In their consciousness God is not as yet conceived as loving them. "As for those who still . . . hover between idolatry and Godlessness, precisely to that extent they do not love God and cannot conceive of God's loving them."[10] Even people who have some consciousness of God or some glimpses of grace cannot be said to recognize God's love for them, because proper development of such a recognition can come only through the ministration of Christ and the Holy Spirit.

Since God's love can be manifested only in God's will for human beings, and since God's will for human beings is manifested only in and through Jesus, God's love (as fully as it can be conceived at present) is expressed only in and through Jesus. Since Jesus is the perfect expression of God's love for the world, and since God's love (intention) and God's work (act) are identical, God's work in history is identical to God's work in Jesus. Since God's wisdom is the principle by which the divine self-impartation or communication takes place, (and self-impartation always implies God's sending of Jesus to effect redemption), and since the whole history of the world is ordered by God's wisdom in such a way as to fashion the point of Jesus' entry into time as the "fullness of time" (in relation to God's self-impartation or redemption), and since fullness of time means that, technically speaking, all the past is purposely made to converge at this point as its fulfillment and all the future is purposely made to flow out of it as its realization in history,[11] God's work in history is identical to God's work in Jesus.

10. Ibid., §166.2, 729. We may well observe here that generally it can safely be taken that God's love for all human beings is a concept alien to every non-Christian religion. One exception may be found in the *Bhagavad Gita*, where the Krishna (the incarnation of Vishnu who is one of the Triad of Hinduism) tells Arjuna the warrior, the following:

> Hear again my supreme word,
> Most secret of all.
> Thou art surely loved by me;
> Therefore, I shall speak for thy good. (*Gita* 18:64)

Strangely enough, this is a verse that is either forgotten or has gone utterly unappreciated in general Hindu thinking. However, we have copious examples in Hinduism where the devotees' uninhibited love for God is expressed in elegant and elaborate terms without ever entertaining a thought of reciprocal love from God to the devotees. We do have the examples of divine grace showered upon the devotee (though in a different sense from that of Christian grace), but God's love for the devotee eludes Hindu thinking as much as in any other non-Christian thinking.

11. I am using the words "past" and "future" in a technical sense here. They are not

It may also be helpful to reiterate that in using "redemption" Schleiermacher is not talking about instantiated instances of individual conversions; it is the big picture of the total work of Christ that is envisaged. "If we should wish to regard the life of the individual as its object but not to sink back into the grossest particularism, we cannot infer the divine love from such advancements of life which are conditioned by restraints against life in others, because then in every instance the opposite of love would be present alongside love itself."[12] The object of redemption, then, is all people of all times embraced as a single unit. The object of God's work is a single unit; that is, the divine love and wisdom are evidenced in the totality of God's work that exists in human beings' absolute dependence on God, facilitating retention of the teaching of the impassibility of God. God's love can then be considered as love of a different nature from human love, a love that is neither counterposed nor defined by the existence of a contrasting feeling within nor ever given over to the vagaries of variability. This is a love that contains the divine wisdom within it. Therefore, there is absolutely no conflict between God's intention and action; they are identical, which creates the condition for us to say that the impassibility of God is intact. The fact of the revelatory nature of God's love and wisdom is no indication that they are revealed in separation from each other, or even that together they are disclosed apart from what is indicated in the rest of God's attributes. In intention and action God is one.

Now, Richard R. Niebuhr has found problems in trying to reconcile Schleiermacher's appreciation for the impassibility of God, on the one hand, and God's intentionality, or divine love and wisdom on the other hand.[13] Niebuhr comments:

> I think one might conceivably get him off the hook by saying that the impassibility he was thinking about was steadfastness of

meant to indicate all the literally preceding and succeeding moments relating to the specific clock-moment under consideration. By past is meant all impulses in history apart from Christ, all of which are created and controlled to proceed to meet in Christ, and by future is meant all impulses proceeding from Christ from His time and until Christianity is consummated.—Here "self-impartation" and (self-) "communication" both translate "*selbstmittheilung.*"

12. *Christian Faith*, §166.1, 728.
13. Niebuhr, "Schleiermacher and the Names of God," 213.

intention. God doesn't change his goal; God doesn't change his mind. That might be one way of doing it, but I am speculating.[14]

However, on his own part Schleiermacher has not gotten entangled on any "hook" from which anyone should strain to release him; in fact, this is one of those instances where it is fundamentally unjust even to fault Schleiermacher for this misunderstanding. It is very clear in Schleiermacher that the impassible God is a God of intentionality. In all the appropriate places, he constantly made it crystal-clear that there cannot be any distinction between the nature and attributes of God. Both refer to the same God, who is simple in nature (or, in my opinion, better put in the negative term "non-complex"), and both impassibility and intentionality are predicated on and only on the basis of our experience of absolute dependence on God. Accordingly, one can say that what we are talking about with regard to God is impassible intentionality. God's love is always a will to love, and it cannot be otherwise; therefore, love is a forceful expression of God's intentionality. The human will to love is always trapped in temporal contingencies and exigencies and therefore always involves a weakened will; and we will not do well to superimpose our weaknesses on God's will (to love). Therefore, no one should have any reason to cast aspersions on God's impassibility due to God's love. By no stretch of the imagination is love a weakness in God. Because of the absolute non-duality of intention in God, one cannot rightly read any emotional variation into God.

The very intelligent and ingenious use of "causality" to explain God's action effectively protects the idea of God from the realm of variation and contrasts. Divine intentionality is in no way indicative of the existence of or possibility of an analogy between divine causality and human causality, and as such analogous relations that are invariably affixed within the realm of human causality are simply not applicable to divine causality. In fact, the relation between absolute dependence and relative dependence can be considered as similar to the relation between divine causality and dependent causality provided that we do not fail to cite that the concept of absolute dependence is our way of understanding our relationship to God, whereas the concept of divine causality is our way of understanding God's relationship to us.

---

14. Ibid.

The intentionality of God's love is identical to the actuality of God's wisdom, which in turn is identical to God's preservation, which is identical to God's creation. Where almighty love is, there absolute wisdom is.[15] Love self-imparts, self-communicates. Even if we do not have any privileged access to the impetus of God's actions, we can read it back through the manifested consequences (which includes all available empirical grounds, scripture, the tradition of the Church within the context of the history of humanity and of the world, and the prophetic perception of our future in communion with God that inevitably occurs in us). Wisdom orders the world to effect that self-imparting and self-communication. Redemption is the consequence. Whereas in its totality the history of the world is itself the product of the divine intentionality, in Christian consciousness it is also and invariably seen both as the stage and as the benefiting object of the practical working out of redemptive history ordered through that same intentionality.

Redemption is the mirror through which Christian consciousness is enabled to understand God's estimation of humanity and history, hence also God's work in, with and for the world in history. Predestination, election and the general upkeep of the world are all of the same divine decree; and since the motive behind the decree is love, God arranges the totality of history towards an eschatological sweep of the whole world into Christian redemption; and that is the final end toward which the world is created.

Redemption and the Contrast between Grace and Sin

Redemption, of course, is the transposition of people from the realm of sin to that of grace. For Schleiermacher, these two realms and the two corresponding doctrines stand back to back, inseparable as they are. However, it is also true that in the way he conceives the scheme of things there is a logical and essential priority of grace over sin, because the doctrine of the latter is and exists only and alone for the doctrine of the former.

> Schleiermacher's entire discussion of sin is ultimately subsumed under grace. Indeed, it must be so, for methodological as well as substantive reasons: the consciousness of sin is an abstraction

---

15. *Christian Faith*, §168.1, 732.

from the Christian consciousness in its entirety, and it presupposes the consciousness of grace (see par. 64).[16]

It is the infusion of grace that informs in us the feeling that life apart from a relationship to God is inadequate and sinful. When we let grace have its say in us, we become dissatisfied with our sinful condition and wish to be possessed by the love and wisdom of God.

Alienation from God (sin) is something that originates in us, as imperfect conditions of humanity are passed on to us; but communion with God is something that is transferred to us from the abundance of the blessedness of the Redeemer according to God's grace. This grace is also the same as the activation of God's electing decree in the sense that it is the particular historical ramification of that decree pertaining to the particular person.

When consciousness of God has not developed in a person, "absolute dependence" in that person is in a state of bondage, which, viewed from a Christian perspective, is the same as alienation from God, or being in a sinful state. Because of the presence and sway of "original sin" (original in the individual by virtue of the deriving of the being of the individual from the commonality of the species, which involves, in itself, corporate sin and corporate guilt), it is our common human experience that the lower power of the soul ("flesh") manifests its prowess and sway over the individual well ahead of the higher power of the soul ("spirit").

If the flesh would have absolute sway over us, we would be in a state of absolute sin. If the flesh would be subject to the spirit, i.e., if the impulses that proceed from the spirit would comprise the active principle within the flesh as well, or if there would be perfect coordination between the spirit and the flesh such that the flesh yields totally to the spirit, we would see an absolute absence of sin. These two scenarios, however, can never happen in real life, except in the case of Jesus, who was without sin. Each individual life at each point in time is a manifestation of the conflict between flesh and spirit, determined by the level of spirituality in which he or she is living at a given point. However, the estate of those on whom the power of flesh has a good grip, and who are still living in a primitive or less than desirable stage of life, Schleiermacher would describe not as one of sinfulness but as a state of crudity and ignorance. It comes to be recognized as sin only when they are enlightened by grace.

---

16. Wyman, "Rethinking the Christian Doctrine of Sin," 209.

Sin is a lower level of existence; and its lowness is a real lowness only in comparison with the state of life in grace.

Apart from the conscientization of life through grace, a human state cannot be recognized as either sinful or lower. Therefore, we can say, sin is ordained by God in relation to redemption, for the sake of redemption; in fact, the two are packed together as a single unit. The more aversion we feel against sin, the more value we attribute to redemption, or the more we value grace. The understanding of God as gracious within the Christian community is commensurate with the feelings sin gives us as the communication of God-consciousness is effected within us through impartation of blessedness wrought through the Redeemer.

Divine "ordination," as we noted in the previous paragraph, should not be given a mechanical connotation; it cannot be construed as a brute force that God employs toward making humans automatons. Rather, the absolute causality of God conditions all time, all space and all other causation; and that includes sin and other evil as well. There cannot be a simple positive description of divine causality, because it lacks an analogue in our mundane experience. Finite causality is what it is only in terms of the contrast between activity and passivity involved in it (and the totality of all such contrasts that constitutes the totality of finiteness). Divine causality is to be understood in contrast with finiteness (both in its parts and in its totality), the former totally conditioning the latter, the latter having no counter-influence on the former, and the two remaining equal in scope.

A doctrine of absolute determinism, the explanation of which is based on the invocation of either natural or supernatural powers, would not find favor with Schleiermacher; rather, within the confines of our natural limitations and our susceptibility to natural influences, humans are free to choose. (If something is imposed upon us against our will, even if it is blessedness, it would cease to be blessedness in the person because it is imposed and thus probably repulsive.) If there is no divine causality, consciousness of sin is a delusion. That which is grounded in human freedom must already be grounded in divine causality. Human freedom and unfreedom are equally grounded in divine causality. So, evil too is grounded in divine causality.[17] "The Church doctrine, as an accurate expression of our self-consciousness, does not exclude the possibility

---

17. *Christian Faith*, §82.2, 339.

of God's being in some sense the Author of sin."[18] Moreover, holiness and justice in God cannot be conceived apart from their relation to evil.[19]

Since sin can be said to exist only where there is consciousness of it, it is always conditioned by a preceding good. That good is present to us not just as an idea or a notion but as flesh and blood, in Christ's original perfection or sinlessness, or in his absolute consciousness of God. (Sin exists where there are interruptions in God-consciousness or the absence thereof.) A notion of an original historical perfection as present in a pre-fall couple is a willing endorsement of a false notion of a fundamental alteration in human nature. The thought of the fall of a sinless couple, in and from a perfect setting, is a thought almost as atrocious as a thought of Jesus' falling! "Now the less we found cause in an earlier passage to ascribe a high degree of religious morality and religious enlightenment to the first pair before their first sin, and the less successful an effort to explain the first sin as proceeding from a perfectly sinless condition, the more decisively does every occasion for claiming that a change in human nature was produced fall away."[20]

The exclusion of sin from the province of human absolute dependence opens the way to Manichaeism. Since there is no division between causing and permitting in divine causality, and since it is against the explicit will of God for people to indulge in sin, and since sin and evil are dehumanizing forces that stand at cross purposes with God's good will for humanity, as an obvious hindrance to the furtherance of God's redemptive activity, we should now explore more fully the nature of God's relation to sin and evil.

Apart from divine causality, human causality is nebulous, unreliable, groundless, anchorless, meaningless and illogical. Sin and evil cannot be thought to have a separate, ultimate anchor apart from that which sustains the interconnected process of nature. Radical separation of sin and evil from the anchor that holds the interconnected process of nature would in effect create an ultimate duality in the Ultimate Reality. Therefore, sin and evil must belong to the same divine causality that we entertain for the totality of the rest of the interconnectedness. So, whether one takes a Pelagian route or an Augustinian route, ultimately the transmundane

18. Ibid., §81.3, 335.
19. Ibid., §167.2, 731.

20. Ibid., §72.3, 298. The earlier passage mentioned here is §61, according to Schleiermacher's note here.

responsibility for these two realities of life lies squarely on God. Then, the dilemma before us is to find a rationale for this apparent display of a contradiction in God's having to work against that (sin and evil) which the same God ordains. Yet, it is not very difficult for Schleiermacher to reconcile these seeming opposites. With regard to the relation between God and evil, Schleiermacher says: "Denn wenn einmal gesagt ist, alles wirkliche müsse durch den schaffenden Willen Gottes gesezt sein, und dann wiederum, Gott dürfe nicht Urheber des Bösen sein: so ist ja beides nur auf die Eine Weise zu vereinsgegen, wenn man sagen kann, daß in Bezug auf Gott das Böse gar nicht ist."[21] The assertion that evil does not exist for God, taken by itself, can be utterly shocking;[22] but since, at this stage, the context and the total framework of Schleiermacher's theological thinking is familiar to us, we are advantageously situated to see the logic of it.

21. *Ueber die Lehre von der Erwählung*, 208. Translation: "Once it is held that everything actual would have to be established by the creating will of God and then, on the other hand, that God could not be conceived as the author of wickedness, the only way to reconcile the two propositions is to be able to say that with reference to God wickedness is non-existent." Here "wickedness" is used for what is sometimes termed "moral evil" (*Böse*) vs. evil in general (*Übel*). *Böse* means human evil of any kind, moral or not.

22. The reality of evil and suffering were all too familiar for Schleiermacher in his personal experience; personal tragedies and pains were constant companions in life. He lived all his life in constant ill-health, and the physical ailments were certainly even more severe than Calvin's. He lost his only nine-year-old son. His estrangement from his father (though they made up later) had an extremely debilitating effect on his spirit as a teenager. Marital bliss, for the sake of which he was willing to sacrifice almost anything he had except his religion, came rather late to him, and that too only after long years of love-disappointments. In spite of his unstinting love for his wife, he was never able to interact very intelligently with her due especially to the intellectual disparity between the two; rather, she had to be treated more like a daughter than anything else, surely something not to his liking as a man who tended to adore women more than men. His later years became more hurtful as his wife fell under the total religious sway of a woman whom he had tried to help, not least by including her and her daughter in his own household, but who became a constant source of irritation for him. He was a direct victim of the highhandedness of Napoleon and at times of the Prussian state and religious establishment. The political misfortunes of Prussian society always bothered him. All his life, he lived under the pain of being misunderstood by most people, even though he always felt he was never to be blamed for that. Recognizing Hegel's ability, he brought Hegel to the philosophy faculty of the University of Berlin, despite knowing Hegel's ill-disposition toward him. True to his premonition, Hegel's extreme unkindness, pugnacity and subversion often made his life at the University a veritable hell. He knew how wicked the human heart could be, nevertheless the religious and the romantic spirit that shaped him constantly prevailed over everything else.

Evil is the result of sin, but certainly not in such a way that any individual's sufferings, pains and misfortunes could be attributed to the individual's sin or the punishment thereof, in this respect, as is done in the Hindu conception of *karma*. Because of our species-nature, each one takes his or her own share of the punishment for the sin of all members of the species as much as each one shares in the blessings that accrue to the species taken as a whole. However, the distribution of pleasure and pain are not in proportion to each one's desert; whatever comes to us comes by virtue of the specific placement of each individual in the whole, coupled with God's wisdom concerning the individual's specific use of endowments received in and through the structure of that individual's relations within the whole. However, we can say this much: The total pain of the whole species is indeed commensurate with punishment for the total sin of the species, though it is distributed unevenly. In other words, this is a doctrine of collective *karma*, as against the atomistic or individualistic *karma* featured in Hindu thought.

In every evil/pain there is some associated good/pleasure and in every good/pleasure there is some associated evil/pain. Were one to accord identical grants to two individuals, the corresponding pleasure-pain proportion to the two recipients will vary according as the two are differently placed and as they receive the accord differently, proving good and evil to be relative to the person's personal existence and peculiar setting. This is not to minimize the terribleness of evil or sin, it is only to place it where it belongs; sin and other evil, notwithstanding their awfulness, are only passing pangs of finiteness.

Since human evil is itself the product of sin, God's relation to that evil is related to God's relation to sin; hence, sin *per se* is also a nonreality with reference to God. The priority given to grace over sin in Schleiermacher's theology is identical to the priority he gives to election over rejection. Without election, there is no rejection. When election is instituted, rejection becomes a reality relative to election; but it is never really real on its own, because it is only for a time, only until divine election pertaining to that person is effected in reality. A sinful state, as a Christian theological doctrine, is likewise a temporal reality, real only relative to grace, and only until and insofar as grace operates in the individual to make the same a person of faith. Sin, not as pangs and privations of finiteness but as a Christian theological concept, exists only in relation to grace, and it exists exactly in parallel relation to the contrast between flesh and spirit, or the world conceived as in need of redemption and the Redeemer. Just as rejection in comparison to election is less real or, from an ultimate point of view, non-real, sin too in comparison to grace is less real, a passing phase, or ultimately non-real. It is in this sense that Schleiermacher can say that sin and evil do not exist for God.

Since sin exists only in contrast to grace, in the pre-grace period nothing that exists (which should eventually become sinful existence individually or collectively, in contrast to grace, when grace is subsequently introduced) is to be called sinful, regardless of the terribleness or dehumanizing oppressiveness or life-hindering dynamic present therein. What needs to be noted is this: "Sin" is a technical theological term used by Schleiermacher in contrast to "grace," as we have explained. So, theologically, even as a concept, sin does not exist apart from grace; and insofar as God's teleological plan for humanity is to wipe out sin through grace (which is already a reality in God by virtue of the omnipotence of God), sin has no ultimate reality for God as well; rather, it is non-real. However, the thought of the non-reality of sin is not an entitlement for us to discount divine causality in relation to it. We will quote here the first half of proposition 80 from *Christian Faith*. "As to the extent that sin and grace are contrasted in our self-consciousness, God cannot be thought of as the Author of sin in the same way as God's being thought of as the author of redemption."[23] This statement is exceedingly useful for explicating our thesis. Divine causality extends to everything in creation. However, sin exists only to be made extinct and be utterly swallowed up by grace; "rejection" exists only in the light of and only to be exterminated by "election," "flesh" exists only to be consumed by "spirit," and the "world" in need of redemption exists only to be swallowed up by the "Reign of God." Therefore, all the first members of these pairs have less reality compared to the second members, or they possess no inherent reality at all for their own sake and before God. So, it can be logically posited here that God's work in the world is identical to God's work in Jesus.

Reinhold Niebuhr has some highly disapproving comments to make against Schleiermacher's teachings on sin and evil.

> It is not surprising that wherever essentially classical views of man prevail, as for instance in both secular and Christian modern liberalism, the bias toward evil should be defined as residing not in

---

23. *Christian Faith*, §80, 326.

> man's will but in some sloth of nature which man has inherited from his relation to the brute creation. This remains true even when, as in the thought of men like Schleiermacher and in the theology of the social gospel, this sloth is attributed to the institutions and traditions of history rather than purely to sensual passion or to the finiteness of the mind. By thus placing the inherited sloth in history rather than in each man's own sensual nature, some justice is done to the actual historical continuum in which every human action takes place, but the bias toward evil is always outside and never inside a particular will.[24]

In a footnote, Niebuhr also quotes two sentences from Schleiermacher's treatment of original sin in *Christian Faith*, ostensibly to make the observation that Schleiermacher, in his treatment of sin, himself admits to emptying "sin" of any content and leaving only "original" in place in "original sin."[25] The third criticism he makes is this:

> Schleiermacher significantly makes no distinction between sin and the consciousness of sin. "We must insist on the fact," he writes, "that sin in general exists only insofar as there is consciousness of it." Pelagianism in short ascribes all sins to "deliberate malice and depravity," to use Calvin's phrase.[26]

The irony of this statement is that, while Niebuhr consigns Schleiermacher to the Pelagian camp, and understandably so from Niebuhr's point of view (and the discussion is under the sub-title, Pelagian Doctrines), Schleiermacher himself calls Pelagianism a natural heresy and conducts his theological thinking and teaching, from one end to the other, as a conspicuous bulwark against it. The problem is easily discerned here: Schleiermacher and Niebuhr have each imbued "Pelagianism" with vastly different content and connotation. This should give us some insight into the conflict that Niebuhr creates between himself and Schleiermacher with regard to sin as well! Obviously, they are talking two different languages. The criticism that Schleiermacher stoops to assigning the human bias toward sin and evil either to the inertia of nature or to inherited sloth needs rethinking. A bifurcation between individual and totality is a clear impossibility in Schleiermacher's scheme

---

24. Niebuhr, *The Nature and Destiny of Man*, 246.
25. Ibid.
26. Ibid., 247.

of things anyway; the relation between the two is organic. Every human being who produces particular evils does so in two capacities: (a) as an individual who, on his/her own, is fully responsible for the action produced, and (b) as an individual in whom the totality of humanity is incarnated in a unique configuration, thus being fully responsible for the evil action he/she produced influenced by and on behalf of humanity as a whole. The totality of humanity as an entity in which an individual act of evil took place through the instrumentality of an individual willing center within itself is also related to that particular evil in two capacities: (a) as an entity whose particular internal configuration has drawn evil into itself and thus takes the total responsibility and due punishment for the evil on itself, and (b) as the entity into which injustice has been done by its own particular configuration, in such a way that the entity holds the offending configuration totally responsible for the same (though due punishment is not always administered to the offending configuration). In other words, the individual who produces evil is one hundred percent responsible for the evil even as the community of humanity itself shares the same identical one hundred percent responsibility and guilt in itself. Organicity requires that there is no essential splitting up of such responsibility. This makes Niebuhr's first criticism invalid.

Niebuhr's second criticism, that in Schleiermacher's explanation of "original sin" Schleiermacher himself admits the barrenness of meaning in the concept "sin," is not a true representation of Schleiermacher's view. It has some truth in that in a postscript to the exposition of §69, and in assessing the suitability of the words enjoined in the expressions "actual sin" and "original sin" as they play out in relation to each other, Schleiermacher does express two reservations. (a) The adjective "actual" in the former expression may give rise to the suspicion that "original sin" is not actual; and (b) since the word "sin" is common to the two expressions, and the second is in apposition to the first, it is easy to superimpose the sense of "sin" in the first onto the second and to perceive what is a mistaken meaning. That is all that Schleiermacher is saying there, and therefore the gravity of the problem is not so disastrous as Niebuhr would have us believe.

The third squabble Niebuhr has with Schleiermacher is that he does not make any distinction between sin and consciousness of sin. This matter too is not exactly as it may appear. Schleiermacher considered reformation to be an ongoing process. Reworking of theology to suit the demands of newer times is both a protestant privilege and a serious responsibility. Considering the amazing scientific advances in the post-Enlightenment world, as well as the crucial intellectual developments occurring in Europe, and considering his contention that traditional theological thinking in his period had not come to grips with the changing times, he believed that there needed to be some paradigm changes in the way theology is thought and taught. Care should be taken to note that the paradigm change he advanced was merely in the structure and content of thought and not in piety, because he believed that what informed his religious being was the unique and uninterrupted supply of Christ-impulses mediated especially through his own Reformed tradition, which supply alone, though with contributions from other traditions, he deemed worthy to determine and define one's adherence to any tradition. To his mind, moreover, there was no longer much reason to separate Lutheran and Reformed within a joint Evangelical theology, despite notable differences in both theology and practice. In accordance with this belief, he thoroughly re-did Evangelical Reformed theology for the united Church in Prussia, and the total outlay was fitted into old categories available especially within this tradition; and in the process, he imbued the old categories with new meaning.

Thus, the category "sin" gets a new meaning; it ceases to be viewed as transgression of the law of God, for transgression of the law of God is seen to be only a ramification of sin. As was noted earlier, in dogmatic language sin is always seen in contrast to grace—two gradients in human spiritual existence, the one existing always in relation to the other. Sin is a comparative category, and the comparison made is always and only to grace. Accordingly, comparison ceases to have meaning at any place and stage where these levels of life are not both present.

If one were to imagine, for the sake of thought, an exclusively placed island somewhere beyond our horizon where there is absolutely no sin, where the species is perpetuated without sin, and where everyone lives in the state of grace, one would have to concede that in that island, the state of grace should be deemed the normal thing. Strictly speaking, since all who would live there would happen to live in absolute blessedness, and since a contrastable state of sin would not be available there, no way could be found for calling that state a state of grace in the same sense. Strictly speaking, the state of grace would always have to be defined in terms of the contrasting relation to redemption and the corresponding state of sin. In spite of the fact that the people of the imaginary island would live in the uninterrupted state of grace, in the absolute maximum experience of God's love, in the conscious enjoyment of the omnipresence of God in all persons, in exactly the same way as an absolutely sinless person would live in our midst, the islanders' dogmatic language could not strictly create a doctrine of grace viewed in terms of redemption and sin. However, their imaginary counterparts who live in identical blessedness, but among us, would have the language of grace in their dogmatics because their state of blessedness would always be viewed in terms of redemption, also because they would always be living in proximity to and in interaction with us sinful people, always in an organic relation with us, from among whom they were redeemed and with whom comparison can be made.

Similarly, even though this is utterly unreal in actuality, imagine for the sake of thought alone, an existence of a group of people who live in a state and stage wherein grace has never made its presence felt, and will never do so in the future, who live in utter ignorance of Jesus, and where it so happens that they do not have any inner thrust toward receiving grace, so that Galatians 4:4 is not applicable to them. Strictly speaking, the inhabitants in this place could not be said to be living in a sinful state, because the counterpoint of grace would not be available there to compare to it and render it conceivable as sinful. It is "sin" viewed in this sense that Schleiermacher is talking about when he says that there is no sin where there is no consciousness of sin. There is no intention in Schleiermacher's thinking ever to trivialize the seriousness of the oppressiveness or dehumanizing forces in life; neither is there any attempt to dilute responsibility for individual actions. One can neither attack nor defend a thinker like Schleiermacher sensibly by picking and choosing pieces from convenient points. His is a well-constructed edifice, the like of which is not found anywhere in the discipline of constructive Christian theology, and it requires that it be understood in its entirety for anyone to reckon with it meaningfully.

Before we move on from this topic, the following comment is apt here. The comparison between the two levels of existence (and by "existence" is meant only the human "spiritual life"), i.e., as between a sinful state and a graceful state, is postulated only to articulate the Christian view of "inner life" or spiritual life. This usage is never intended to invalidate analogous comparisons practiced by other religious adherents, even in their depicting their spiritual experiences as more noble than others' experiences. Others can assume as much freedom to do such things as Christians assume, and as much privilege to present apologies for their case, and in their own scheme to consign Christianity to a lower level. For example, similar to the claims made in favor of Christianity by Schleiermacher, Swami Vivekananda is entitled to make and does make claims for the advaitic point of view that Vedanta is the universal religion, and that it is the highest spiritual or religious experience possible to human beings, one to which all other faiths in the world (all of which do have valid spiritual experiences, but at a lower level) are traveling and are destined to be dissolved in.[27] Yet, strictly speaking, from the Christian perspective even the highest level of vedantic spiritual experience is still immersed in the realm of sin and therefore, like others, the vedantins too are in need of redemption.

God's Work in the World in and through the Church

The church is a visible entity, existing in the world but ideally over against that part of the world that is alienated from God and gradually expelling it. Thus, Schleiermacher will certainly refuse to join company with any rhetoric that articulates an uncompromising contrast between the world and the Church. Even the minutest of a compromise on the foundational doctrine of God's working in and through the *Naturzusammenhang* (interconnected process of nature) cannot be made, for Schleiermacher, without fundamentally destroying both the fabric of this modern scientific view of the world and the basis of our absolute dependence. The church, even at its best, is still a part of the world, and an organic part at that. The new creation is not a second creation; it is not the insertion of something alien into the world from outside of its confines, it is only the becoming patent of what was latent in the world; it is the blossoming, at the fullness of time, of the idiosyncratic potentiality of the original creation. Nature, being an infinitely complex entity within, is mutable and is subject to infinite combinations and limitless relative contrasts from within. On the other hand, as a totality it is a single existence, with nothing (which means not even emptiness) alongside it. This means that no evolvement of the Church from within the confines of nature, nor any fruitioning of the creative possibilities from within it, has either added

27. Swami Vivekananda, *Vedanta: Voice of Freedom*, 275–301.

anything to or subtracted anything from what can be enabled within the total complex of nature.

So, the reality of the relative contrast between Church and non-church is only a freshly formed configuration of the world at its divinely appointed time, related to each other like, say, a geographical location, or a national or political entity standing face to face with the rest of the world, though each in its own way. So, in this sense, the Church is in the world and of the world, and if the case were otherwise and the Church and the world were radically different, the Church would have had no ministry in the world! The Church must be sufficiently of and like non-Church to be able to make its influence on the world and thus change the world in accordance with the order of redemption. On the other hand, the world must have sufficient inherent susceptibility and adaptability within itself to take whatever influence peculiarly flows from the distinctiveness of the Church if the two are to work in the way they are meant to function. Furthermore, it is only logical that this be the situation, because it is the world that provides the conditions for the Church's existence and growth within its confines. Since its inception the Church has been feeding on the world to grow into what it is today.[28]

On the other hand, the peculiarities of the Church as a community of faith separate it from the world in such a way that it can be described as "not of the world." "If we consider it simply in its co-existence with the rest

---

28. If the world can be compared to a huge reservoir of milk to which there is attached an active inlet and outlet respectively representing the births and deaths that occur in the world of humanity, and if Jesus can be compared to an ounce of curd that is poured into this reservoir at a particular point in history, this illustration can efficiently explain the relation between the Church and the world. The original insertion, that of the ounce of curd, should be thought of as a supernatural work, the way we have explained it in chapter III. Just as curd is produced only from milk, Jesus should be thought of as having been produced from humanity, albeit in a way unknown to us. He was produced from the total strength of humanity, though somehow concealed in it. Once some curd is introduced into a mass of milk, that curd immediately starts the process of converting, through its bacterial action, each particle of milk in the reservoir into pure curd. This occurs in an ever expanding process until all the milk in the reservoir is converted into curd. This is exactly what Jesus is doing in the world in and through the Church. The Church is similar to the expanding curd, and the world is similar to the receding milk. The reverse process is impossible, just as curd cannot be reconverted into milk. The eschatology envisaged is the conversion of every particle of milk into curd, but because there is a constant inflow of milk, an absolute conversion of every particle of milk in the reservoir is almost a practical impossibility. The same is the case with the relation between the Church and the world of humanity.

of contemporary human existence, which is in Scripture condensed into the term 'world,' it is indeed permissible to say, as it seems, that the Church can just as well be recognized by its being different from the world as the world can be recognized by its being different from the Church."[29]

In the Christian scheme, humanity (that is, human beings of all times and of all places) may certainly be divided into two groups, namely, the Church and the non-Church or "the world." The Church operates on the non-Church and grows at its expense while humanity remains a constant. The plan is that the Church is to eliminate the non-Church by absorbing it steadily, progressively and completely over the course of time, into the Church, in such a way that the Church could become identical to humanity, regardless of the question of whether what is envisaged is historically achievable or not. Church is the operating field of grace and in that conception the world is the field of sin. The boundaries of the Church are visible to everyone; therefore the Church is visible and visibly separated from the world. Yet, the situation is not such that there is no sin in the Church and no grace in the world. Roughly speaking, the differentiating mark is that insofar as a preponderance of grace exists in the visible Church, grace is the operating fuel within the Church, while in its particular relation to redemption, sin may be said to fill the corresponding spot for the world.

However, particles of grace exist also in the world, and particles of sin exist also in the Church, so that, even given this somewhat confusing distinction, we can say that there is Church in the world and the world in the Church, no matter however large or small the measure may be. If someone dares to deny even a minimal sprinkling of grace in the world, that person will have the onerous and impossible task of explaining the Christian concept of the "fullness of time."

On the other hand, no one who is serious can object to the fact that sin is present within the Church, hence the presence of the sin-tainted "world" in the Church. Inasmuch as a redeemed person's or community's actual life contains the vestiges of the sinful world, there is an incessant struggle of flesh against spirit, hence the life of such a person or community is an admixture of spiritual life and worldly life; and inasmuch as the effects of the work of the Holy Spirit in its purity should be isolated for understanding, Schleiermacher makes a distinction between the visible

---

29. *Christian Faith*, §126.1, 582.

Church and the invisible Church, the former being the actual concrete living Christian community and the latter being "the totality of all the workings of the Spirit in their interconnectedness."[30] Thus, the Spirit's (that is, the Spirit of Jesus Christ and the common Spirit of the Church) prodding of people outside the visible Church toward regeneration must also be considered part of the "totality of all the workings of the Spirit," even as the sinful worldly elements within the visible Church in both their individual and their collective forms are counted out. In this respect, it is the invisible Church that "extends the Christian's awareness of God's active presence in all the world, even beyond 'Christianity'."[31]

Schleiermacher's "invisible Church" is very different from the common understanding of the expression in the Church, the latter understanding referring as it does to the mental construction of a conglomeration of all the born-again faithfuls of all places or to the membership as oriented to individuals as such. This sort of "invisible Church" is impure; it is a mixture of the world of sin and the Church as there is always a struggle between flesh and spirit within it. Schleiermacher's "invisible Church" is the interconnected whole of all the workings of the Spirit; therefore, it is singular, as against the divided, quarrelsome visible Church. The visible Church is sin-infested and fallible in all its manifestations and expressions, but the invisible Church is always infallible.

God's Work in the Church and in History through the Holy Spirit

The growth of the invisible Church always results in the growth of the visible Church, which can generally be defined as a concretely organized visible form of the invisible Church. The Church maintains itself in whatever purity exists within it, and grows and expels "the world" only by the workings and extensions of the Spirit.

During the days of Jesus' life on earth, everything that marked out the circle of friends around Him as participants in the blessings of the Reign of God was totally Jesus' gift to them; in other words, His friends had no spontaneous activity with regard to this particular matter, they only had a holy susceptibility to Jesus, so that the Reign of God, in a strict sense, was confined to Jesus and the shared communion with God

---

30. Ibid., §148.1, 677.
31. Tice in a communication to Kunnuthara, 4/28/96.

effected through Him. The basis of the common life totally depended upon Jesus, and therefore there was nothing common between Jesus and anyone else that could be isolated as the common spirit of the Reign of God; everything distinctive belonged to that one individual, Jesus. Living in the shadow of the absolute spiritual perfection of Jesus, they had absolutely no counter-influence on His spirituality or uninterrupted consciousness of God.[32] (In fact even the totality of the power of the world, conceived as apart from himself—which would be sinful in comparison to Him—would have had no capacity to make any improvement on or make any dent on His consciousness of God.)

As a household might scatter at the departure of its head, the disciples of Jesus scattered at his death. Yet, according to tradition their common bond in the Holy Spirit, "sent" to them and present among them after Jesus' ascension, kept them together. For the friends of Jesus, once Jesus departed from the world it was no more a direct receptivity to the person of Jesus that kept them spiritually enlivened; it was no more the case that just the influence of Jesus was passing through them; rather, there was an emergence of the spontaneous activity of their memory of Jesus and, hence, of a following and imitation of Him.

Ever since, it has been the case that each individual Christian's spontaneity is corrected and conditioned by the influence of all, which is the common spirit of the Church, and by the individual's corresponding receptivity. The omnipresence of God in Jesus continues in the world, not as though it were converted to the omnipresence of God in the person of

---

32. The absence of counter-influence that we are talking about is only with regard to the distinctive spirituality pertaining to the Reign of God. Had Jesus been sinfully counter-influenced in this realm, He would not have been perfect, because such counter-influence would bring change of a sinful nature. Then we would not have been able to claim that He had either absolute consciousness of God or absolute sinlessness. However, in every other aspect of life, Jesus was certainly susceptible to counter-influence because He was a human being like anyone else; and it could not be otherwise.

One further remark: Since God's presence is in the world, and God's revelation is in the world, and since consciousness of God's revelation is in the world, and since consciousness of God in anyone can arise only through that individual's relation with the world, even Jesus' absolute consciousness of God arose in Him only through His relations with the world of humanity and the larger world of God's creation. On the other hand, since Jesus recognized God's omnipresence within Him at every stage of His life, the consciousness of it being commensurate with the capacity for it at each stage of His development, in absolute terms He lacked receptivity for any sinful impress of the world or any sinful counter-influence on Him.

the Holy Spirit but as the omnipresence of God in Jesus Himself and in the interconnected whole of all the Christian spiritual particles, thus as the common, spiritual and infallible bond that exists within the Church, as the Holy Spirit. "Hence, taking everything together, we are able to say that after Christ's departure the disciples' common apprehension of Christ's activity changed into their own continuation of His community-forming activity, and that it was only through this process of their settled apprehension of Christ having come to be referred to the imperishable common spirit that the Christian Church arose."[33]

Now, when preparatory grace is at work in a person, the efficacy of Christ is making itself felt in that person through the activity of others in their Christian life. This happens in such a way that the person can be said to participate in the Christian common spirit through that person's own receptivity. Subsequently, when that person readily and actively re-fashions his or her relation to Christ to suit a mode that has currency within the Church, the person becomes a Christian, comes under the sway of the Reign of God present by faith within that person. Then the communication of the divine Spirit to that person can be said to have taken place. The result is the continuing indwelling of the Spirit in the person, which in actual terms is identical to the expressions "assumption into the living community of Christ" and "the bond of the community of the faithful." Therefore our communion with Christ is the same as our communion with the community of the faithful, both of which are constituted by our communion in and with the Holy Spirit.

By now it should be obvious that by Holy Spirit Schleiermacher is not talking about the third person of the Trinity as in the doctrine's classic formulations. The nature of God's self-subsistence is a useless thought for Schleiermacher; even Calvin's contention of God's accommodating Godself to human capacity is not particularly helpful.[34] God is neither personal nor impersonal but is non-personal, though God may well be perceived as relating person-to-person by persons, and God's communion with the faithful does occur through Christ and other persons. Internal distinctions within God are definitely not proper to the domain of dogmatics. The Trinitarian form adopted in Schleiermacher's dogmatics is not about a status of God in Godself; it is about the divine economy of

---

33. *Christian Faith*, §122.3, 568–69.

34. For Calvin's thought of God's accommodation, see Battles, *Interpreting John Calvin*, 117–37.

redemption; it is a Christological postulate, and it simply helps to explain the nature of God's dealing with us. It is, and can only be, a theological construct. God in Godself cannot be said to be either Unitarian or Trinitarian, and it is not in our interest to waste time on such useless speculation over unreachable ranges; therefore, the Trinitarian teaching of the Constantinopolitan creed, with or without the filioque, is not a matter of dogmatic interest for Schleiermacher. He might well have asserted that his Christological trinitarianism is, as it were, a trinitarianism of a higher order. In Schleiermacher's usage, the Holy Spirit is "the unity of life shared in the Christian community viewed as a moral Person."[35] The Holy Spirit, or the common Spirit of the Church, is the Being of God within the Church, and as such is a continuation of the presence of God in Jesus.

The consciousness of God that Christ imparts to the Church through the instrumentality of the Holy Spirit, active in the common life of the Church, makes Christ equidistant, or better, equiclose to all Christian communities both near and far, past, present and future, in such a say that Christ ever remains the Church's contemporary; and by way of individual participation in the relationship to His eternal blessedness, all believers ever share or remain in that contemporaneity. There is an unbridgeable philosophical gap between Schleiermacher and Søren Kierkegaard, in that the former is a product and proponent of that outlook of the West which regards humanity to be ever in immediate relationship with God, while the latter is a firm believer in the position that human sin absolutely forecloses any logical possibility of communication between God and human beings. However, both believe that in the aftermath of one's initiation into the redemptive influence of Christ, the person of faith exists in relationship with Christ and all the Christian faithful of all times.[36] From the flipside of this entry into contemporaneity with Christ, we surmise that the work of God in Christ is identical with the work of God in all faithful persons, which is, in turn, identical with the work of God in history.

---

35. *Christian Faith*, §116.3, 535. Here "moral" means entirely human in all its functions, not just in one's morals, this, as in Jesus, contrasted with being a merely physical receptacle for God.

36. See Kierkegaard, *Philosophical Fragments*, 72–110.

God's Work in History Thought through the Church's Doctrine of Eschatology

The consummation of the Church as an event in history is practically unattainable to us, as that would require the world to reach a perfect state of affairs wherein redemption is no more necessary. In contrast, it is a fact of life that sin will develop anew in each generation as the propagation of the species goes on.[37]

Since in Christian faith Christ is indisputably regarded as the end of prophecy, and since no more perfect form of inner life is ever to be expected, also since all who attain blessedness must invariably be blessed only with the impulse that uniquely emanates from Christ, and since the completion of God's work with regard to redemption is displayed in its entirety in Christ, Christ, in a certain sense, is also the consummation of the Church. As long as human life lasts, the essence of human history will lie in attempts to appropriate this consummation to itself. Hence, the climax for Christian faith is not sometime in the future, it is Christ. God's work in Christ is identical to God's work in history!

Any deliberation on life after death, it has to be pointed out, is not very relevant to Christian dogmatics, interlocked with Christian ethics, because the concern of both remains strictly with the "inner and outer life" of persons in this life alone and not with any supposed extension of life beyond death. Further, in a sermon Schleiermacher affirms:

> The divine decree regarding everything that lies between the moment when each of us departs this life and the great day of our common reunion with the Redeemer is a sealed book. We are not able to read this book, not to know when the time is coming when it will be opened to us.[38]

We may quote a similar passage from *Christian Faith* as well.

> The question as to the conditions of existence after death, of information about which would have to underlie any clear notion, is a purely cosmological question; and space and spatialities are so closely connected with times and seasons that they likewise lie

---

37. *Christian Faith*, §157.1, 696.

38. Schleiermacher, *Servant of the Word*, 62–63. This sermon was preached on March 18, 1821.

> outside the range of communications that the Redeemer had to make to us.[39]

Since we have no access to what is outside time and space, and since there is no revelation related to life after death, as that is something outside the range of what can possibly be communicated to us, even the idea of a possibility of some continuation of our existence after death puts some concrete content into that which cannot be assumed to have a concrete, earthly character. It is impossible for serious thought to transport experiences within the framework of the confines of a physical estate, and suited only for that, to a state after one is deprived of any physicality. There is a finality with regard to death. One may be able to speculate about some sort of continuation of an individual's history beyond that, but such an idea, being mere speculation, has no contribution to make to dogmatics. Moreover, it fits well with the Christian's trust and confidence in God that persons of faith would surrender their personal existence to God in gladness for God to do what is in the divine good pleasure. From a different angle, we can also say that the significance of anyone's life on earth is never lost to the world, because that individual's spirit gets absorbed by the living community; due to the organic nature of humanity, each one's impression on the world is indelible, and each one's indispensability is such that the world as it is just could not have existed apart from that same self.

However, anything within time and space and natural causality is finite. Outside the confines of these factors, thought becomes impossible.

> What can be said of an afterlife is only "prophetic" in nature. It cannot describe our consciousness of being in communion with God in the way other doctrines do, but it does not deny (because it would have no grounds for doing so) that the communion continues. Whether it does or not is entirely up to God, but the God in whom we have faith extends the one divine decree to all.[40]

Thus, apart from all the other reasons we have elicited earlier against an after-life partition of humanity into two groups, here is yet another reason why such a division should not be made, according to Schleiermacher. It is untenable because a thought leading to such a

---

39. *Christian Faith*, §158.3, 702.
40. Tice in a communication to Kunnuthara 4/28/96.

division is itself untenable. Further, inasmuch as God is love, God's love extends equally to all eternally.

Because of the limit and finality of present existence and because of the interconnectedness of the individual with the whole and *vice-versa*, future and past must be thought to be organically present in the present. Individual consciousness must be able to relate to the totality of history, staying within the confines of its appointed finite consciousness (because of its awareness of the interconnectedness of the parts and the whole). Every moment is a product of the past in its totality and simultaneously is related organically to the totality of the future; and the corresponding spatial and causal relations must also be predicated. (It should be noted that this is so not because of Schleiermacher's prior trust in any sort of "deterministic" theories but because it comes as a natural corollary to his belief in the interconnectedness of all finite causes and effects.) Further, a Christian's taste of eternity within the confines of mundane life privileges the Christian into an experience of being contemporaneous with the total work encased in redemptive history and hence also with the total work of God in history, thus relating each to feelings and perceptions of organicity and belonging in relation to everything by way of the experience of eternity.

7

Christian Consciousness of God's Government of the World

OUR CONSIDERATION IN THIS CHAPTER WILL BE GENERALLY CONFINED TO the matters covered in Part I of *Christian Faith*. However, we must start with a candid admission that our attempt here is only a recapitulation of certain salient elements chosen from what we have already covered in the previous chapters, in order to indulge in further exposition or explication of the same; we are not going to encounter anything entirely new in this chapter. Once the Christology and Ecclesiology of *Christian Faith* are reckoned with, a comprehensive coverage of the material in Part I of *Christian Faith* is rendered redundant, except as aids to understanding those in Part II, as "presuppositions" to which they lead. After all, the first part is only an abstraction from the second part! Ample warning to the same effect had been issued sufficiently early by Schleiermacher himself, stating that this would be a concomitant consequence of the particular method we have adopted, which of course is a reverse organization of the manner in which *Christian Faith* is actually arranged.[1] On the other hand, this final chapter is the "coping stone" of our treatment of Schleiermacher's theological thought, a necessary round up without which a first-time student of Schleiermacher may well evince a tendency to misunderstand a great many of the materials covered in the first six chapters.

1. "After a complete discussion of the doctrines of redemption and the kingdom of God, there would have been scarcely any other option than to deal as briefly as possible with all those doctrines now contained in the first part. And there can be no doubt that this would have been detrimental not only to the book itself, nor just as it pertains to me personally, i.e., as a reflection of my point of view, but also as it relates to the present needs of our church. I would not be convinced that I had done justice to my calling if I had eliminated anything significant in this part." Schleiermacher, *On The Glaubenslehre*, 60.

The Absolute Dependence of the World on God

For Schleiermacher, in the Christian view of things (and for that matter for almost any such view), it can be demonstrated that God is the vital foundation of all impulses and all formations within the world.[2] It is in this sense that the world is taken to be the revelation of God, but by virtue of this revelation, the conception we make of God cannot be surmised as in actual correspondence to the actual Being of God. The world's dependence on God is non-reciprocal. It is not a juxtaposition of two entities, nor is it a union between them of any kind. Since this relation is of such a unique nature that no analogy from our earthly experience is possible, we should just indicate that this relation is ultimately unexplainable, or undefinable; or, to put the matter positively, we employ the term "absolute" and say that the world is in absolute dependence on God.

Because of the interconnected process of nature, which also involves each individual's inescapable connection with everyone else and the whole, the self-consciousness that we possess toward our individual absolute dependence on God is identical to the self-consciousness we possess with regard to our consciousness of the absolute dependence of the world. The Christian view of the absolute dependence of the world on God is traditionally apportioned to two doctrines, namely, creation and preservation, the predominant denotation in the former being the dependent origination of the world and the predominant denotation in the latter being its dependent subsistence. However, since both creation and preservation are functions attributed to God, and since any act in God is essentially eternal, and therefore non-dual, on serious consideration any difference between creation and preservation must fall away; rather, they are the same thing viewed from two different angles. If creation is seen to be the divine work of the origination of the world, including successive origination of all the dynamic emergences of animate and inanimate compositions that occur in the history of the world, and if preservation is considered to be the divine upkeep of these same emergences, each of these concepts can comprehensively be subsumed under the other. "Thus, the concept of creation if taken in its entire compass makes the concept of preservation superfluous,"[3] and *vice-versa*. Subscription to ei-

---

2. For a brief discussion of pertinent issues and directions for further study, see Tice, "Editor's Introduction," in Schleiermacher, *Dialectic*, xxii–xxv.

3. *Christian Faith*, §38.1, 147.

ther creation or preservation as a non-dual act in God is a simultaneous expression of the feeling of absolute dependence.

> Every notion of the origin of the world by which anything whatever is excluded from origination by God, or by which God is placed under those conditions and contrasts that have arisen in and through the world, is contradictory to that religious self-consciousness which is our basis here.[4]

The Divine Act of the Origination of the World or Creation.

If there were anything in the world that originated apart from God, or if there were anything around that could be conceived as sneaking into the parameters of the world subsequent to God's creation, that extra would act as a limiting adjunct to God. Since that extra, in some proportion, should have entered into our constitution as well, that part of us would then remain apart from God, so that a consciousness of absolute dependence would become impossible.

The doctrine of creation is one place where the "eternal covenant"[5] between Christian faith and completely free scientific inquiry must be respected *sans* reservation. Karl Barth certainly respects this "covenant" in what he writes to his grandniece.

> The creation story is a witness to the beginning or becoming of all reality distinct from God in the light of God's later acts and words relating to his people Israel—naturally in the form of a saga or poem. The theory of evolution is an attempt to explain the same reality in its inner nexus—naturally in the form of a scientific hypothesis. The creation story deals only with the becoming of all things, and therefore with the revelation of God, which is inaccessible to science as such. The theory of evolution deals with what has become, as it appears to human observation and research and as it invites human interpretation. Thus one's attitude to the creation story and the theory of evolution can take the form of an either/or only if one shuts oneself off completely either from faith in God's revelation or from the mind (or opportunity) for scientific understanding.[6]

---

4. Ibid., §40, 149–50.
5. *On the Glaubenslehre*, 64.
6. *Karl Barth Letters 1961–1968*, 184.

A scientific explanation of the origin of the world is just not in the domain of dogmatics. In thinking of God and creation, the following rules must be observed. First, the scope of the originating activity of God with regard to the world must be exhaustively the world's entirety. There are no pre-existing materials for God to work on and no other force to co-operate with God in creation. Subsequently, no one can insert anything into God's creation, and no one can ever tamper with God's work at any time. Genetic engineering, or any future scientific inventive genius of humanity would not have added anything to, or taken away anything from, God's creation. Second, the nature of God's work must be understood to be in consonance with the nature of God's realm and never as analogous to human work. Temporal accretions into that realm should be counted as nonsensical. Third, God's work must be conceived in such a way that all the temporal activities, movements, creativities, and the infinite interrelations within nature, i.e., in time and space, should be comprehensively conditioned by it. In fact, God's act[7] must be thought to intimate the bringing into being of the totality of "time" and "space" but never in such a way that God's act is judged to occupy either time or space. Inasmuch as "time" and "space" are created categories, and inasmuch as there cannot be posited a multiplicity in eternal activity without dragging it down to the mundane level, the creation and preservation of time and space, and the creation and preservation of nature or the world, are one and the same divine act.

Even the notion of a pre-existence of "form" or "idea" within God before creation must be guarded from two possible mistakes. First, the prefix "pre" should not facilitate a subjection of God to the temporal terrain. Second, the bifurcation between "form" and "matter" must not be such as to denote that God is having differing relations with them.

Therefore, the doctrine of *creatio ex nihilo* can be accepted only with precautions. First, as was stated above, God must not be subjected to time and space; and second, God cannot be conceived as an existence alongside creation, in a way so as to predicate a reciprocity of relationship

---

7. The limitation of the verb "act" must be conceded here. In normal parlance, it is used only to denote the practical working out of the decision of some willing-center, within time and space, toward some end such as some desired change that is brought forth within the interconnected process of nature. Since God's realm transcends time and space, and since God does not do things the way we do, our use of the term is anthropomorphic. It is part of our human limitation that we have to use such anthropomorphic expressions in detailing doctrines even while fully realizing their inadequacies.

between God and creation at any time. In other words, *creatio ex nihilo* can be accepted only when its content is suitably shaped to signify the absolute dependence of creation on God. Since the adjective "absolute" functions to indicate its transcendence of time, a two-stage theory in which the stages are marked apart at the point of the origin in time of this absolute dependence postulates a contradiction in terms.

Christian orthodoxy cherishes the doctrine of *creatio ex nihilo* for its inherent vitality to vouch for the absolute freedom and impassibility of God. *Creatio ex nihilo* played a crucial role for Indian Christian Theology during its early days. The most extensive use of this was made by P. Johanns in his attempt to rethink Christian thinking in terms of the Vedanta.[8] His argument is that if one could only supplement all the prominent and diverse Vedantic philosophies with the Christian doctrine of *creation ex nihilo*, it would then be possible to harmonize all of those Vedantic schools by choosing all of their positive elements on the groundwork of *creation ex nihilo*; and the product would be Thomistic metaphysics.

Brahmabandhab Upadhyaya's attempt, however, was a much more successful one than that of Johanns. He argues that *creation ex nihilo* is already present in the *advaita* school of Vedantic thought, thus he confines himself to Sankara's system alone and tries to prove that Sankara's doctrine of *maya* is an adequate expression of the Christian doctrine of *creation ex nihilo*.[9] *Maya* is the inscrutable power of Brahman (God) by which the world is created or preserved. From the *paramarthika* (ultimate or intrinsic ontology) point of view, Brahman alone is real, and the world is unreal; however, from the *vyavaharika* (relative point of view) the creation is real; or the creation is a contingent reality, it is real in its own level, but compared to the reality of the Brahman, the creation is absolute nothingness. Upadhyaya argues that *maya* and the Thomistic doctrine of creation are identical in essence. Both teach that creation is the overflow of the abundance of God and that creation is nothing in

---

8. This is a very long series of articles by the Belgian Jesuit and Oxford scholar, Fr. P. Johanns in *The Light of the East*, under the title "To Christ through the Vedanta," from 1922 onwards in Kolkatta. Collected works are now available under the title *To Christ Through the Vedanta*, U.T.C., Bangalore. A synopsis of these long articles was later published in four small volumes: *To Christ through the Vedanta: A Synopsis. Part 1, Samkara; Part 2, Ramanuja; Part 3, Vallabha; Part 4, Chaitanya*. 3d ed. Ranchi, 1944.

9. For an extremely good and fairly comprehensive analysis of Upadhyaya's theological writings, see Aleaz, "Theological Writings of Brahambandhav Upadhyaya," 55–77.

and of itself, and therefore the claim of intrinsic permanence to creation is a falsity. The word *maya,* Upadhyaya says, comes from the root *ma,* which means "make" and is more conducive to explaining the Christian doctrine of "creation" than the latin root *creare.*

> ... the term *"maya"* is more expressive of the doctrine of creation than the Latin root "creare." Whenever we speak of creation we should be careful to make explicit three factors implied in the creative act. First: there is no necessity on God's part to create. Second: the coming into being of finite objects with the implication that they did not exist. Third: the finite perfections are contained in the infinite in a pre-eminent way. Now the term "Creation" expressed only the second significance, while "maya" conveys ... all the three."[10]

Both Johanns and Upadhyaya realize the cruciality of the proper articulation of having a Christian view of the God-world relationship for Indian Christian Theology. Moreover, both are methodologically at one with the *Vedantic* philosophers in pegging their starting point of theological thinking at the Ultimate Reality (God), in such a way that they can reason out the reality and the relevance of the creation therefrom. Schleiermacher's theological method requires the exact opposite route. "Christian doctrines of faith are conceptions of Christian religious mental states presented in the form of discourse."[11] Any affirmation of the reality of Ultimate Reality apart from the relatively real world, to him, is meaningless. A detached (i.e., apart from the feeling of absolute dependence, which is the same as being in relationship to God, which in turn arises in oneself as the highest level of self-consciousness, originated from one's relation to the world) indulgence in thinking of/on God is mere speculation and is absolutely bereft of any underpinning. In fact, we are not in a position to entertain seriously the notion of seizing or sizing up that Being on whom we are *absolutely dependent*; we cannot have such control over God. Even the notion of a special revelation (a conception of which both the Vedantins and the orthodox Christian theologians have in common) does not take one very far, because whatever is claimed to have come from that extraordinary act is still within the realm of creation. The divine "insertion" of a special work of God into the already

---

10. Brahmabandhav Upadhyaya, "Vedantism and Christianity," 6.
11. *Christian Faith,* §15, 76.

created creation only engenders further problems for thought: (1) there is the necessary depiction of God's original work as defective, insofar as God had to supplement it with a subsequent special work of revelation; and (2) there is the problem of leaving a gap or void in God between God's two separate acts, whereby passivity is introduced into the concept of God.

In a worldview where the creation of the world is assigned in an absolute manner to God, the relation between God's creation and God's time has always been a very difficult problem to handle.[12] If time in itself is a constructed category, and if time cannot be thought of as having been created within time, the question of the "whenness" of the creation is just absurd. The view represented by William Lane Craig is that God created (i.e., originated out of nothing) time and everything within time together as though at the one creative instant, with the result of "time" having a nature that would give the observer an appearance of having no limits at either end, past or future. He holds to a relational view of time, which claims that time does not exist apart from events and that "God exists changelessly and timelessly prior to creation and in time after creation."[13] Schleiermacher would sympathize with Craig on this much, that time and events are integrally related, although even he would certainly prefer to substitute "space and spatialities" for the word "events."[14] Finite causalities vary in intensity depending upon their position and strength, in such a way that some causalities cannot be called events. However, even where space is occupied exclusively by "dead" forces, the

---

12. The relation between God and time is not an issue for Vedantins because they consider creation to be always in process and therefore regard the question of the beginning or end of creation to be utterly irrelevant. In Sankara's philosophy, Brahman is the Ultimate Reality and the world is an illusion compared to the Brahman, or a relative Reality. God is related to the world just as the *atman* (the innermost reality within each human being) is related to the body. However, immediately this idea must be balanced by saying that *atman*, or the innermost reality within each individual, is identical with the Brahman, in Sankara's philosophy. That being the case, the Brahman's relation to the world is identical with the *atman's* relation to the outer reality of the person or to the world. The relation between God and the World being what it is, i.e., permanent and unchangeable, the question of a beginning or an end for the creation is an utterly unacceptable question. For a competent treatment of Sankara's thought, see Sharma, *Critical Survey of Indian Philosophy*, 252–89.

13. Craig, "God, Time, and Eternity," 503.

14. *Christian Faith*, §158.3, 702.

minutest effect and value that they possess therein for the totality of finite causality must not be overlooked.

That aside, Schleiermacher would argue that the thrust of Craig's argument is hopelessly untenable. Craig appears to have conquered the unconquerable, but it is itself a grand illusion. We cannot shape the nature of realities to harmonize with the given limits of our capacity for thought. To say that this is a truth revealed to us by God through the Bible also would not appeal to Schleiermacher, because the Bible is not the best guide to matters of physics. The purpose of the Bible is not to impart scientific knowledge; it is to promote Christian piety.

In the modern world, one must not force oneself to live in the thought-structures developed in times of old, when even the materials for scientific thought were taken mostly from the scriptures. In large part, these structures were suitable only for those times. Craig's argument, Schleiermacher would respond, proceeds only from the selfish desire (unwitting, though) to have our own control over God's "acts." It is a lack of willingness to leave to God and trust in God concerning things with regard to which we are not endowed with the capacity to penetrate and understand. He would also say that no amount of intellectual gymnastics would suffice to cover up the logical contradiction involved in thinking of a thought or a state of affairs "prior to creation" when time and events are taken to have been intricately connected.

What applies to the "whenness" of the creation (time) applies also to the "whereness" of the creation (space). In order to arrive at his own conclusion, what Craig does is provisionally to split the space-time continuum into events and time, so as to contend that insofar as events can have a beginning, and in so far as time and events are always related, time ought to have its temporal beginning in creation. Two problems arise here. First, if time and events are always related, a hypothetical split between the two does not serve any purpose. Second, there is no basis for one to say that events ought to have a beginning; rather, if time cannot be thought to have a beginning on its own merit, events also ought not to be thought to have a beginning on their own merit. Further, Craig's subjecting of God to time, once the creation of time is an accomplished fact, propagates two further mistakes: (1) it indicates a change in God in relation to creation, thus foundering the divine attribute of immutability; and (2) in spite of time's being a construct, it cannot be thought to be in absolute dependence on God after its inception if God is in any way subject to or dependent on it. Yet another serious problem with Craig's position is that, insofar as God is thought of as existing along with the creation after the event of creation, though in a different status, it goes without saying that before the creation (which awkwardly means "before time was created"), there was a void in God.

Even Augustine's suggested solution to the problem is not satisfactory to Schleiermacher.

> Augustine is hardly more satisfactory when, in order to avoid this position, he sets forth only a single act of divine will for both the earlier non-existence and the later existence of the world. The reason is that if an equally effectual act of the divine will is required to explain the prior non-existence of the world, then we must assume that without this divine will the world would have come into existence earlier and consequently that there was a capacity for its coming into existence independently of God. However, if that same single divine will is deemed to be ineffectual prior to the existence of the world, in that God would have been no more producing than preventing, then the transition from inaction to action remains, even though it may be differently expressed as a transition from willing to actualizing; while, on the other hand, it is impossible to see how the notion that God does not exist without anything's being absolutely dependent on God should either weaken or confuse religious self-consciousness. Just so, a tracing of the Word by which God created the world—a subject not at all to be considered here—back to the Word that was with God from eternity cannot be brought to proper clarity unless there is an eternal creation through the eternal Word.[15]

In other words, if God is eternal, God's activity is eternal. The question of the temporal beginning of the creation is a matter beyond us; and in any case, that is a question of no direct interest to Christian theology as far as Schleiermacher is concerned; it is the concern of science and not of doctrine. As long as the divine causality and absolute dependence are intact, Christian doctrines too are intact, though they themselves continually change, just as external science does, and thus they carefully borrow from external science in such a way as not to compromise genuinely Christian doctrine, which indeed has its own pertinent scientific findings and procedures.

15. *Christian Faith*, §41.2, 155–56.

The Christian consciousness is that the world is "the absolutely harmonious work of the divine art."[16] In the divine government of the world everything is "inseparably conditioned by everything else."[17] It is a disruption of harmony when there is even the minutest violation of this principle. Schleiermacher's unflinching loyalty to the concept of *Naturzusammenhang*—which he interprets as a "dynamic aspect of nature," a knowledge of which was not available to earlier generations[18]—is in part a "Romantic" response to the post-Newtonian physics of his time, and in part it prefigures certain aspects of the process theology of the twentieth century. Moreover, it is so crucial to Schleiermacher's theological way of thinking that if one were to raise reasonable doubts against this theory, the nature of those doubts would then dictate the nature of any reworking required in the system; it could lead to a mere readjustment or to a total collapse.

In Schleiermacher's view, either God's making special miraculous interventions against the interconnected process of nature, or the occurrence of any disruption of this harmonious relation (that is, of the *Naturzusammenhang* or conditioning of everything by everything else) would be because of an original defect, to begin with; it would also be a testimony to the weakness of the original planning and to the lack of efficiency in the original planner. This would destroy the feeling of absolute dependence. However, that cannot be the case; the world is the absolute revelation of the Supreme Being.[19] The consciousness of the regularity of the world process and the consciousness of absolute dependence on God are complementary; they are inseparable.

There cannot be any dispute with regard to the purpose of creation and preservation, or of the divine activity as a whole; it is the redemption of humankind.[20] Neal Keesee elegantly argues that in *On Religion* God's purpose is viewed as divine self-manifestation; redemption is subsumed under this wider purpose.[21] This rhymes well with Calvin's position; however, when one considers the style, stuff and dynamic of the thinking

16. See ibid., §168.1, 732–33.
17. Ibid., §163.P.S., 721.
18. Ibid., §41.2, 155.
19. See ibid., §169, 735–36.
20. See the whole of the third section of the second part of *Christian Faith* (§§164–69).
21. Keesee, "Divine Purpose in Schleiermacher's *Speeches*."

executed by Schleiermacher, this interpretation leads to problems. *On Religion* is not a book about God and God's purposes but about human piety and its concrete expressions in life; hence, to discern the divine purpose therein, we have to divine it from between the lines. Keesee himself acknowledges that the movement of thought in both *On Religion* and *Christian Faith* moves from abstract to concrete progressively[22] and that the most concrete is always the climax. That being the case, it is the fifth discourse on "Religion in the Religions" that should be consulted as the basic text if one wanted to look for and discern the divine purpose in the book. Since humanity's redemption is the more concrete of the two, it is wiser to construe that as the final divine purpose rather than divine self-manifestation. Logically, one cannot subsume human redemption under divine self-manifestation in Schleiermacher's style of thinking, because the very expression "divine self-manifestation" begs for an answer to the question, "What for?" Certainly, it is not something for God's own sake; it has to be for the sake of the creation. Further, inasmuch as Schleiermacher does not evince any interest in an integral evolution, God's self-manifestation must be for the sake of humanity alone; it is for humanity's redemption, and God's self-manifestation is just a necessary concomitance to human redemption. It is both how God achieves God's purpose and the ongoing achievement itself. A few lines from the conclusion of Keesee's paper suffice to make the issue clear.

> But what, finally, of the fact that Schleiermacher describes the divine activity which directs history to life as "redemptive love?" Surely an act so described has as its purpose the well-being of its recipient, so that to describe the divine work as redemptive love indicates that the divine purpose is the redemption of humanity. Schleiermacher does not in the *Speeches* provide us with a definition of love, and it is less than prudent to assume that he means simply this by his use of the word. In fact, his use of the term "love" in the *Soliloquies* supports the conclusion I have reached. There he opposes love to sensitivity. Love is the self-disclosing activity, a pouring out of the self which expresses creative freedom. It is genuine love in that it benefits the other by enriching her life, providing another manifestation of the variety of the whole which helps the other to better discern her individuality. But its enrichment of the other occurs precisely through self-manifesta-

22. Ibid., 1.

tion. Certainly the working out of the divine purpose achieves human well-being by redemption, and thus it is a loving, beneficent process. But that single purpose is self-manifestation.[23]

Yet, again, what is this self-manifestation for? It is for human redemption; God's love, the only attribute that is predicated for God as Godself, works toward not self-manifestation in and of itself but human redemption; God's self-manifestation certainly does occur in the process, in the entirety of it in fact. God's love is directed not toward Godself, however, but toward humanity and toward human beings' communion with God. That is why the meaning and purpose of history should be seen in the light of human redemption, the planting and extending of the Christian Church to its ultimate completion, and not divine self-manifestation as such. This tallies with our thesis that God's work in history is identical with God's work in Jesus. History, viewed either as a totality or as in isolable parts, finds its meaning in and through Jesus; everything, sparing nothing, is summed up in Him and in Him alone.

The Divine Preservation of the World and the Continual Entering of the Infinite into the Finite.

The object of the divine preservation is the world, and by "world," of course one means more than the mechanism of nature. Rather, it involves "the interaction of that mechanism and of free agents, so that in each of these factors the other is taken into account."[24] Internally each free agent can be said to be God's object of preservation only in the sense that the person is patterned, in the divine scheme of things, to find exactly his or her place within the larger complex of human relations. Each free agent's sphere of freedom is as wide as, and simultaneously as limited as, the total compass of the world. This point must be further qualified: Each free agent's exercise of freedom, or ability to exercise it, is promoted as well as constricted especially by the person's human relations and all other relations within the person's immediate community and physical environment wherein the person is located. The immediate context, in turn, is related to its larger context, just as the individual is related to its larger context and just as the individual is related to the immediate one; and

23. Ibid., 23–24.
24. *Christian Faith*, §47.1, 180.

similar circles of relations must continue to be predicated as the compass is necessarily expanded stage by stage so as to reach the uttermost reaches of the "world" and to include the entirety of creation.

In the pious mind, the doctrine of divine preservation coheres with the idea of the interconnected process of nature provided by God. If religion is the "sense and taste for the infinite," such sense and taste are evoked only through the instrumentality of the stimulation of self-consciousness coming from the impulses that affect us from around ourselves. Consider the following two statements from *On Religion:*

> To seek and to find this infinite and eternal factor in all that lives and moves, in all growth and change, in all action and passion, and to have and to know life itself only in immediate feeling—that is religion.[25]

> Your feeling is your piety, with two qualifications: first, insofar as that feeling expresses the being and life common to you and to the universe in the way described and second, insofar as the particular moments of that feeling come to you as an operation of God within you mediated through the operation of the world upon you.[26]

In other words, God's work in any person is the individuated representation in that same person of God's work in the world, in and through the interconnected process of nature. God's work in the individual is never executed in an isolated person-to-person or piecemeal fashion. The order that exists in the interconnected process of nature, as viewed in a pious way distinctive to the Christian religion, is viewed as the divine preservation of the world. Thus, the noncontradictory, internal relation between divine preservation and *Naturzusammenhang* is uncompromisable in Schleiermacher's view.[27]

> It is said that the more clearly we consider something in its being completely conditioned by the interconnected process of nature, the less can we arrive at the feeling of its absolute dependence upon God; and conversely, the more vivid this feeling is the more must we leave its relation to the interconnected process of nature indefinite and undecided. However, it is manifest based on our

---

25. *On Religion*, trans. Tice, 79.
26. Ibid., trans. Tice, 89–90.
27. *Christian Faith*, §46.2, 174.

> standpoint and in accordance with all what we have already said on the matter that we cannot admit such a contrast between the two concepts. This is so, for otherwise, because everything would always present itself to us as within the system of nature, once our knowledge of the world reached completion the development of religious consciousness in life as we know it would cease, and this is quite contrary to our presupposition that piety is of the essence of human nature.[28]

This outlook cannot but remind one of Dietrich Bonhoeffer, who, though thinking and writing in a very different context, talks of God's "beyondness" in the midst of our life.[29] The notion of a "God of the gaps" is totally useless to him as well.

> Religious people speak of God when human perception is (often just from laziness) at an end, or human resources fail: it is really always the *Deus ex machina* they call to their aid, either for the so-called solving of insoluble problems or as support in human failure—always, that is to say, helping out human weakness or on the borders of human existence. Of necessity, that can only go on until men can, by their own strength, push those borders a little further, so that God becomes superfluous as a *Deus ex machina*.[30]

Rather, God is the God of the totality of our existence. Similarly, for Schleiermacher the division of preservation into *generalis*, *specialis*, and *specialissima* should be avoided, in the interest of religion.

In the Christian's consciousness, God is the one who gives sense to the orderly flow of history and to management of the world. Events are connected with each other and moments are related to each other by virtue of the Infinite entering into the finite in a continual fashion. That is, every point in the past and every point in the future are equi-distant and equally related to the Infinite. Any gap between moments is filled by the Divine. All sentient and nonsentient entities at all places in all time are absolutely dependent on the eternal God; or, all entities are equally related to eternity. The idea that the world constitutes an orderly whole is inseparably linked with our consciousness of absolute dependence.

---

28. Ibid., §46.1, 171.
29. Bonhoeffer, *Letters and Papers from Prison*, 166.
30. Ibid., 165.

Divine causality, directed in real space and time, and dependent causality, exhibited in the totality of creation, are co-extensive.

The nature of the continual entering of the Infinite into the finite can be further clarified by highlighting the difference between much traditional Reformed theology and Schleiermacher with regard to the divine decree. For the former,

> The decree is not eternal in exactly the same sense that God is eternal. The decree results from the free, sovereign will of God; it must be distinguished therefore from the necessary acts of God within the divine Trinity. The decree of God must also be distinguished from its execution in history. The decree to create is not the actual creation of the world "in the beginning" (Gen. 1:1).[31]

Schleiermacher would disagree with all the three points above. Since God is simple and pure activity, one cannot imagine any gap between God's eternal nature and the eternal nature of God's decree. Second, we are not privy to God's internal activities; the very thought of that is unwarranted speculation, and it does not belong to the realm of dogmatics. Third, only by a thorough misunderstanding of the nature of eternity can one possibly posit a distinction between God's decree and its execution in history; temporal tenses do not apply to God or to God's deed.

Our consciousness cannot posit divine causality as more extensive than mundane causality, because one without the other at any point is impossible for thought to entertain; invariably, an activity in God within the reach of our knowledge or sense perception is or becomes mundane. We are mundane, our knowledge is mundane and the reach of our perception is mundane. Ontology and epistemology are coextensive in scope because the ontology that we can talk or think of is only an ontology that is within our perceptual reach. Apart from the arena of the operation of the world (by which Schleiermacher means the created universe of space and time), there is no space where God can be reflected upon or understood; apart from God, there is no way in which the absolute dependence we may feel with regard to both individual and collective existence can be understood. History too cannot be understood apart, without the doctrine of the divine government of the world, within Christian consciousness.

---

31. Klooster, "Decrees of God," 303.

Our consciousness of the continual entry of the Infinite into the finite, or of the occupation of the gaps between moments, is the groundwork from which we elicit the understanding of the organicity of history. It is the same groundwork that guides us to an understanding of the teleological nature of history, particularly the motif of divine love in creation, preservation and redemption, and the final summing up of the creation in Jesus. History is Christo-centric. This is true, given that the fullness of time converges only in Christ. In that the existence or the omnipresence of God is focally present only in Christ, and in that the eternal life that constitutes the children of God brought into God's Reign is being made to proceed only from Christ, we must see the continual entry of the Infinite into the finite as the direct ramification of God's work in Christ.

Spatiality and the Divine Omnipresence

The foregoing depiction of the Infinite's continual entry into the finite is conspicuously a representation of God's relation to the world through the metaphor of physical movement. Here, however, a reminder is in order that the absolute causality of God must also be delineated as absolutely spaceless. When the divine causality is portrayed as pertaining to that attribute in God which conditions all spatialities and space itself, it is called God's omnipresence. Internally, God's presence strings together all the indivisible particles that compose what is known as space. Externally (a thought which makes no sense, if taken literally, but which we use here in a metaphorical way), God's omnipresence creates the facility for the sustaining of space; put another way, it makes "space" for space, or it absolutely conditions the very being of space.

Such being the case, it must also be said that the divine omnipresence must be absolutely spaceless because, as that entity which absolutely conditions space, it cannot in the least be thought to be conditioned by space. Therefore, its presence "everywhere" cannot be judged to vary in intensity from place to place, or from time to time. In contrast, variability can certainly be observed in the receptivity accorded to God's omnipresence among finite entities. "Dead" forces cannot be said to have any receptivity to God. In general, the same could be asserted with regard to sub-human species too, but with a caution that we have no way of assessing their inner life. "In this way, the receptivity of human beings for

God's omnipotent actions is greater than that of any other earthly being, but among human beings it looms greatest among people of piety."[32] In Jesus we see receptivity to the divine omnipresence at its unparalleled best, in pristine purity. The reason Schleiermacher affirms the "existence of God" in Jesus is that this is the only instance, and will be the only instance in history, where receptivity to the divine omnipresence is met with a receptivity of total constancy at uttermost maximum intensity. This is the reason that the divine omnipresence also has a wholly representational character, such that one could reasonably claim that God's work in Jesus is identical to the work of God historically effected, i.e., in time and space.

Poetical and popular language constantly depict the space-conditioning causality of God in the figure of unlimited spatiality, but omnipresence is to be considered in actual terms as the negation of both remoteness and nearness. A mixing of the Divine Being with space smacks of pantheism. A space-filling by God must be thoroughly avoided; God produces or provides space, but never occupies it. So God is related equally to all places, collective and individual, so that omnipresence occurs in the finite "everywhere selfsameness" wrought by divine causality.

Omnipresence is also not the extension of God's power apart from God's nature. Such a bifurcation is possible only within the realm of finite beings. God's own mode of existence is so incomprehensible to us that we can, in our thinking, only remove the spatial element from our concept of God and say that God is in Godself! This is not as though we are ascribing a temporal precedence to God ahead of creation. Rather, it is an assigning of the issue to a range beyond our faculties. Omnipresence is that attribute we ascribe to God in our absolute dependence on God as individual pious centers of perception; in this capacity we identify ourselves to be part of the same nature. This we do by virtue of our acknowledging our spatial existence, both in and of each self and in utter coincidence in and of the whole of nature, as created and preserved by the vital being associated with the omnipresence of God.

Temporality and the Divine Eternality

The words that were set between spatiality and omnipresence to indicate their idiosyncratic relation can be used in the exact same form and

---

32. *Christian Faith*, §53.1, 208.

arrangement to set forth the connection between temporality and eternality. However, in practical terms, the divine causality pertaining to the former combination evokes more religious moments than the same pertaining to the latter. Yet at the same time, the time and effort usually expended on the latter in terms of thinking and reflecting, overwhelmingly out distances that of what is accorded to the former.

For Schleiermacher, whatever attributes can be predicated of God can be so applied only in or with reference to divine causality. Proposition 52 of *Christian Faith* states: "By the Eternity of God we understand the absolutely timeless causality of God, which along with its conditioning all that is temporal also conditions time itself."[33] Since divine causality cannot but be presented as activity, any predication of a lifeless or still or inert attribute to God is devoid of any significance; God's eternity ought to be portrayed as active; it is power; more, it is the administered act of divine power, it is *eternal power*.

We may sympathize with the sentiment behind the notion of God's eternity as existing before time, but the harm it entails must not be overlooked. However elevated or lofty our calibration of God's eternity may be, once it is put parallel to our temporality, or once a single similarity is found between them (even if we temper it by positing the former as some sort of transcendental reality), the two are called to exist in comparable relation. This is illogical because, in our conception, all moments of time and time itself in its totality are absolutely dependent upon, or conditioned by, eternity. Even by the standards of a traditional understanding of *creatio ex nihilo*, the intrinsic reality of creation's being having been issued from total nullity compared to the pure reality of God, there cannot be any meaningful comparison between God and creation, and therefore between God's realm and the realm of creation.

The contrast between eternity and time must be identical in nature to the contrast between God and the world. Even though the world is the revelation of God, and the only tools or data available for us by which we are given to effect an understanding of God, it also remains true that the knowledge it gives us of God is at best indirect, or negative.[34]

---

33. Ibid., §52, 203.

34. We may leave aside the theological and philosophical differences between Aquinas and Schleiermacher for the present and see some similarity here. In Aquinas' thinking: "The distinction between Creator and creatures is of an unique kind. It is unlike any distinction we are familiar with, because these always hold between creatures. In other

The best that can be asserted of God's eternity, therefore, is that it is that active power of God that causes temporality and time *to be*. Since time itself is utterly conditioned by the divine causality pertaining to temporality, God's eternity must be related to all points of time and temporality in a manner that transcends the nature and limitations of time. This relation is somewhat similar to the contemporaneity of Christ with the people of faith of all times that we talked about earlier. It is also similar to the presence of God that we also talked about earlier, at all points of space, facilitating the being of spatiality once and everywhere. We may pictorially express this matter by saying that God connects all actual moments in history by occupying all the gaps between all the moments in time by a single or identical, spaceless presence, and strings them into a coherent, singular, organic unity. Therefore, "temporal contrasts of before and after, older and younger are overcome in reference to God" by their being assigned the same status.[35]

So, Schleiermacher's view of the divine "eternity" places him in a neutral zone between those who join issue on the length of the temporal extension of the world; whether it is limited or unlimited, the relation between time and eternity is a constant.

---

words: God differs differently. This fundamental insight of faith dominates Aquinas' theological reading of the Scriptures and is reflected in the second characteristic of his theology: its negativity." Goris, *Free Creatures of an Eternal God*, 11.

Advaita Vedanta explains the relation between God and the world through the term *maya*. Once the Atman (the innermost reality of the individual) attains the intuitive realization that it is identical with Brahman (God), it simultaneously comes to the realization also that the world is unreal. Consequently, with regard to the relation between God and the world, based on this ultimate point of view (of intrinsic ontology), what happens is that in the light of the Absolute reality of God, the world is seen to be a falsity, a lie, a grand illusion. Therefore, the question of the relation between "time" and the Brahman's realm is a matter of disinterest. Neither a comparison nor a contrast is possible between that which is ultimately real and that which is unreal. See Sharma, *Critical Survey of Indian Philosophy*, 275–77.

35. *Christian Faith*, §52.1, 204. This relation is not necessarily, and is perhaps never, the same as a "coincidence of opposites"; thus, we may do well here to note that in its presentation it is a necessary corollary of Schleiermacher's systemic thinking. From what we know, it is highly unlikely that Schleiermacher had ever had any knowledge of Nicholas of Cusa, who built his doctrine of God around the expression, "coincidence of opposites." For a comparison of Nicholas of Cusa and Schleiermacher on this issue, one may refer to Williams, *Schleiermacher the Theologian*. This is a very helpful study, though I must admit that I cannot accept Williams' easy identification of Nicholas and Schleiermacher with regard to their doctrine of God.

> Just as what now arises in time is nevertheless also grounded in the omnipresence of God and is consequently willed and enacted by God in an eternal, *i.e.* timeless, manner, the world could also be timelessly willed to emerge at the beginning of time. On the other hand too, we need not have any concern that if the world is given no beginning or end, the difference between divine causality and causality within the interconnected process of nature would be overcome and the world would be eternal as God is. Rather, the eternity of God would still remain unique in that the contrast between the temporal and the eternal is not in the least diminished by the infinite duration of time.[36]

Eternity invades time always, but eternity is neither timelessness (in the sense of having only instantaneous temporaneous location) nor boundless time; it is utterly timeless or absolutely untime-bounded. The sketching of eternity as endless time, or as something similar to it, by simply eliminating the terminal points of time reduces the existence of God to a temporal one; consequently, "temporality in itself and the mensurability of the Divine Being, and thus of God's activity through time as well, are none of them denied but, on the contrary, are indirectly affirmed."[37] Instead, eternity must be understood as that which is utterly unlike temporality, as existing in contrast to endless duration and instantaneity but identically related to both and identically causing both simultaneously. This conception needs to be further qualified and amplified by saying that there is no dialectical relation between eternity and time or temporality. The latter two, whether as a single unit or in isolated particles, have their being in and only in their contrast to eternity. This is a contrast of a very different kind from that of any available contrast discernible in the mundane world, a contrast that gives an address, being and legitimacy to what is temporal. Time and temporality are absolutely dependent upon eternity, whereas eternity is absolutely free from anything temporal, or, to put it differently, eternity and time are neither two nor one, neither distinct realities nor identical.

Nelson Pike, in his ground-breaking work, *God and Timelessness*, devotes a full chapter to Schleiermacher's doctrine of timelessness. Pike does not seem to rate Schleiermacher's logical consistency very high. He remarks:

---

36. *Christian Faith*, §52.1, 204–5.
37. Ibid., §52.2, 205.

Schleiermacher also seems to have been alert to the internal friction involved in the claim that a timeless being is omnipotent. It is not at all obvious that a timeless individual can be consistently characterized as having *any* creative power, let alone creative power that is unlimited or "infinite." We must add that there appears to be no obvious way of understanding the idea that a being existing "outside of time" sustains or preserves the temporally extended universe of objects.[38]

Pike seems to make two mistakes here. One, he depicts Schleiermacher's God as a being like us who just happens to be "timeless." Then he proceeds to reason that, inasmuch as God is timeless, God cannot have any power or knowledge, because power and knowledge must necessarily be timeful in our experience. However, it is fundamental to Schleiermacher that God is God and not human, also that humans lack the ability to present a definite and exhaustive description of God, and that God-in-Godself is utterly inaccessible to us. Therefore, for Schleiermacher, it is beyond us to say that there is a logical contradiction between the concept of a timeless God and God's ability to know or to exert power; rather absolute knowledge and power are essential postulates of the One who causes the existence of all manifested power and knowledge; one may not be able to understand or explain how those fit into God, but that should not matter—the fit is there.[39] Divine knowledge and divine power are to human knowledge and human power what divine causality is to human causality, as we have explained earlier. Second, Pike superimposes his own meaning and definition of "timelessness" on Schleiermacher. "Timelessness" as attributed to God is only a negative concept employed in Schleiermacher, as certainly as it is in Anselm[40] and Aquinas,[41] in order to distinguish God from the limits of creation and from the creation itself; but in Pike's thinking "timelessness" seems to assume a positive description, a state of an explainable reality. Schleiermacher does not give "timelessness" a content, as he recognizes that we can never transcend

---

38. Pike, *God And Timelessness*, 173.

39. Alan Padgett also argues that there need be no logical necessity that an agent who causes an effect in time must be bound by time. See Padgett, *God, Eternity And The Nature Of Time*, 57.

40. See Rogers, "Eternity has no Duration," 1–16. Also see Craig, "Boethius on Theological Fatalism," 324–47.

41. See Goris, *Free Creatures of an Eternal God*, 34–52.

the limitations of time in our mundane thinking. The nearest possible positive description of God's estate is an indirect one, expressed in terms of causality, namely, that God is the total and absolute cause of time and space and everything that exists within the confines of those categories. Pike's assumption that Schleiermacher is aware of the internal friction between timelessness and omnipotence is, in all probability, because of Schleiermacher's doctrinal argument that it is necessary in Christian theology to redeem the doctrine of "eternity" from its being a limiting adjunct of temporality of any sort and to combine it with "omnipotence" to make sense, which to him also gives the added advantage of addressing the apprehension of certain people who fear that if eternity is thought of as timelessness, "nothing would be posited by it."[42] However, Pike's reading of Schleiermacher is less than adequate. He seems to think that Schleiermacher is giving respective definitions for "timelessness" and "omnipotence" and then fusing them together; but that is simply the reverse of Schleiermacher's method. His starting point is the feeling of absolute dependence, and, therefore, the correlate of our absolute dependence, God, must be the causal ground of time and everything within time. It is that causal demand that generates the need to posit God as simultaneously and equally both timeless and omnipotent.[43] "Timelessness" as applied to God is just a testimony that that which conditions time/space cannot be conditioned by time/space.

Divine causality cannot have any analogue, because it is a non-plural act and is non-enumerable at that. Comparing it with the finite and tem-

---

42. *Christian Faith*, §52.2, 205.

43. Pike has a footnote on page 188 (note 23) that presents a certain amount of sarcasm at the expense of Schleiermacher. He says: "Schleiermacher cites one passage from the New Testament in support of the claim that God is timeless. The passage in question is from Peter II, Ch. 3, verse 8. It reads: 'But beloved, be not ignorant of this one thing, that one day is with the Lord as a thousand years, and a thousand years as one day.' I leave it to the reader to decide the extent to which this passage suggests the idea that God is timeless."

However, one must respond that Pike is thoroughly misrepresenting Schleiermacher. (1) Schleiermacher does not advocate Pikian "timelessness." (2) The use of 2 Pet 3:8 by Schleiermacher is not to argue for any type of timelessness but only to point out that within the New Testament itself there is the acknowledgment that the biblical poetical representation of eternity as unending time (e.g., Job 36:26, Ps 102:28) needs to be supplemented for didactic purposes. (3) While one need not hesitate in saying that Schleiermacher believes that his view of eternity is perfectly within the tradition of Augustine and Boethius and that it is scriptural, nowhere does he argue that scripture itself explains the meaning of "eternity" as Pike, Augustine and Boethius do.

poral, with or without terminal points, duration made into an absolute minimum or an absolute maximum is impossible, because divine causality and human causality are opposed in kind. Therefore, divine causality can be explained only negatively. We can know it only by its fruits.

Divine Causality and God's Absolute Sovereignty over Creation

We have now come to a final round up of our study of Schleiermacher's theology and a concluding attempt to explain the nature of God's work in history, or, more accurately, what its nature is not, so that we can sense God's sovereignty over the world in our innermost being. God is God, and we are only women and men; we are equipped neither with the ability to explain nor with the strength to understand the way in which God executes God's work; rather, we can only feel and taste it as our absolute dependence on God takes our being in that direction.

As human beings, our thoughts, knowledge and even the uttermost reaches of our senses and imagination are circumscribed by the uttermost reaches of nature. Time, space, and causation are the characteristic dimensions of nature, and our faculties cannot ever hope to transcend them, because the very attempt to do so must always be rooted within them, must take shape within them, and must necessarily grow and have its being within them, so that it can never outgrow their confines or stand apart from them even to the minutest degree. Even our knowledge of God, the creator and the preserver of this nature, has to take place within the confines of that same nature. We live, move, and have our being within the parameters of nature; we are produced by it, each one of us is a unique configuration within it. Comprehensively we belong here, and there is nothing in us that comes from outside it.

Within the interconnected process of nature, we, as products and participants within it, observe its inner dynamics; we compare and contrast the individual properties of things and forces, relate things and forces one to another and to ourselves, make observations, name things and relations, learn, interpret, adapt ourselves and live our lives. Language and thinking are created and cultivated in the process. Thus, language and thinking always exist in a symbiotic relationship. So, we cannot produce thought, understanding, or language apart from and outside of the range of *Naturzusammenhang*. Therefore, everything that can be thought of or known or is inherently language-producing, must necessarily exist in relation to us. Even the God that we know of must be known, therefore, in relation to us, within the boundaries of the interconnected process of nature (boundaries, of course, which we cannot reach). Moreover, by virtue of the fact that God-knowledge and God-language must be just like any other knowledge or language we possess, it should be just like any other language or knowledge we have; but, on the other hand, by virtue of the fact that the "object" of our knowledge is the creator and preserver of the *Naturzusammenhang*, on whom it depends absolutely, in a non-reciprocal way, and is therefore utterly unlike any other object we know of, this knowledge should be utterly unlike anything else we know of.

The life and living from which we experience absolute dependence on God is composed of moments, from one end to the other, and each moment is shaped in association with a feeling of either partial or conditioned dependence and hence with a partial passive state or a feeling of partial or conditioned freedom and hence partial self-initiated activity. Furthermore: "Whenever dependence or a passive state is posited in some part of finite existence, spontaneity and causality are then posited in another part to which the first is related, and this being-reciprocally-related-to-each-other of differently distributed causality and passivity shapes the interconnected process of nature."[44] Therefore, every natural effect is produced by the exactly needed cause or causes required for that effect to come in to being and by nothing more and nothing less. This does not mean that the world is a juxtaposition of innumerable natural cause-effect series, each of which flows in parallel pipelines, without any intermingling. Rather, the truth is that each effect is usually created by a unique convergence of an indeterminable number of causal fibers, each of which coming into the union in strength unique to itself, thus in as much variety as there are fibers themselves. This effect, thus produced, then scatters itself into innumerable causal fibers, each of which could connect with other such causal fibers proceeding from countless neighboring effects in ingeniously new and creative configurations to produce the next generations of effects.

Therefore, we will be looking in vain if we want to find one cause for one effect; each formation is a complex process with each effect having exactly sufficient preceding cause, not needing any special additional

---

44. *Christian Faith*, §51.1, 201.

factor from outside the causal nexus. This is the dynamic of natural causality, the working out of the interconnected process of nature, and this is one reason why Schleiermacher has concern for the tendency of people to wonder at apparent big effects from small or no special causes. Our ineptitude for discerning all the causal connections that produce particular effects is no excuse for calling any of them miracles, in the sense of their bypassing the causal nexus of nature.

Now, natural causality explains only those natural relations, both cooperative and contrastive, that exist within the interconnected process of nature. Two observations, the contents of which are identical in actuality, must be made before we proceed further. (1) People are spiritual beings, and consciousness of God is ingrained in the constitution of highly developed self-consciousness. (2) For the sake of oneself, as well as for the sake of humanity and of the nature of which each one is part, in each person individually, and in the individual togetherness of one's spiritual association with any and all, there can arise a feeling of absolute dependence, and a sense of divine causality as the ground of this absolute dependence. Recognizing this effect is especially evident in Christianity.

The world "as the theater of redemption is the absolute revelation of the Supreme Being."[45] The consciousness of the regularity of the world-process and the consciousness of absolute dependence on God are complementary and are inseparably so. Since we are one with nature, nothing in nature is left out of this divine causality. If something were left out, as was said earlier, the organic portion that is ours, ingested in us from what was left out, would be bereft of absolute dependence, and that cannot be the case. Therefore, the scope of divine causality must be registered as identical to that of total finite causality, though of themselves they are not identical.

On the other hand, the scope of divine causality also cannot be thought of as more than the scope of finite causality, because, among other reasons, a superimposition of "more" and "less" (which are temporal and spatial qualifications) would make divine causality the same in kind as finite causality. However, divine causality must be utterly unlike finite causality for it to be absolutely dependent on divine causality. If divine causality were taken to be reduced to the nature of finite causality, as it were interfering with the mechanical-dynamical process of

---

45. Ibid., §169, 735.

the world, finite causality within the world would then be able to resist that particular divine causality, so that absolute dependence would be compromised. God would be dragged down to the mundane level and counter-influenced in two ways: (1) by the aforementioned resistance, and (2) by necessity's being imposed on God or by some persuasive influence from the world made on God to meddle with the natural process, apart from which God would have had no reason to do so. When there is thought to be a counter-influence on God, this tampers with the idea of God's absolute sovereignty over the world.

The relation, then, between finite causality and divine causality requires careful clarification. "Causality" is the common term in the two expressions. Since the world is the only medium for the revelation of God that we have, and since all knowledge and experience of God for us has to be stimulated from, and appropriated in and through, the means and terms of our mundane experience, Schleiermacher borrows words that signify the most vital human positive experiences, releases them from the quagmire of worldly contrasts, and transposes them for the use of theology by translating the "feel" of mundane vital experiences to the divine realm, to stand as vehicles for expressing the experiences of the divine. "Activity," "dependence," "love" and "wisdom" are some of the other important words Schleiermacher adopts for the purpose along with "causality."

Just as the world is rooted in God and finds its legitimacy, address and reality in differentiation from God, or just as time is rooted in as well as differentiated from eternity, so too does finite causality, wholly and in its parts, find its address, reality, and legitimacy only in relation to and in differentiation from divine causality. Confusing finite causality with divine causality is like confusing the world with God.

Finite causality is what it is only in the contrastive but interactive and complementary relation between finite activity and finite passivity. Divine causality is what it is only in differentiation from the total compass of finite causality. Yet, we must also remember that just as the differentiation between time and eternity is not in the least affected by finite or infinite duration in time, so too the differentiation between finite causality and divine causality is not in the least affected by the compass of finite causality. Just as God's non-dual, non-temporal eternity fills the gaps between moments and God's non-dual, non-spatial presence fills the gaps between all particles of space, so too does God's non-dual, non-physical causality cause all finite causality, in its parts and as a whole, and all relations between them. So, God's care for the particular is identical with God's care of the general. That is why statements such as the following should be considered misleading. "Because nature is a closed causal system, and because God is ground but not participant in the system, the unit of divine care is necessarily the whole, rather than individual parts, of the world."[46] Instead, the unit of divine care is equally individual and equally whole at all times, in all places. This has to be so both because of the interdependence of the system of nature and because of the nature of God's causality. If God does not or cannot take care of the individual, God cannot take of anything. It is true that in our general perception of individual happenings or mishappenings, we would not be able to understand and isolate the inner dynamics of the peculiar relatedness of a particular event in view to the totality of the nexus of interrelation and thus expose a cause-effect series. However, that inability does not call for desperation. Rather, we have to look at the big picture (of the totality of events and moments) and let the rough edges of individual events (which come as a mixture of pleasures and what is lacking in pleasure or positives and negatives) to cancel out each other, and trust in divine causality. Our inability to isolate the causal connections of individual events does not grant grounds for dismissing God's care for the individual. We must also add here that everything in the world, in its parts and as a whole, must be uniformly related to God; if some things are thought to be more related than some others, absolute dependence is made faulty.

Divine causality cannot be conceived as anything but the divine decree in eternity, and its fulfillment cannot be conceived otherwise than from an historical perspective, as actualized in time;[47] and that perspective results in the understanding of God as Immanuel.

The word "sovereignty" does not seem to make any impression on Schleiermacher in talking about God's relation to the world. However, I do not find any harm in using it on his behalf, since he makes constant reference to God as Lord and to the Reign of God. In his view, God's sovereignty over the world is absolute; God is ultimately responsible for the "devil" and all devilishness as well as all the best things of life, but in God's own way. If anything should happen within the world that is not in some fashion willed by God, then God would be limited by that

---

46. Fox, "Dogmatic Function of Election in Schleiermacher's Theology," 7.
47. *Christian Faith*, §172, 750–51.

clear opposition, and that cannot be the case. Therefore, no opposition to good that one finds in the world is to be considered as an ultimate opposition to God. Further, whatever good may fight against evil in this world also must not be considered to be in special relation to God, as though God is struggling along with the struggles of the world as a finite participant in them. God's sovereignty is identical with God's eternal will. God's sovereignty is the absoluteness of the sway of divine causality over finite causality.

Yet, God's absolute detachment from the natural dynamics of the world must not prompt us to take it that God is incapable of activity in mundane existence and is limited in this way; nor should anyone ever employ the defense on God's behalf that God is capable of such activity but is only abstaining from it based on God's own will. We are not imbued with the capacity to penetrate the mind of God; we can work only on the data given to us through the world in which we exist. The very thought of an attack on God's ability, or the defense thereof, can occur only on a presupposition that requires God to be reduced to the mundane level. "Capability" is a characteristic of finite limitation; it is in the realm of "more" or "less," and, as such, it is inapplicable to the divine realm. Even when the word "sovereignty" is used with respect to God, this fact must be kept in mind.

True to the spirit of the above observation, yet another point must be made here. Any attempt to defend God against the accusation of creating an imperfect and evil world, by suggesting either that what God did is to produce the best of all possible worlds or that God by God's nature could even have chosen not to create, is also utterly out of place. If God deliberates and then chooses, then there is a contrast in God between freedom and necessity,[48] and this would implicate our understanding of the perfection of God as untenable. The absence of options in God must not induce us to take the divine Mind to be still or to hold that God's action is determined robotically. First, then, Schleiermacher maintains a resolute refusal to speculate on God's capacities or modes of action or to offer any anthropomorphic portrayal of God except as an inescapable practical aid. For one thing, choice or lack of it is anthropomorphic and is thus inapplicable to God's realm. Second, choice always implies imperfection; if there are two perfects, either it is the case that each perfect will limit the other and thus

---

48. *Christian Faith*, §41.P.S., 156.

both will become imperfect, or it is the case that both should be identical and hence choice as a thought becomes superfluous. If there is one perfect, and one or more imperfects to choose from, the imperfect loses its relevance, and hence choice too loses its relevance. If there are two or more imperfects to choose from, whichever choice is made, both the choice and the act of choice will be imperfect, and it will not be a good testimony for God's perfection. Third, supposing unrealized options within God opens God to the charge of having a void in God. Fourth, who are we to stand in judgment of God's so-called choices, or lack thereof! Surely this would be the highest height of stupidity!

Since the world in which we are absolutely dependent is itself absolutely dependent on God, God's sovereignty over it must be absolute. In our consciousness, as Christians at least, the running of the writ of God's absolute sovereignty covers as extensive an area as the totality of the world. Yet, it must also be remembered that the extent of God's sovereignty is also limited by the extension of God's creation, since we cannot have any consciousness of an existence apart from the creation that we are part of. Since God's sovereignty cannot be reduced to the realm of contrasts, of choices and of reciprocity, and since it must be placed beyond all casual, spatial and temporal limitations, "sovereignty" must be conceived as such to suit its peculiar trans-mundane status. Attribution of any worldly character to God's sovereignty is a surrender of God's sovereignty to the exact measure of such attribution.

For example, the view that God exists timelessly before the creation of time, but within time after the creation of time, practices such surrender with serious consequences, though perhaps unwittingly. We will illustrate it thus: Considering only the duration of the temporal existence of creation, since God would at this stage be in time, God would have a past, a present and a future. Thus, God is brought down to the mundane levels of natural relations and contrasts. Even if one should concede God's absolute sovereignty over the present and future, since God would be in time, and since the past is something that has already expired, God's sovereignty over all the events of the past is already past, which means that there is no scope for God's sovereignty to alter or modify the past in the present or future. In other words, it is utterly impossible for God to redo history or to change the past, say for example, to nullify a shameful portion of human history like the holocaust.

Therefore, our concept of God's "sovereignty" must not be conceived so as to corner us in the ridiculous position of having to invent ways (which will in any case be untenable in the final analysis) to redeem God from such utter trivialities. Divine sovereignty must be explained in terms of divine causality, which is equal in scope to the totality of finite causality and utterly opposite in kind. (If we leave aside all the differences between Schleiermacher and Kierkegaard for a moment, something interestingly similar can be observed between them here. The relation between God and the world, and between eternity and time, is one of utter opposition in Schleiermacher, whereas in Kierkegaard, it is an absolute paradox!)[49] To the exact measure of any portion of the divine causality that is conceived as similar in kind to finite causality, divine sovereignty is compromised, and God is reduced to a human status, and as a result absolute dependence is rendered impossible.

The world is God's work, nature is God's art. God is the ultimate causal source of everything there is; God's non-spatial presence is everywhere connecting everything to everything else. A matching receptivity to this presence could exist, among the whole creation, only in human beings. However, the incapacitating force of sin has effectively seen to it that generally there is very little activation of this receptivity in human beings. In contrast to other human beings though, in Jesus we find an unfailing receptivity continually activated and at full capacity. This is why one should say that the Being of God is in Jesus, or that God is omnipresent in Him.

The distinguishing mark of Christianity is that "everything in it is referred to the redemption accomplished through Jesus of Nazareth."[50] Redemption is the peculiar work of God in and through Jesus. By extension, the redemption of the redeemed, and therefore the redeemed themselves, are God's work in Jesus. By further extension, the rest of humanity are all potential recipients of the full fruits of redemption through Jesus and are therefore objects of divine good pleasure. The totality of creation exists to facilitate the spread of Jesus' consciousness of God into the self-consciousness of all remaining centers of self-consciousness. If Jesus, as the center of the absolute consciousness of God, can be compared to the light rays beaming out of the sun in straight lines, the spiritual life of the

---

49. Kierkegaard, *Philosophical Fragments*, 42–48.
50. *Christian Faith*, §11, 52.

redeemed can be compared to the light particles that wave out of those straight lines to lighten all shades and darkness within their reach.

The rest of humanity can be viewed as the prospective receiving agents of these light waves and the rest of the sentient and insentient entities of creation as facilitating agents, in their own endowed capacities, for the spreading of the light waves conveying the consciousness of God that has the particular modification emanating from Jesus into all the potential receiving centers. With respect to human beings, this spreading of redemption and the corresponding consciousness is the purpose of creation, and this is why we can say that God's work in Jesus is identical to God's work in history.

Conclusion

OUR ATTEMPT AT A REVERSE PRESENTATION OF THE THEOLOGY OF CHRISTIAN *Faith,* building it all around the theme of God's work in Christ, is now complete. Since this is only a work of moderate proportion, I hope that others will come along soon and so further comprehensive, thoroughgoing work along the same lines as those emphasized here, thus fulfilling a cherished dream of Schleiermacher himself.[1] I believe I have shown that for Schleiermacher God's work in Christ is identical to God's work in history, having highlighted the matter at regular intervals, from one end to the other of this work.

Through it all we have found an edifice developed with amazingly consistent adherence to the basic principles of dogmatic construction, as he understood them and elegantly articulated them. If logical impeccability, architectonic precision, and sharpness in thinking were the main criteria, one would not find anything that can excel Schleiermacher's systematic, critical work on dogmatics in Christian history. Once one has accepted his Christological definition of dogmatics, the basic presuppositions regarding the one divine decree, the interconnected process of nature and the species nature of human beings the way Schleiermacher sees them, one can see all the pieces of his overall system neatly interlocking.

However, in the building of his edifice Schleiermacher starts with a tremendous advantage over orthodox theological thinking. He starts with the premise that since dogmatics is a scientific enterprise, a probing systematic presentation of teachings of faith that have currency in the Church at a given time and place, an appropriate scientific method must be adopted in its development. Since knowing and thinking are possible only in terms of some dialectical process, viewed as the art of coming to know, the scope of knowing, and therefore that of dogmatics, must be limited to a range wherein both analogy and dialectic are possible and suitable. The fundamental source in religious consciousness, or piety, or

---

1. *On the Glaubenslehre,* 59.

being in communion with God in Christ is evoked, therefore, always through the stimulations coming from the world of multiplicity. Thus, God is known only in our pious experience, generally emanating from the influence of the particular modification of religion found in the pious association one is part of. Therefore, a literally, exclusively supernatural revelation, as any sort of arbitrary insertion into the interconnectedness of the physical and human world, in verbal or any other form, is ruled out. That being the case, there is no chance of a knowledge of a divine causality or a divine "isness" apart from what is related to the interconnected process of nature. The realm of the "absolute," which is in utter contrast with the world of multiplicity, is beyond the range of our knowledge. God in Godself is utterly inaccessible to us in this respect. Likewise, a knowledge of life after death is placed beyond the scope of dogmatics.

Therefore, the area of operation for dogmatics, in Schleiermacher's view, is substantially smaller than that of traditional orthodox Protestantism. All the complexities and complications of difficult doctrines like those on the "two natures" of Christ, the "Trinity" and such are either totally eliminated or considerably trimmed, though critically examined with care. This is the reason he is able to produce what appears to be a virtually impeccable system, though he also leaves it open for further reflection, critical examination and revision as time goes on and does not attempt to account for doctrine in every religious community.

Christian Faith is conceived and constructed especially against the backdrop of the Reformed orthodoxy of Schleiermacher's time; at almost all points, it is presented at least in interaction with that orthodoxy, its precedents and its contemporary counterparts, for example, Augustinian and Lutheran. The criticisms he makes of traditional orthodox thinking are relentless, penetrating, and passionate; this is done in zeal for his "father's house." In part, he also wants to see this work to be presented in a defendable shape, not only on behalf of the community of faith but also in response to seekers among the cultured critics of religion. Above all, it must be made inviting to all of these so as to spread the aroma of Christ, on the one hand, and to arrest and reverse the growth of blatantly negative atheism, on the other hand. Schleiermacher holds that the inadequate, misleading, or faulty thinking shown in the various orthodox and heterodox positions he critiques and abandons throughout comprise a major reason for repulsion against religion in the minds of many cultured critics, even despisers and detractors in his day. In order to help correct that situation, as well as to lead people of faith to attain a finer, clearer understanding, he was willing to pay any price that could be taxed on his own reputation, personal comfort, time or energy or on his total being.

In concluding an essay on Schleiermacher's Christology, Professor Richard Muller makes the following remarks.

> Those who have labeled his thought as heterodox or unsuccessful and incapable of sustaining a genuine Christology or genuinely Christocentric approach to theology have greatly overstated their case, if only to defer inquiry into the problematic elements in their own Christologies. Those who have asked objectively the question of the success or failure of his approach in the context of traditional Christological language encounter the difficulty of Schleiermacher's acknowledgment, on the one hand, of the intention behind the traditional language, and his rejection, on the other, of the language itself—on precisely stated and very cogent theological grounds, indeed, for the sake of the profoundly biblical and traditional intention that Jesus Christ be understood as an individual subject. The final verdict has not been pronounced on Schleiermacher's Christology. We are left both with a renewed sense of the difficulty of formulating a Christology in contemporary language and with the distinct impression that the century and a half separating us from Schleiermacher has in no way diminished the importance of his contribution to the discussion.[2]

I want to echo the spirit of Muller's words. There is no hiding the radical revision of earlier Christian doctrines at the hand of Schleiermacher, but those who want to take umbrage at his revisions and at the severe criticisms of much theological thinking in both traditional and modern Christianity, not just of Christology but of a great many other orthodox doctrines as well as of non-orthodox and heterodox doctrines, must first come to terms with those criticisms and then make a considered response of equal care. So far that has rarely taken place. Along with the criticisms he made, Schleiermacher has produced an alternative, consistent, and viable theological system true to the religious faith and experience he observed within the confines of his community of faith. That system being what it is, it will be possible to make a really valid criticism of Schleiermacher's thought only by contributing to a systematic account

2. Muller, "Christological Problem as Addressed by Friedrich Schleiermacher," 162.

of theological thinking as a teaching tool for the Church, one that appropriately answers all his criticisms, and one that will also be able to stand as an edifice presenting the same or nearly the same interlocking consistency and logical precision as *Christian Faith* does. Such a system must also be in accordance with the religious faith and experience of the faith community with which the producers identify. That is the minimum required if we are genuinely to reckon with the father of modern theology. The onus is on the critic.

Bibliography

Works by Schleiermacher

Schleiermacher, Friedrich. *Brief Outline on the Study of Theology Field of Study.* Translated, with Introduction and Notes by Terrence N. Tice. Atlanta: John Knox, 1977. [A new edition by Tice of the 1811 and 1830 texts, with Essays and Notes, appeared under the title *Brief Outline of Theology as a Field of Study,* Edwin Mellen, 1990.]

———. *The Christian Faith.* Translated from the 2d German edition. Edited by H. R. Mackintosh and J. S. Stewart. Edinburgh: T. & T. Clark, 1928. [A new translation by Tice is in process.]

———. *The Christian Household; A Sermonic Treatise* (1820, 1826). Translated by Dietrich Siedel and Tice. Lewiston, NY: Edwin Mellen, 1990.

———. *Christmas Eve: Dialogue on the Incarnation.* Translated with Introduction and Notes by Terrence N. Tice. Richmond: John Knox, 1967. [A presentation by Tice of both editions, of 1806 and 1826, is forthcoming.]

———. *Dialectic: or, The Art of Doing Philosophy: A Study Edition of the 1811 Notes.* Translated with Introduction and Notes by Terrence N. Tice. Atlanta: Scholars, 1996. [A translation by Joseph Eckenrode and Tice is in process.]

———. *Fifteen Sermons of Friedrich Schleiermacher Delivered to Celebrate the Beginning of a New Year.* Translated and edited by Edwina Lawler. Lewiston, NY: Edwin Mellen, 2003.

———. *Hermeneutics: The Handwritten Manuscripts.* Edited by Heinz Kimmerle. Translated by James Duke and Jack Forstman. American Academy of Religion Texts and Translation Series 1. Missoula, MT: Scholars, 1977. [A newly arranged translation of all the hermeneutic materials by Tim Clancy and Tice is forthcoming, in two volumes.]

———. *Introduction to Christian Ethics.* Translated by John C. Shelley. Nashville: Abingdon, 1989. [A long-term project to issue the 1826/27 text in German, edited by Hermann Peiter, and to translate that text and all the rest is underway.]

———. *The Life of Jesus.* Edited with an Introduction by Jack C. Verheyden. Translated by S. Maclean Gilmour. Lives of Jesus Series. Philadelphia: Fortress, 1975.

———. *Luke: A Critical Study.* Translated by Connop Thirlwall, newly edited by Terrence N. Tice. Lewiston, NY: Edwin Mellen, 1992.

———. *On Creeds, Confessions and Church Union: "That They May Be One."* Edited and translated by Iain G. Nicol. Lewiston, NY: Edwin Mellen, 2004.

———. *On Election* (1819). Translation by Iain G. Nicol and Allen Jorgensen. In preparation.

———. *On Freedom.* Translated, Annotated and Introduced by Albert L. Blackwell. Lewiston, NY: Edwin Mellen, 1992.

———. *On Religion: Addresses in Response to its Cultured Critics.* Translated, with Introduction and Notes by Terrence N. Tice. Richmond: John Knox, 1969. [A critical edition of all three editions of 1799, 1806, and 1830 by Tice is forthcoming.]

———. *On Religion: Speeches to its Cultured Despisers.* Translated and edited by Richard Crouter. Cambridge: Cambridge University Press, 1996.

———. "On the Discrepancy between the Sabellian and Athanasian Method of Representing the Doctrine of Trinity." Translated by Moses Stuart. *Biblical Repository and Quarterly Observer* 6 (1935) 1–116. [This essay, with other related writings on *The Triune God,* translated by Tice and Edwina Lawler, is forthcoming.]

———. *On the Glaubenslehre: Two Letters to Dr. Lücke.* Translated by James Duke and Francis Fiorenza. American Academy of Religion Texts and Transmissions Series, no. 3. Chico, CA: Scholars, 1981.

———. *On the Highest Good* (1789). Translated by Victor Froese. Lewiston, NY: Edwin Mellen, 1992.

———. *On What Gives Value to Life.* Translated with an Introduction and Notes by Edwina Lawler and Terrence N. Tice. Lewiston, NY: Edwin Mellen, 1995.

———. *Reformed but Ever Reforming: Sermons in Relation to the Celebration of the Handing over of the Augsburg Confession* (1830). Translated, with introduction and notes, by Iain G. Nichol. Lewiston, NY: Edwin Mellen, 1997.

———. *Selected Sermons of Schleiermacher.* Translated by Mary F. Wilson. New York: Funk and Wagnalls, 1890.

———. *Servant of the Word: Selected Sermons of Friedrich Schleiermacher.* Translated with an introduction by Dawn De Vries. Philadelphia: Fortress Press, 1987.

———. *Schleiermacher's Soliloquies.* An English translation of the Monologen, with a critical introduction and appendix by Horace Leland Friess. Chicago: The Open Court Publishing Co., 1957. (A new translation of both editions by Tice is in process.)

———. "Ueber die Lehre von der Erwählung: besonders in Beziehung auf Herrn Dr. Bretschneiders aphorismen." *Kritische Gesamtausgabe* pt. 1, vol. 10, 147–222. Berlin, New York: Walter de Gruyter, 1990. [A translation is in process, see *On Election* above.]

Secondary Sources

Aleaz, K. P. "The Theological Writings of Brahmahandhav Upadhyaya Re-Examined." *Indian Journal of Theology* 28 (April–June 1979) 55–77.

Allen, Diogenes. *Philosophy for Understanding Theology.* Atlanta: John Knox, 1985.

Augustine, Saint. *Confessions.* Translated by William Watts. Cambridge, MA. Harvard University Press, 1977–1979.

———. *On Genesis: Two books on Genesis against the Manichees.* Translated by Roland J. Teske. Washington, D.C.: Catholic University of American Press, 1991.

Avis, Paul D. L. "Friedrich Schleiermacher and the Science of Theology." *Scottish Journal of Theology* 32 (February 1979) 19–43.

Barth, Karl. *Church Dogmatics,* Vol. 3. Edited by G. W. Bromiley and T. F. Torrance. Translated by G. W. Bomiley and R. J. Erlich. Edinburgh: T. and T. Clark, 1960.

———. *Protestant Thought: From Rousseau to Ritschl, being the Translation of Eleven Chapters of Die Protestantische Theologie im 19. Jahrhundert.* Translated by Brian Cozens. New York: Harper, 1959.

———. *The Theology of Schleiermacher.* Edited by Dietrich Ritschl. Translated by Geoffrey W. Bromiley. Grand Rapids: Eerdmans, 1982.
Benson, John E. "Schleiermacher on God and the Self: The Witness to Transcendence in Feeling." *Dialog* 16 (Summer 1977) 174–81.
Berkhof, Hendrikus. *Two Hundred Years of Theology: Report of a Personal Journey.* Translated by John Vriend. Grand Rapids: Eerdmans, 1989.
Birkner, Hans Joachim. "Beobachtungen zu Schleiermachers Programm der Dogmatik." *Neue Zeitschrift fur systematische Theologie und Religionsphilosophie* 5 (1963) 119–31.
Blackwell, Albert L. "The Antagonistic Correspondence of 1801 between Chaplin Sack and his Protegé Schleiermacher." *Harvard Theological Review* 74 (1981) 101–21.
———. *Schleiermacher's Early Philosophy of Life: Determinism, Freedom and Phantasy.* Harvard Theological Studies 33. Chico, CA: Scholars, 1982.
———. "Schleiermacher's Sermon at Nathanael's Grave." *Journal of Religion* 57 (1977) 64–75.
Boethius. *The Consolation of Philosophy.* Translated with an Introduction and Notes by Richard Green. New York: Macmillan, 1989.
———. *The Theological Tractates.* With an English translation by H. F. Stewart, E. K. Rand and S. J. Tester. (new ed.) Cambridge: Harvard University Press, 1973.
Bonhoeffer, Dietrich. *Letters and Papers from Prison.* New York: Macmillan, 1966.
Boyd, Robin H. S. *An Introduction to Indian Christian Theology.* Madras: Christian Literature Society, 1969.
Boyer, Bruce L. "Schleiermacher on the Divine Causality." *Religious Studies* 22 (1986) 113–23.
Brandt, James M. *All Things New: Reform of Church and Society in Schleiermacher's Christian Ethics.* Louisville: Westminster John Knox, 2001.
Brandt, Richard B. *The Philosophy of Schleiermacher: The Development of His Theory of Scientific and Religious Knowledge.* New York: Harper, 1941.
Brown, Colin. *Christianity and Western Thought.* Vol. 1. Downers Grove, IL: InterVarsity, 1990.
Brunner, Emil. *Dogmatics.* Translated by Olive Wyon. Philadelphia: Westminster, 1950.
Calvin, John. *Institutes of the Christian Religion.* Edited by John T. McNeill. Translated and indexed by Ford Lewis Battles. Philadelphia: Westminster, 1977.
Christian, C. W. *Friedrich Schleiermacher.* Makers of Modern Theological Mind. Edited by Bob E. Patterson. Waco, TX: Word, 1979.
Clements, Keith. *Friedrich Schleiermacher: Pioneer of Modern Theology.* The Making of Modern Theology: 19th and 20th Century Theological Texts. London: Collins, 1987.
Clendenin, Daniel B. "A Conscious Perplexity: Barth's Interpretation of Schleiermacher." *Westminster Theological Journal* 52 (1990) 281–301.
Collins, Alice. "Barth's Relationship to Schleiermacher: A Reassessment." *Studies in Religion* 17 (1988) 213–24.
Copleston, F. C. *A History of Philosophy.* Vol. 7. New York: Image, 1963.
Corliss, Richard L. "Schleiermacher's Hermeneutics and its Critics." *Religious Studies* 29 (1993) 363–97.
Craig, William Lane. "Aquinas on God's Knowledge of Future Contingents." *Thomist* 54 (1990) 33–79.
———. "Boethius on Theological Fatalism." *Ephemerides Theologicae* 64 (1988) 324–347.

———. "God and Real Time." *Religious Studies* 26 (1990) 335–47.
———. "God, Time, and Eternity." *Religious Studies* 14 (1978) 497–503.
Craver, Bennie Dale. "The Divine Government of the World: The Function of Providence in the Theology of Friedrich Schleiermacher." Ph.D. diss., Southwestern Baptist Seminary, 1994.
Crouter, Richard. "Hegel and Schleiermacher at Berlin: A Many-sided Debate." *Journal of the American Academy of Religion* 48 (1980) 19–43.
———. "Rhetoric and Substance in Schleiermacher's Revision of *The Christian Faith*." *Journal of Religion* 60 (1980) 285–306.
Dayton, Wilbur T. "A Weslyan Note on Election." In *Perspectives on Evangelical Theology*, ed. Kenneth S. Kantzer and Stanley N. Gundry, 95–103. Grand Rapids: Baker, 1979.
Devadutt, V. E. "Augustine and Sankara on Time." *Indian Journal of Theology* 33 (January-September 1984) 24–34.
DeVries, Dawn. *Jesus Christ in the Preaching of Calvin and Schleiermacher*. Louisville: Westminster John Knox, 1996.
———. *Servant of the Lord: Selected Sermons of Friedrich Schleiermacher*. Philadelphia: Fortress, 1987.
Duke, David N. "Schleiermacher: Theology without a Fall." *Perspectives in Religious Studies* 9 (1982) 21–37.
———. "Schleiermacher and the Theology of the Bourgeois Society: A Critique of the Critics." *Journal of Religion* 66 (1986) 285–306.
Duke, James O., and Robert F. Streetman, eds. *Barth and Schleiermacher: Beyond the Impasse?* Philadelphia: Fortress, 1988.
Durant, Will. *The Story of Philosophy*. New York: Washington Square, 1961.
Ebeling, Gerhard. "Schleiermachers Lehre von den gottlichen Eigenschafter." *Zeitschrift für Theologie und Kirche* 65 (1968) 459–94.
Fantino, Jacques. *La théologie d'Irénée*. Paris: Cerf, 1994.
Ferguson, Duncan S. "Augustine on History: A Perspective for our Time." *Evangelical Quarterly* 58 (1986) 39–52.
Feuerbach, Ludwig. *The Essence of Christianity*. Translated by George Eliot. Introduction by Karl Barth. Foreword by H. Richard Niebuhr. New York: Harper & Row, 1957.
Fluckiger, Felix. *Philosophie und Theologie bei Schleiermacher*. Zollikon-Zurich: Evangelischer Verlag, 1947.
Ford, David. ed. *The Modern Theologians*. Cambridge, Mass: Basil Blackwell, 1990.
Foreman, Terry H. "Schleiermacher's 'Natural History of Religion': Science and the Interpretation of Culture in the Speeches." *Journal of Religion* 58 (1978) 91–107.
Forstman, H. Jackson. "Barth, Schleiermacher and the Christian Faith." *Union Seminary Quarterly Review* 21 (1966) 305–19.
———. *A Romantic Triangle: Schleiermacher and Early German Romanticism*. American Academy of Religion Studies in Religion, 13. Missoula, MT: Scholars, 1977.
———. "Understanding of Language by Friedrich Schlegel and Schleiermacher." *Soundings* 51 (1968) 146–65.
Fox, Charles W. "The Logic of Schleiermacher's Interpretation of Religion." Harvard University Relig./Philos. Diss., 1979. Abstract in *Harvard Theological Review* 72, (1979) 315.

Funk, Robert W., ed. *Schleiermacher as Contemporary.* New York: Herder and Herder, 1970. [With contributions by Gerhard Ebeling, H. Jackson Forstman, Hans-Georg Gadamer, Richard R. Niebuhr, Wilhelm Pauck, Gerhard Spiegler, and Others.]

Gerrish, Brian. *Continuing the Reformation: Essays on Modern Religious Thought.* Chicago: University of Chicago Press, 1993.

———. "The Doctrine of Faith." *Princeton Seminary Bulletin* 16 (1995) 205–215.

———. "Nature and the Theater of Redemption: Schleiermacher on Christian Dogmatics and the Creation Story." *Ex Auditu* 3 (1987) 120–36.

———. *Old Protestantism and the New: Essays on the Reformation Heritage.* Chicago: University of Chicago Press, 1982.

———. *A Prince of the Church: Schleiermacher and the beginnings of Modern Theology.* Philadelphia: Fortress, 1984.

———. "Schleiermacher and the Reformation: A Question of Doctrinal Development." *Church History* 49 (June 1980) 147–59.

———. "Theology within the Limits of Piety Alone: Schleiermacher and Calvin's Doctrine of God." In *Reformatio Perennis: Essays on Calvin and the Reformation,* edited by B. A. Gerrish in collaboration with Robert Benedetto, 67–87. Pittsburg: Pickwick, 1981.

———. *Tradition and the Modern World: Reformed Theology in the Nineteenth Century.* Chicago: University of Chicago Press, 1978.

Goris, Harm J.M.J. *Free Creatures of an Eternal God: Thomas Aquinas on God's Infallible Foreknowledge and Irresistible Will.* Leuven: Peeters, 1996.

Graby, James K. "The Question of Development in Schleiermacher's Theology." *Canadian Journal of Theology* 10 (1964) 75–87.

———. "Reflections on the History of the Interpretation of Schleiermacher." *Scottish Journal of Theology* 21 (1968) 283–99.

Graham, Terry. "The Dual Aspect of Hermeneutics." *Studies in Religion* 22 (1993) 105–116.

Grenz, Stanley J., and Roger E. Olson. *20th Century Theology.* Downers Grove, IL: InterVarsity, 1992.

Hamilton, Kenneth. "Schleiermacher and Relational Theology." *Journal of Religion* 44 (1964) 29–39.

———. "Under Schleiermacher's Banner." *Religion in Life* 32 (1963) 564–73.

Harshaw Dumas Alexander Jr., "Theology of Engagement: Schleiermacher on the Relation of God and the World." D. Min. Project. Claremont School of Theology, 1978.

Harvey, Van A. "A Word in Defense of Schleiermacher's Theological Method." *Journal of Religion* 42 (1962) 151–70.

Hegel, G. W. F. *Reason in History.* Translated by Robert S. Hartman. Indianapolis: Bobbs-Merrill, 1981.

Heppe, Heinrich Ludwig Junius. *Reformed Dogmatics Set out and Illustrated from Sources.* Forward by Karl Barth. Revised and edited by Ernst Bizar. Translated by G. T. Thomson. Grand Rapids: Baker, 1978.

Herms, Eilert. "Schleiermachers Eschatologie nach der zweiten Auflage der "Glaubenslehere."" *Theologische Zeitschrift* 42 (1990) 97–123.

Heron, Alasdair I. C. *A Century of Protestant Theology.* Philadelphia: Westminster, 1980.

Hick, John. *Philosophy of Religion.* Englewood Cliffs, NJ: Prentice-Hall, 1963.

Irenaeus, Saint. *The Writings of Irenaeus.* Translated by Alexander Roberts and W. H. Rambant. Edinburgh: T. & T. Clark, 1874.

Jantzen, Grace M. "Could There Be a Mystical Core of Religion?" *Religious Studies* 26 (1990) 59–71.
Johnson, Charles Michael. "Schleiermacher's God as Contemporary." *Encounter* 38 (1977) 245–72.
Kant, Immanuel. *Foundations of the Metaphysics of Morals.* 2d ed. Translated with an introduction by Lewis White Beck. New York: Macmillan, 1990.
———. *Religion Within the Limits of Reason Alone.* 2d. ed. Translated with an introduction and notes by T. M. Greene and H. H. Hudson. New York: Harper & Row, 1960.
Keesee, Neal K. "Divine Purpose in Schleiermacher's *Speeches.*" In *Working Papers,* edited by David F. Klem, 1–26. Papers of the International Schleiermacher Society and Schleiermacher Group. American Academy of Religion, New Orleans, 1995. Iowa City: University of Iowa Press, 1995.
Kelsey, Catherine L. *Thinking about Christ with Schleiermacher.* Louisville: Westminster John Knox, 2003.
Kennedy, Henry A. "The Eschatology of Friedrich Schleiermacher." *Southwestern Journal of Theology* (1994) 22–23.
Kierkegaard, Soren. *Philosophical Fragments.* 2d. ed. Translated and introduced by David F. Swenson. New Introduction and Commentary by Niels Thulstrup. Translation revised and commentary by H. V. Hong. Princeton, NJ: Princeton University Press, 1962.
King, Robert H. "Models of God's Transcendence." *Theology Today* 23 (1966) 200–209.
Kinlaw, Jeffery, ed. *Schleiermacher's Reformed Doctrine and Ethics and his Contributions to Liberation/Feminist Theology Today.* Papers presented at the 1995 annual meeting of the American Academy of Religion. Philadelphia, 1995.
Klooster, Fred H. "Predestination: A Calvinistic Note." In *Perspectives on Evangelical Theology,* ed. Kenneth S. Kantzer and Stanley N. Gundry, 81–94. Grand Rapids: Baker, 1979.
Krieg, Carl E. "Schleiermacher: On the Divine Nature." *Religion in Life* 42 (1973) 514–23.
Küng, Hans. *Does God Exist? An Answer for Today.* Translated by Edward Quinn. New York: Vintage, 1981.
Lamm, Julia A. "The Early Philosophical Roots of Schleiermacher's Notion of Gefühl." *Harvard Theological Review* 94 (1994) 67–105.
———. "Schleiermacher's Post-Kantian Spinozism: The Early Essays on Spinoza." *Journal of Religion* 74 (1994) 476–505.
Leftow, Brian. "Eternity and Simultaneity." *Faith and Philosophy* 8 (1991) 148–79.
Lewis, Delmas. "Eternity, Time and Timelessness." *Faith and Philosophy* 5 (1988) 72–86.
Liebing, Heinz. "Ferdinand Christian Baurs Kritik an Schleiermachers Glaubenslehre." *Zeitschrift für Theolgie und Kirche* 54 (1957) 225–43.
Lienhard, Joseph T., ed. *Collectanea Augustiniana: Augustine.* New York: Lang, 1993.
Locher, Gottlieb Friedrich Daniel. "Die Beziehung der Zeit zur Ewigkeit bei Augustin." *Theologische Zeitschrift* 44 (1988) 147–67.
Mackay, Donald M. "The Sovereignty of God in the Natural World." *Scottish Journal of Theology* 21 (1968) 13–26.
Mariña, Jacqueline, ed. *The Cambridge Companion to Friedrich Schleiermacher.* Cambridge: Cambridge University Press, 2005.
Marshal, Bruce D. "Hermeneutics and Dogmatics in Schleiermacher's Theology." *Journal of Religion* 67 (1987) 14–32.

Martin, William C. "Religion for Its Cultured Despisers—A Study in the Theological Method of Schleiermacher." *Restoration Quarterly* 13, (1970) 91–105.
Marty, Martin E., and Dean G. Peerman, eds. *A Handbook of Christian Theologians*. Nashville: Abingdon, 1984.
McGrath, Alister E., ed. *The Blackwell Encyclopedia of Modern Christian Thought*. Oxford: Blackwell, 1996.
McMahon, John. "The Influence of the Rise of Classical Science on the Theology of Freidrich Schleiermacher." *Colloquium* 25 (1993) 20–28.
Mednieta, Eduardo. "Metaphysics of Subjectivity and the Theology of Subjectivity: Schleiermacher's Anthropological Theology." *Philosophy and Religion* 6 (1992) 276–90.
Moore, Walter L. "Schleiermacher as a Calvinist: A Comparison of Calvin and Schleiermacher on Providence and Predestination." *Scottish Journal of Theology* 24 (1971) 167–83.
Muller, Richard A. "The Christological Problem as Addressed by Friedrich Schleiermacher: A Dogmatic Query." In *Perspectives on Christology*, edited by Marguerite Shuster and Richard Muller, 141–62. Grand Rapids: Zondervan, 1991.
Musser, Donald W. and Joseph L. Price, eds. *A New Hand-Book of Christian Theology*. Nashville: Abingdon, 1992.
Newman, Amy. "The Death of Judaism in German Protestant Thought from Luther to Hegel." *Journal of the American Academy of Religion* 61 (1993) 455–84.
Nicol, Iain G. "Schleiermacher and Ritschl: Two Nineteenth-Century Revisionary Christologies." In *The Christological Foundation for Contemporary Theological Education*, edited by Joseph D. Ban, 137–57. Macon, GA: Mercer University Press, 1988.
Niebuhr, Richard R. "Karl Barth's "Schleiermacher" A Review Essay." *Union Seminary Quarterly Review* 39 (1984) 129–36.
———. "Schleiermacher: Theology as Human Reflection." *Harvard Theological Review* 55 (1962) 20–49.
———. "Schleiermacher as Prophet: A Reckoning of his Christian View of History." *Springfielder* 32 (1969) 7–14.
———. *Schleiermacher on Christ and Religion*. New York: Charles Scribner's Sons, 1964.
———. "Schleiermacher on Language and Feeling." *Theology Today* 17 (1960) 150–67.
Nowak, Kurt. "Romanticism—Religion—Utopia: Schleiermacher's and Chateaubriand's Interpretation of Religion about 1800." *Neue Zeitschrift für systematische Theologie and Religionsphilosophie* 33 (1991) 44–58.
———. *Schleiermacher: Leben, Werk und Wirkung*. Göttingen: Vandenhoeck & Ruprecht, 2001.
O'Connor, Don Thomas. "Schleiermacher and Kierkegaard: 'The Odd Couple' of Modern Theology." *Religion in Life* 41 (1972) 8–17.
Padgett, Alan G. "God and Time: Toward a New Doctrine of Divine Timeless Eternity." *Religious Studies* 25 (1989) 209–15.
Pannenberg, Wolfhart. "Hermeneutics and Universal History." Translated by P. and J. Achtemeier. *Journal for Theology and the Church* 4 (1967) 122–52.
———. *Human Nature, Election, and History*. Philadelphia: Westminster, 1977.
Parekh, Manilal C. *Bramarshi Keshub Chunder Sen*. Rajkot: Oriental Christ House, 1926.

Paul, William W. "What Can Religion Say to its Cultured Despisers? A Comparison of Schleiermacher (1799) and Tillich (1959)." *Reformed Review* 23 (1970) 208–16.
Pelikan, Jaroslav. "Creation and Causality in the History of Christian Thought." *Southwestern Journal of Theology* 32 (1990) 10–16.
Penzel, Klaus. "A Chapter in the History of the Ecumenical Quest: Schelling and Schleiermacher [Influences of Romanticism and Idealism]." *Church History* 33 (1964) 322–37.
Pickle, Joseph W. "Schleiermacher on Judaism." *Journal of Religion* 60 (1980) 115–37.
Quinn, Philip L. "Does Anxiety Explain Original Sin?" *Nous* 24 (1990) 227–44.
Redeker, Martin. *Schleiermacher: Life and Thought.* Translated by John Wallhausser. Philadelphia: Fortress, 1973.
Richardson, Ruth, ed. *New Athenaeum/Neues Athenaeum: A Scholarly Journal Specializing in Schleiermacher Research and Nineteenth Century Studies,* vols. 1–3. Lewiston, NY: Mellen, 1989, 1991, 1992.
―――, ed. *Friedrich Schleiermacher's "Toward a Theory of Social Conduct" and Essays on Its Intellectual Cultural Context.* New Athenaeum/Neues Athenaeum, 4. Lewiston, NY: Mellen, 1995.
―――, ed. *Schleiermacher on Workings of the Knowing Mind: New Translations, Resources, and Understandings.* New Athenaeum/Neues Athenaeum, 5. Lewiston, NY: Mellen, 1998.
―――, ed. *Schleiermacher in Context: Papers from the 1988 International Symposium on Schleiermacher at Herrnhut, the German Democratic Republic.* Lewiston, NY: Mellen, 1991.
Roberts, Robert. "Feeling of Absolute Dependence." *Journal of Religion* 57 (1977) 252–66.
Rogers, Katherin A. "Eternity has no Duration." *Religious Studies* 30 (1994) 1–16.
Root, Michael. "Schleiermacher as Innovator and Inheritor: God, Dependence, and Election." *Scottish Journal of Theology* 43 (1990) 87–110.
Russell, S. H., "Punishment in Schleiermacher and Hegel." *Theology* 76 (1973) 21–27.
Scaer, David P. "The Doctrine of Election: A Lutheran Note." In *Perspectives on Evangelical Theology,* edited by Kenneth S. Kantzer and Stanley N. Gundry, 105–15. Grand Rapids: Baker. 1979.
Schleiermacher Society and Schleiermacher Group. Working papers for the 1996 Annual Meeting. American Academy of Religion. New Orleans, 1996.
Schultz, Werner. "Schleiermachers Theorie des Gefühls und ihre theologische Bedeutung." *Zeitschrift für Theologie und Kirche* 53 (1956) 75–103.
―――. "Die Transformierung der theologia cruces bei Hegel und Schleiermacher." *Neue Zeitschrift für systmatishche Theologie und Religionsphilosophie* 6 (1964) 290–317.
Scott, Charles E. "Schleiermacher and the Problem of Divine Immediacy." *Religious Studies* (1968) 499–512.
Selbie, W. B. *Schleiermacher: A Critical and Historical Study.* The Great Christian Theologies. New York: Dutton, 1913.
Sen, Keshub Chunder. *Keshub Chunder Sen's Lectures in India.* 2 vols. London: Cassell, 1901–4.
Sharma, Chandradhar. *A Critical Survey of Indian Philosophy.* Delhi: Motilal Banarsidass, 1973.
Sherman, Robert J. "Shift to Modernity: Christ and the Doctrine of Creation in the Theologies of Schleiermacher and Barth." PhD diss., University of Chicago, 1992.

Smart, Ninian, ed. *Nineteenth Century Religious Thought in the West*. Cambridge: Cambridge University Press, 1985.
Sockness, Brent W. "The Ideal and the Historical in the Christology of Wilhelm Herrmann: The Promise and the Perils of Revisionary Christology." *Journal of Religion* 72 (1992) 366–88.
Sonderegger, Katherine. "The Doctrine of Creation and the Task of Theology." *Harvard Theological Review* 84 (1991) 185–203.
Sorrentino, Sergio, ed. *Schleiermacher's Philosophy and the Philosophical Tradition*. Lewiston, NY: Mellen, 1992.
Spiegler, Gerhard. *The Eternal Covenant*. New York: Harper and Row Publishers, 1967.
———. "Schleiermacher and the Problem of Kulturtheologie." *Religion in Life* 35 (1966) 417–32.
Streetman, Robert F. "Friedrich Schleiermacher's Doctrine of Trinity and Its Significance for Theology Today." (Dissertation abstract.) *Drew Gateway* 46 (1975–76) 118–19.
———. "Some Later Thoughts of Otto on the Holy." *Journal of the American Academy of Religion* 48 (1980) 365–84.
Sykes, Stephen W. *Friedrich Schleiermacher*. Makers of Contemporary Theology. Richmond: John Knox, 1971.
———. "Theological Study: The Nineteenth Century and After." In *The Philosophical Frontiers of Christian Theology*, edited by Brian Hebbelthwaite and Stewart Sutherland, 95–118. Cambridge: Cambridge University Press, 1982.
Thandeka. "Schleiermacher's Dialektik: The Discovery of the Self the Kant Lost." *Harvard Theological Review* 85 (1992) 433–52.
Thangasamy, D. A. *The Theology of Chenchiah, with selections from his writings*. Bangalore, India: Christian Institute for the Study of Religion and Society and the Literature Dept. of the National Council of Y.M.C.A's of India, [1966].
Thiel, John. *God and World in Schleiermacher's Dialektik and Glaubenslehre: Criticism and the Methodology of Dogmatics*. Bern: Lang, 1981.
Thielicke, Helmut. *Modern Faith and Thought*. Translated by G. W. Bromiley. Grand Rapids: Eerdmans, 1990.
Thiemann, Ronald F. "Piety, Narrative, and Christian Identity." *Word and World* 3 (1983) 148–59.
———. *Revelation and Theology: The Gospel as Narrated Promise*. Notre Dame, IN: University of Notre Dame Press, 1985.
Thomas, M. M. *The Acknowledged Christ of the Indian Renaissance*. Madras: Christian Literature Society, 1970.
Tice, Terrence N. "Indications of What Schleiermacher's Thought is Good for Today." In *Understanding Schleiermacher: From Translation to Interpretation: A Festschrift in Honor of Terrence Nelson Tice*, edited by Ruth Drucilla Richardson and Edwina Lawler, 605–15. Lewiston, NY: Mellen, 1998.
———. "Interviews with Karl Barth and Reflections on his Interpretation of Schleiermacher." In *Barth and Schleiermacher: Beyond the Impasse?*, edited by James O. Duke and Robert F. Streetman, 43–62. Philadelphia: Fortress, 1988.
———. *Schleiermacher*. Abingdon Pillars of Theology. Nashville: Abingdon, 2006.
———. *Schleiermacher Bibliography: With Brief Introduction, Annotation, and Index*. Princeton, NJ: Princeton University Press for Princeton Theological Seminary, 1966.

———. *Schleiermacher Bibliography (1784–1984): Updating and Commentary.* Princeton, N.J.: Princeton University Press for Princeton Theological Seminary, 1985. [This and other further updates by Tice are available in *New Athenaeum/Neues Athenaeum*, a scholarly journal specializing in Schleiermacher research, published periodically from 1989 by Mellen.]

———. "Schleiermacher on the Scientific Study of Religion." In *The Founding of the University of Berlin and the Scientific Study of Religion*, edited by Herbert Richardson, 45–82. Lewiston, NY: Edwin Mellen, 1988.

———. "Schleiermacher Yesterday, Today and Tomorrow." In *Cambridge Companion to Friedrich Schleiermacher*, edited by Jacqueline Mariña. Cambridge: Cambridge University Press, 2005.

———. "Schleiermacher's Conception of Religion: 1799 to 1831." *Archivio de Filosofia* 52, N. 1–3. (1984) 333–56.

———. "Schleiermacher's Interpretation of Christmas: Christmas Eve, the 'Christian Faith', and the Christmas Sermons." *Journal of Religion* 47 (1967) 100–126.

———. *Schleiermacher's Sermons: A Chronological Listings and Account.* Lewiston, NY: Mellen, 1997.

———. "Schleiermacher's Theological Method: With Special Attention to his Production of Church Dogmatics." Th. D. diss., Princeton Theological Seminary, 1961.

———. "Schleiermacher's Theology: Ecclesial and Scientific, Ecumenical and Reformed." In *Probing the Reformed Tradition: Historical Studies in Honor of Edward A. Dowey, Jr.*, edited by Elsie Anne McKee and Brian G. Armstrong, 386–407. Louisville: Westminster John Knox, 1989.

———. "Themes in Schleiermacher's Early Theology." In *Papers of the Schleiermacher Seminar, American Academy of Religion, Chicago, 1989*, edited by Terrence N. Tice, 1–26. Ann Arbor: University of Michigan, 1989.

———. "Themes in Schleiermacher's Later Theology." In *Papers of the Schleiermacher Seminar, American Academy of Religion*, edited by Robert F. Streetman, 32–49. Fairfield, CT: Fairfield University Press, 1988.

Tice, Terrence N., et al., eds. *Schleiermacher and Contemporary Theology.* Papers presented in the Schleiermacher Group at the 1994 annual meeting of the American Academy of Religion. Chicago, 1994.

Tillich, Paul. *A History of Christian Thought.* Edited by Carl E. Braaten. New York: Simon and Schuster, 1968.

Torrance, James B. "Interpretation and Understanding in Schleiermacher's Theology: Some Critical Questions." *Scottish Journal of Theology* 21 (1968) 268–82.

Torrance, Thomas F. "Hermeneutics according to F. D. E. Schleiermacher." *Scottish Journal of Theology* 21 (1968) 257–67.

Vance, Robert L. "Sin and Consciousness of Sin in Schleiermacher." *Perspectives in Religious Studies* 13 (1986) 241–62.

———. *Sin and Self-consciousness in the Thought of Friedrich Schleiermacher.* Lewiston, NY: Mellen, 1994.

Van Ness, Peter H. "Apology, Speculation, and Philosophy's Fate." *Philosophy and Theology* 5 (1990) 3–17.

Verheyden, Jack. "The Knowledge of the Existence of God in Protestant Theology." *Dialogue and Alliance* (1987) 27–40.

Vivekananda, Swami. *Vedanta: Voice of Freedom.* Edited with an Introduction by Swami Chetananda. New York: Philosophical Library, 1986.

Ward, Daryll. "The Doctrine of Election in the Theologies of Friedrich Schleiermacher and Karl Barth." Ph. D. diss., University of Chicago, 1989.

Watts, Craig M. "The Intention of Schleiermacher in *The Life of Jesus.*" *Encounter* 46 (1985) 71–86.

Weborg, John. "A Study of Schleiermacher's Concept of Faith." *Covenant Quarterly* 36 (1978) 39–48.

Welch, Claude. *Protestant Thought in the Nineteenth Century.* Vol. 1. New Haven: Yale University Press, 1972.

West, Cornel. "Schleiermacher's Hermeneutics and the Myth of the Given." *Union Seminary Quarterly Review* 34 (Winter 1979) 71–84.

Wilburn, Ralph G. "Role of Tradition in Schleiermacher's Theology." *Encounter* 23 (1962) 300–315.

Wilkin, Robert L. "The Resurrection of Jesus and the Doctrine of the Trinity." *Word & World* 2 (1982) 17–28.

Williams, Robert R. "Schleiermacher and Feuerbach on the Intentionality of Religious Consciousness." *Journal of Religion* 53 (1973) 424–55.

———. "Schleiermacher, Hegel, and the Problem of Concrete Universality." *Journal of the American Academy of Religion* 56 (1988) 473–96.

———. *Schleiermacher the Theologian: The Construction of the Doctrine of God.* Philadelphia: Fortress, 1978.

———. "Theodicy, Tragedy, and Soteriology: The Legacy of Schleiermacher." *Harvard Theological Review* 77 (1984) 395–412.

Wyman, Walter E., Jr. "The Historical Consciousness and the Study of Theology." In *Shifting Boundaries: Contextual Approaches to the Structure of Theological Education,* edited by Barbara G. Wheeler and Edward Farley, 91–117. Louisville: Westminster John Knox, 1991.

———. "Rethinking the Christian Doctrine of Sin: Friedrich Schleiermacher and Hick's 'Irenaen Type'." *Journal of Religion* 74 (1994) 199–217.

Index

Names, Places and Titles

Aleaz, K. P., 131n
Anselm, St., 147
Aquinas, Thomas, 144n, 145n, 147
Arjuna, 102n
Augustine, St., 82, 135n, 148n
Augustinian, 81, 160
Aurabindo, 37n, 38

Bangalore, 131n
Barby, Germany, 62
Barth, Karl, 8, 14, 27n, 31n, 81, 87, 95n, 101n, 129n
Church Dogmatics, xi, 8n, 14, 66, 81n
Barthian, 38
Battles, Ford Lewis, 121n
Bergson, Henri, 37n
Berkof, Henrikus, 1
Berlin, University of, 109n
Bhagavad Gita, 102n
Blackwell, Albert, 62n
Blaising, Craig, xii
Boethius, 147n, 148n
Bonhoeffer, Dietrich, 140
Boyd, Robin H., 56n
Bretschneider, Karl, 81, 82
Brief Outline, 17n, 19n
Buddha, Gautama, 47
Burns, Lanier, xii

Calvin, John, 11, 12, 13, 14, 82, 90n, 101n, 112, 121, 136
Chaitanya, 131n
Chardin, Teilhard de, 38
Chenchiah, Pandippedi, 36, 37, 38, 39, 59

Church, Marthoma, ix
Church of England, ix
Church of South India, ix
Coleridge, Samuel Taylor, 43n
Craig, William Lane, 133, 134, 147n
Craver, Bennie Dale, 87
Cusa, Nicholas of, 145n

Dallas Seminary Foundation, xiv
Dallas Theological Seminary, ix, xiii, xiv
Dialectic, 7n, 15, 128n
De Vries, Dawn, 45, 46n
Dowey Jr., Edward A., 12

Ebeling, Gerhard, 99n
Emerson, Ralph Waldo, 43n
Europe, 114
Evangelicalism, ix
Fantino, Jacques, 34n
Fox, Charles W., 153n

Gandhi, 36, 47
Gerrish, Brian, xiii
Goris, Hamm J.M.J., 145n, 147n

Hegel, Friedrich, 109n
Heppe, Heinrich Ludwig Junius, 79n
Hermeneutics, xiii, xi(n), 3m

India, 37, 39, 56
Irenaeus, 33, 34, 35

Job, 37n, 38n
Johanns, P., 131

Keesee, Neal, 136

Kelsey, Catherine L., xv
Kerala, South India, ix
Kierkegaard, Søren, 122, 156
Klooster, Fred, 141n
Kolkatta, 55n, 57n, 131n
Kraemer, Hendrick, 38

Landsberg an der Warthe, xiv, 62
Life of Jesus, 31n, 49n

Mohammed, 59
Moses, 59
Muller, Richard, 161

Napoleon, 109n
Niebuhr, Reinhold, 111–3
Niebuhr, Richard R., 43n, 103

Oman, John, xiii
On Religion, (*Speeches*), x, xiii(n), 1, 2, 15, 20, 136, 137, 139
On the Glaubenslehre, 1n, 2n, 3, 11n, 15n, 24n, 127n, 129n
Otto, Rudolf, xiii

Padgett, Alan G., 147n
Palestine, 54
Parekh, Manilal C., 56n
Pauck, Wilhelm, xiii, 17n, 19n
Pickle, Joseph, 29n
Pike, Nelson, 146, 147
Pudukottai, 36
Prussia, 109n
Pune, Maharastra, India, ix
Radhakrishanan, xiii
Ramanuja, 131n
Ranchi, 131n
Reden (On Religion), xiii
Reeves, Jerry, xiv
Rogers, Katherin A., 147n
Roman Catholic, xiii
Rome, ix
Sages, Hindu, xiii
Sämmtliche Werke 17n

Sankara, 82, 131
Schelling, Friedrich Wilhelm Joseph, 43n
Sen, Bramarshi Keshub Chunder, 55, 56n, 57n, 58, 59
Servant of the Word, 45n, 46n, 123n
Sharma, Chandradhar, 133n, 145n
Soliloquies, 137
Spencer, Stephen, xiii, xiv
Spinoza, Baruch, xiii

Thangasami, 37n, 59n
Thomas, M. M., 55n, 56n
Tice, Terrence N., xiii, xiv, 2, 6, 15, 43n, 45n, 90n, 119n, 124n, 128n, 139
Tillich, Paul, 58, 66
Turretin, Francis, 79n

Union Biblical Seminary, ix
United States, 2
Upadhyaya, Brahmabandhab, 131, 132

Vivekananda, Swami, 116

Ward, Daryll, 95n
Williams, Robert R., 145n
Wingren, Gustav, 34n
Wyman, Walter E., Jr., 106n

Subjects and Concepts

abstraction, 3, 10
act, arbitrary divine, 25; creative divine, 36; God's eternal, 77; God's justifying, 77; non-dual, 129; non-plural, 148; original divine, 49
activity, a carrier of the divine, 45; Christ's, 26; creative, 64; creative divine, 66; God's redemptive, 38, 63, 108; initial divine, 36; multiplicity in eternal, 130;

Index   177

nature of God's eternal, 54; pure, 42; self-disclosing, 137; sovereign eternal, 53
Adam, 24, 34, 49; and Eve, 108; descendants of, 91; second, 24, 26, 32-4, 48, 49
adi-purusha, 37
Advaita, 131
aesthetic, 1
analogy, 34, 83, 97, 159
analysis, elemental, 13; phenomenological, 29
animals, 60
anthropomorphism, 12, 34n, 54, 82, 84, 99, 130n, 154
anti-Semitism, 29, 37n
apologetics, 2, 15
arbitrariness, 91
art, divine, 136
asceticism, 56
associations, religious, 30
atheism, 11, 13, 99
atman, 133, 145n
atomistic, 93, 101
attributes, 100–101; divine, 99n; holiness and justice, 32
automatons, 107
avatara, 38

becoming, in process of, 16
Being, Absolute, 7; absolute revelation of the Supreme, 136, 157; mensurability of the divine, 146
being, sinless human, 42; ideal human, 42
being-reciprocally-related-to-each-other, 150
beyondness, 140
Bible, the, 134
bifurcation, methodological, 58
blessedness, 18, 89, 123; absolute, 114; corporate life of, 66; impartation of, 107
Böse, 109n

Brahman, 131, 133, 145n
Buddhism, 13

called, the, 81
Calvinism, 11, 81
capriciousness, divine, 25
catalytic, 65
causality, 12, 148-150; finite, 107, 133, 151, 152, 154, 156; human, 5; absolute, 107, 142; absolutely timeless, 144; creational, 97; divine, 5, 18, 31, 42, 46, 82, 94, 95, 97, 98, 99, 104, 107, 108, 111, 135, 141, 143–47, 148-56, 160; human, 82, 99, 104, 108, 147, 149; mundane, 18, 141; natural, 95, 124, 151; nexus of, 150-1; non-physical, 152; relative, 96, 97, space-conditioning of, 143; totality of finite, 134; ultimate, 43
ceremonies, 37
changes, paradigm, 114
character, representative, 45
Christ, advent, 31; as high priest, 73; contemporaneity, 122, 145; created, 56; cultic, 57; dignity, 26; freedom of, 64; God's work in, ix, 159; influences of, 31, 70; kingly office of, 74–5; mediation, 27; ministration, 102; obedience, perfect vicarious of, 73; originality and uniqueness of, 23–4; person and work of, ix, 27, 41, 63, 122; raw fact of, 37; spirit of Jesus, 119; two natures of, 42, 160; uncreated, 56
Christians, 28; early, 7; Indian, vii, 36; potential, 70
Christian faith, God of the, 2
Christianity, xii, 27, 29; germ of, 30; meaning of, ix
Christ-impulses, 67, 68, 114

Christology, 27, 37, 41, 49, 58, 127; genuine, 161; Schleiermacher's, 64, 161
Church, 116-18; Christ-centered, 94; common spirit of, 119, 120, 122; consummation of, 123; historical, 35; invisible, 119; missionary thrust of, 15, 90; of the New Dispensation, 57; princes of the, 19; visible, 44n, 118-19
communion, active relationship of, 5, 46; religious, 6; with God, 106
communities, literate, vii; religious, 15, 30
community, Christ's communion with the, 67; Christian, xi, xiv, 107; monotheistic, 11; new, 80; organic, 74; original Christian, 80, redeemed, 73
compulsion, divine, 31
condemnation, divine, 13
connections, causal, 151, 153; organic, 6
conscientization, 107; communal, 39
consciousness, animal, 9; Christian, 2, 5, 19, 27; fundamental source in religious, 159; historical, 17; human, 8; innate, 12; nature of, 6
constancy, inviolable, 23; receptivity of total, 143
contextualization, 11
contingencies, historical, 84
continuum, space-time, 134
contrasts, eternity and time, 144; freedom and necessity, 154; God and the world, 144; level of, 12; realm of, 15, 155; relative, 9, 29
contrastive, cooperative and, 151
conversion, 77, individual, 95, 103
correlation, method of, 66
counter-influence, 42, 97
Covenant, eternal, 15, 129

creation, 25, 62, 105, 128, 130, 136, 142; crown of its, 62; *ex nihilo*, 89, 130, 144; arbitrary, 94; being of the, 42; brute, 112; completed, 48; doctrine of, 129; elevation of, 39; first, 33; God's ultimate purpose for and in, 65; limits of, 147; nature of human, 26; new, vii, 23, 24, 28, 29, 31-35, 36, 38, 39, 46, 48, 80,116; old, 23, 28, 29, 31, 32, 80; perfecting of, 35; second, 33, 116; totality of, 7, 53, 54, 141; Thomistic doctrine of, 131; totality of the old, 80; "whenness" and "whereness" of the, 133-34
Creator, nature of the, 42
creatures, rational, 31
creed, xi, 53; Constantinopolitan, 122
criticism, historical, 19
cross, 37n, 38, 42

damnation, everlasting, 80, 92
death, life after, 124, 160; world of, 34
decree, absolute singleness of God's eternal, 49, 79-80, 82; divine, 54, 78, 82, 83, 97, 105, 123, 153, 159; electing, 106; general and special, 79; justifying, 77; plurality of, 79
decisions, *ad hoc*, 88
defect, original, 136
deism, 10, 87
deity, 57, 59; sense of, 11
demythologizing, 84
dependence, absolute, 10, 11, 97, 104, 106, 116, 128, 139, 149-50, 156; absolute feeling of, 97, 100; consciousness of absolute, 14, 140; feeling of absolute, 12, 13, 83, 129, 132, 136, 148; one-way,

5; partial, 9, 13, 150; relative, 83, 104
determinism, absolute, 107
deus ex machina, 140
development, human, 13, 47
devil, 153
devilishness, 80, 153
dialectic, 8, 20, 159, interior, 9, 11
dialogue, xi, 6; inter-faith, x; openness to, xii
didactic, 85
difference, infinite (unbridgeable) qualitative, 31
discrimination, divinely ordered, 93
dispensation, pre-determined, 56
divine, the, 140; good pleasure, 53, 73, 95, 94, 96, 124, 156; government of the world, 78, 80, 85, 90-92, 94, 101, 136, 141
divinity, emanation from, 57; filling of the, 55; in a person, 45; perfect, 63; pristine, 51; sense of, 12
docetism, 52, 63
doctrines, xi, 37; Christian, 3; "frozen" set of, 11; non-orthodox and heterodox, 161; prophetic, 20; system of, 54n; traditional orthodox, 50
dogmas, 37
dogmatic, xi, 15
dogmatics, 2, 14, 18, 121, 130, 141; Christian, 51, Christological definition of, 159
duration, 82, 101; endless, 146

ecclesial, x; cf. church
ecclesiology, 81, 127; Schleiermacher's, 80
election, 79, 81, 85, 88, 90, 91, 94, 100, 110-11; arbitrary, 94; doctrine of, 77, 81; primordial, 94
embodiment (of ideal human nature), 44

emotions, religious, 6
energy, cosmic, 37-8
entity, non-dual, 96
environment, human, 25
epistemology, 141
equality, absolute, 90
equiclose, 122
Erregungen, 6n
eschatology, 123
essence, 100
eternality, 144; divine, 143
eternity, xii; God's, 5, 144-45; nature of, 141; time and, 145
ethics, Christian, xi, 123
evangelicalism, ix, 11
evil, 41, 110; moral, 109n
evolution, 31, 38; aimless, 60; cosmic, 39; chain of, 59; integral, 137; spiritual, 57; theory of, 129
existence, of God (in Christ), 52, (in Jesus), 59; order of, 38
experience, interiority of Christian, 3; vedantic spiritual, 116
expiation, temporary, 32

faith, Christian, 24, 26, 27; community of, 15, 67, 99, 161; living, 15; non-Christian, 30; Reformed, xiv; religious, x; seeking understanding, 14
faithful, inner vital relationship of the, 74
fall, the, 38
feeling, province of, 10
fetishism, 13
fibers, innumerable causal, 150
finiteness, passing pangs of, 110
flesh, 106, 111, 118; and blood, 54, 108
flow, free, 64
forces, dehumanizing, 108, 115
freedom, absolute, 9, 10, 96, 97; creative, 137; dependent, 97; human, 64; partial, 9

fruits, final, 39, first, 37
fulfillment, 39, perfect, 73
fullness of time, 7, 25, 44n, 54, 56, 88, 102, 118, 142

Gemeinshaft, 69n
God, xi, 160, 172; absolute consciousness of, 108, 120n, 156; absolute dependence on, 128; absolute detachment, 154; absolute freedom of, 131; absolute reality of, 145n; active receptivity for, 44; alienation from, 106; and evil, 109; as the Absolute, 45; as Immanuel, 153; the being of (in Jesus), 51, 65, 67-68; comprehensiveness of Christ's consciousness of, 64, 156; constant perfect consciousness of, 49, 51; foreknowledge, etc. of, 34, 95; impassibility of, 103, 131; internal acts in, 79; Jesus-mediated consciousness of, 46; knowledge of, 15, 150; language of, 43n; living, 58; love and wisdom of, xi; mercy and justice of, 92; mind of, 54; omnipotence, 111, 148; omnipresence, xii, 120, 142-3, 146, 148, in Jesus, 52, 60, 63, 98; overflow of the abundance of, 131; penetrating the mind of, 154; pure reality of, 144; receptivity to, 142; simplicity, 42; singularity, 79; sinless consciousness of, 53; son of, 38, 45; sons of, 38; triune, xi, 45, 58; will of, 54n
God, bracketed work of, 85
God-consciousness, 9, 11, 15, 19, 24, 25, 27; absolute, 6, 20, 36, 45, absolutely powerful, 42, 46; Christian, 14; communication of, 107; communicator of perfect, 59; constancy and intensity of, 63; fragmented, 32; full, 55; immutability of, 134; impassibility of, 104; interruptions in, 108; less perfect, 55; non-Christians', 46; on behalf of all, 54; perfect, pure, 44, 48, 53; progressive actualization of, 20; trinitarian, 14; ultimacy of, 19
Godhead, distinctions within the, 14, 42
God-in-Godself, 14, 83, 97, 100, 147
God of the gaps, 140
godliness (in its perfect form), 51
God-Man, 38
Goodness, absolute, 20
good-pleasure, God's, 94, 95
gospel, 39; social, 112
government, civil, 74
grace, ix, 105, 107, 111; consciousness of, 106; enabling, 66, infusion of, 106; justifying divine, 89; operating field of, 118; preparatory, 89, 90; state of, v, 114-15
ground, causal, 83, 100, 148
guilt, corporate, 106
gustus divinitatis, 12

heresies, natural, 82, 112
heritage, Hindu, 59; Reformation, 11
hermeneutics, 3; and criticism, 17
higher life, 24, 66, 68, 69, 70
highest intuition, xiv, 62
Hindu, ix, 91; seeker, 55n
Hinduism, 37, 39, 55n, 102n; Triad of, 102n
history, xiii, 7, 16, 141; as chronicle of cause and effect series, 17; as Christo-centric, 142; Christian view of, xiv; consummation of, 87; contingency of, 92; end-point of, 20, 87; God's work in, xi, xii, 2, 5, 41, 77, 96, 98, 99, 125, 157, 159; invading, 38; meaning of, ix;

organicity of, 142; redemptive, 5, 105, 125; teleological nature of, 142
holiness, 108
holocaust, 20, 155
Holy Spirit, xiii, 38, 45n, 58, 102
hope, Christian, 20
humanity, xiv(n), 26, 31, 43, 81; common, 24; divinely apportioned to represent, 47; divinity and, 55; enfleshment of perfect, 63; existence of God in, 44; fulfilled destiny of, 63; imperfect conditions of, 106; of Jesus, 41, 44, 62, 63; organic nature of, 124; partition of, 124; redemption of, 137; regenerated, 58; species, 159; steady evolution of, 59

ideas, 55n, 130
ideality, 26, 42
imagery, guiding, xiv; legal and biological, 37
impeccability, logical, 159
imperfects, a corpus of, 44
impulses, Christ-created, 73; Christian, 67; human, 67; kindred, 80; spiritual, 35, transmittal of the, 67
incarnation, 38, 50; true doctrine of, 56
inclusiveness, gender, 2
infinite, into the finite, 138, 140-42; sense and taste for the, 139
influences, 42; conditioning, 96; pagan, 50; transforming, 96
insentience, 43, 157
instantaneity, 146
intention, steadfastness of, 103-4
intentionality, divine, 103-105
interconnected process of nature, xii, 2, 6, 8, 12, 14, 16, 65, 83, 88, 108, 116, 128, 130n, 136, 139, 146, 149-51, 159-60; see *Naturzusammenhang*
interconnectedness, 89, 119, 125; of parts and whole, 125; of physical and human world, 160
interrelation, nexus of, 5, 18, 153
intervention, divine, 86; extra-terrestrial, 24; miraculous, 136; theory of, 38

Jainist, 13
Jehovah, the Supreme Brahma, 57
Jesus (of Nazareth), 29, 94, 98; absolute spiritual perfection of, 120; ascension, 120; Being of God in, 41, 156; birth of, 35, 38; calling, 61; divine humanity of, 25, 46, 51, 54, 57; divinity of, 42; God's work in, 41; God-consciousness of, 28; omnipresence of God in, 68, 69, 70; person of, 25; redemption accomplished through, 156; uniqueness of, 55; see Christ
Jesus-worship, 45n, 59n
Judaism, 20, 29, 30, 39; doctrines, 72; historical connections with, 70
justice, 108
juxtaposition, 128, 150

Kantian thought, 97
karma, collective and individual, 110
kenosis, 55
Kingdom of God, 37, 39, 127
knowing, boundaries of our, 7
knowledge, religious, 12; scientific, 11

language, Christology in contemporary, 161; dogmatic, 114, poetical and popular, 143
life, inner, 99, 123, 142; new corporate, 35, 80; outer, 99; universal spiritual, 25

Lila, Bhagavan's, 91
lives, pre-natal, 93
location, 16, 82; instantaneous temporaneous, 146; locationless, 82
logos, 57
love, divine, 100, 101, 103; redemptive, 137
Lutheran, xiii, 23, 81, 114, 160

magical, 78
man, elected, 81; new, 37; the old and new, 66; son of, 38
Manichaeism, 82, 92, 95, 108
maya, 131, 132, 145n
miracle, 24–25, 72, 151; the greatest, 56
monism, 10
monotheism, 11; Christian modification of, 13
mortifications, 32
mysteries, 37
mystical, xiii, 78
myth, 71

natural, 6, 7, 31
nature, 7, 100; "original creation" of human, 63; communication of the divine, 101; derangement of human, 28; disturbance of, 41; God's eternal, 141; human, 27; infinite interrelations within, 130; interdependence of the system of, 153; original act of human, 49; perfect specimen of human, 62; romantic, 43n; spatio-temporal rules of, 68; totality of, 16, 43; uttermost reaches of, 149; see interconnectedness
natures, three divine, 50; two, 50
Naturzusammenhang, xii, 2, 10, 14, 83, 86, 89, 116, 136, 139, 149, 150
necessity, biological and divine, 38-39

New Testament, 7, 29, 30, 39, 57, 72;
noetic, 10, 13
non-causative, 52
non-church, 117, 118
non-dual, 83, 84, 87, 152
non-duality, absolute, 84, 104
non-enumerable, 148
non-locational, 83
non-multiple, 84
non-mundane, 52
non-pagan, 29
non-real, ultimately, 111
non-reciprocal, 128
non-redeemed, 18
non-spatial, 101, 152, 156
non-temporal, 83, 87, 101, 152
nothingness, absolute, 131
numinis, 12

obeisance, 59n
Old Testament, 29, 30, 37, 39, 73
oneness, metaphysical, 38
ontology, 141; intrinsic, 145n
opposites, coincidence of, 145n
organicity, 1, 5, 18; self-perpetuating, 69
orthodoxy, 14; Christian, 131; Reformed, 160; Syrian, ix
outflow, 64–5

paganism, 29, 39
pantheism, xiii, 2, 10, 100, 143
paradox, 20; absolute, 156
Paramarthika, 131
passivity, 86
Pelagianism, 82, 92, 95, 112
penances, 32
perception, 12; individual pious centers of, 143
perfect, imperfect to, 30
perfection, 26, Christ's original, 108; God's, 155; original historical, 108

period, pre-grace, 111
permanence, intrinsic, 132
person-forming activities, 47, 67, 68, 69
philosophy, Sankara's, 133; Vedantic, 131–32
physics, post-Newtonian, 136
piety, xii, 159; Christian, 134; human, 137
polemic, 82
polytheism, 11
potentiality, fullest blooming of humanity's ultimate, 65; spiritual, 49
power, eternal, 144; inscrutable, 131; maximum, 90; perfect spiritual, 28; natural or supernatural, 107
predestination, 79, 88-90, 94, 100, 105
predictions, apostolic, Jesus', 72
pre-reflective, 12, 13
presence, spaceless, 145
present, organically, 125
preservation, divine, 105, 128, 130, 136, 138, 139, 142,
privilege, Protestant, 11, 50, 114
problem, juridical, 37; in genetics, 37
process, dialectical, 8, 159; mechanical-dynamical, 151; reversing of a thinker's, 4
prophecy, 30, 59, 70, 124; climax and fulfillment of all, 72, 123
propitiation, 37
purifications, 32, 73

reality, intrinsic vs. transcendental, 144; ultimate, 108, 132, 133
realm, God's, 130, 144
recapitulation, theory of, 33, 34
receptivity, 49; absolute, 45, 53; patchy active, 44; perfect vital, 44, pure; 43
redeemed, 18; yet to be, 73

Redeemer, 6, 14, 25, 28, 41, 51, 59, 61, 123, 124; blessedness of, 106
redeemers, 23; plurality of, 26
redemption, xi, xii, 18, 29, 36, 101, 103, 105, 114, 117, 123, 127, 136, 142; author of, 111; divine economy of, 46; estate of, 54n; furtherance of, 99; glimpses of, 67; humanity's, 137–38; means in, 99; possibility of, 44; theater of, 151
reformation, 11, 50, 113
Reformed, ix, xiii, 11, 114; faith, 23
regeneration, 77, 89
reign of God, 18, 19, 20, 35, 54n, 66, 71, 72, 74, 89, 94, 95, 111, 119, 120, 121, 142, 153
rejection, 90, 92, 110, 111
relation, non-reciprocal dependent, 83
relationship, God-world, 132; reciprocity of, 130; symbiotic, 149
religion, 11, 27, 31, 37, 52, 139; cultured critics of, 160; ethos of a, 54n; monotheistic, 13; non-Christian, 54n, 102n; refinement of, xii; teleological, 54n; Vedanta is the universal, 116
religiosity, human, 13
religious *a priori*, 12
reprobation, 79
resurrection, doctrine of, 57
revelation, 6; divine, 25, 120n; original, 71; subsequent special work of, 133; supernatural, 160
rhetoric, 1, 116
rituals, 37
romantic, 43n, 136

sacrifice, 32, 37
sakti, 37
sanctification, 77
sastras, Hindu, 39

science, xii, xiv, 15, 35, 129, 159
scripture, 105, 118; see Bible, New Testament, Old Testament
Selbstmittheilung, 103n
self, xi; self-abnegation, 55, 59; self-communication, 103n, 105; self-consciousness, 9, 11, 12, 27–29, 111; Christian religious, ix; highest level of, 132; highly developed, 151; individualized religious, 43; Jewish, 29; religious, 23; sensory, 43
self-emptying, 59; self-impartation, 103n; self-impartation, God's, 102, 105; self-manifestation, divine, 136–38; self-pride, 73; self-redemption, 65; selfsameness, everywhere, 143; self-surrender, 56
sensation, 12, 43n
sensoriness, 49
sensory, sensuous, 43n
sensuousness, 49n
sensus, 12; *sensus divinitatis*, 11–13
sentience, 157
series, cause-effect, 150, 153
sin, 105, 107, 118; actual, 113; Adamic, 73; author of, 108, 111; consciousness of, 28, 107; corporate, 106; disturbance of, 48; incapacitating force of, 156; misery of, 32, 33; non-reality of, 111; original, 28, 106, 112, 113; state of, 115; state of absolute, 106
sinfulness, 90; congenital, 28; corporate life of, 24; state of, 55; universal, 26
sinlessness, 6, 28; absolute, 28; total, 20
sinnlich, 43n
Sinnlichkeit, 49n
sloth, 112

sovereignty, 153–55; Divine, 156; God's absolute, 149, 155
space, 18, 130, 141, 149; absolute cause of time and, 148
spacelessness, absolute, 142
spatiality, 142–43, 145; space and, 123
spatio-temporal, 101
specialis, specialissima, 140
species, 26, 87, 89; commonality of the, 106; new, 38; permanent split of the, 92; sub-human, 43, 142; species-consciousness, 92, 93; species-nature, 110
speculation, 8; unwarranted, 141
spirit, 106, 111, 118; communication of the divine, 121; continuing indwelling of the, 121; divine, 35; Holy, 118, 120–22
spirituality (Jesus'), 47
spontaneity, 64, 150
stirred, stirrings, 6, 15
sub-Christian, 37
sub-culture, 47
subjective/objective, 3–4
substrata, 43
supernatural, 6, 7, 8, 24, 25, 36, 68
superstition, 58
synchrony, 47

teleology, 18, 62; Christian, 5; Schleiermacher's, 35
telos, 20, 63
temporal, eternity in the, 69
temporality, 16, 18, 34n, 53, 130, 143–46; limiting adjunct of, 148
theologian, amateur, 36, Evangelical Reformed, xi; orthodox Christian, 132
theology, viii, 28; liberal, xi; Christian, 18, 64, 135, 148; Christocentric approach to, 161; dogmatic, x; Evangelical Reformed, 114; father of modern, ix, 162;

Indian Christian, 36, 55n, 131, 132; joint Evangelical, 114; natural, 71; nineteenth century Protestant, xiii; popular Western, 57; process, 136; to redeem dogmatic, 50; Reformed, 79; Scholastic, 51; systematic, x; traditional Christian, 53; traditional Reformed, 141
thinkers, Indian, xi, 5
thinking, Hindu, 102n; language and, 149; ongoing tradition of religious, 53; sharpness in, 159
thought, as language-producing, 149; flow and production of, 4; Schleiermacher's, ix
time, 130, 141, 147, 149; eternity invades, 146; terminal points of, 146
timelessness, 147, 148; doctrine of, 146
tradition, xiv, 5; church's, 70; dogmatic, xiv; non-Christian, 36; orthodox, 45; orthodox Reformed, 79; standard Reformed, 79; Western and Eastern, ix
trans-conceptuality, 10
trans-phenomenal, 6
trans-spatial and temporal, 10
trinity, 50, 51, 59, 122, 127, 141; orthodox doctrines of, 65; second person, 33; third person, 121

Übel, 109n
union, Lutheran/Reformed, xiv
union, mystical, 55
Unitarians, 57n, 122
unity, organic, 35, 145
Universum, 8, 15
unreal, world as, 145n

values, 47
variation, emotional, 104
vedanta, 131; advaita, 82, 145n

vedas, 57
vishnu, 102n
vocation, 61
void, 55
Vollkommenheit, 47
Vyavaharika, 131

Wesen, 100
wholesomeness, 33
wickedness, 109n
will, divine, 50, 73; human, 50; perfect fulfillment of the divine, 73
wisdom, absolute, 105; divine, 99-101, 103
world, xi, 9, 111, 116, 118; as the revelation of God, 128; fallen, 33; government of the, 75, 127; imperfect and evil, 154; origin of, 129, 130; totality of, 155
world-consciousness, 9, 11
world-process, regularity of, 151
worship, 37; of either Jesus or the Holy Spirit, 45

Bible References

Job 36:26	148n
Ps 102:28	148n
John 11:42	72
Rom 2:11	30
Rom 2:12	30
Rom 3:21	30
Rom 3:24	30
Rom 7:7	27
1 Cor 15:25	34
2 Cor 5:16–17	30, 33n
Gal 4:4	7n, 25, 31, 115
Eph 2:13	18, 30
Phil 2:6	45
Phil 2:7	45
2 Pet 3:8	148n
1 John 4:16	100n

www.ingramcontent.com/pod-product-compliance
Lightning Source LLC
Chambersburg PA
CBHW062041220426
43662CB00010B/1597